THE JEWISH WORLD
in the
MIDDLE AGES

THE JEWISH WORLD
in the
MIDDLE AGES

by
JON BLOOMBERG

KTAV PUBLISHING HOUSE, INC.
New York
2000

Library of Congress Cataloging-in-Publication-Data
Jon Irving Bloomberg
Copyright©2000

Bloomberg, Jon Irving.
   The Jewish world in the Middle Ages / by Jon Bloomberg.
      p. cm
   Includes bibliographical references (p.) and index.
      ISBN 0-88125-684-6
      1. Jews--History--70-1789. 2. Judaism--History-- Medieval and early modern period,
425-1789. 3. Jewish women--History I. Title.

DS124.B73 2000
909'.04924--dc21

                                                                00-034049
                                                                CIP

Distributed by
Ktav Publishing House, Inc.
900 Jefferson Street
Hoboken, NJ 07030
(201) 963-9524 Fax (201) 963-0101
Ktav@compuserve.com

Contents

Maps and Illustrations

Acknowledgments

We acknowledge the inclusion of selections from

Ancient and Medieval History. Ed. L. Feldman. New Brunswick: Rutgers University Press, 1972.

Agus, I. *Rabbi Meir of Rothenburg.* New York: Ktav Publishing, 1970.

Baer, Y. *A History of Jews in Christian Spain.* Philadelphia: Jewish Publication Society, 1962.

Brody, R. *The Geonim of Babylonia and the Shaping of Medieval Jewish Culture.* New Haven: Yale University Press, 1998.

Chazan, R. *European Jewry and the First Crusade.* Berkeley: University of California Press, 1987.

Church, State and Jew in the Middle Ages. Ed. R. Chazan. New York: Behrman House, 1980.

The Expulsion 1492 Chronicles. Ed. D. Raphael. North Hollywood: Carmi House Press, 1992.

Finkelstein, L. *Jewish Self-Government in the Middle Ages.* New York: Jewish Theological Seminary, 1924.

Freehof, S. *Treasury of Responsa.* Philadelphia: Jewish Publication Society, 1963.

Gerber, J. *The Jews of Spain.* New York: Free Press, 1992.

Goitein, S.D. *A Mediterranean Society.* Berkeley: University of California Press, 1983.

Ibn Daud, Abraham. *Sefer ha-Qabbalah.* Ed. Gerson Cohen. Philadelphia: Jewish Publication Society, 1967.

Letters of Jews through the Ages. Ed. F. Kobler. Philadelphia: Jewish Publication Society, 1952.

Maccoby, H. *Judaism on Trial*. Washington: Littman Library, 1993.

Marcus, J.R. *The Jew in the Medieval World*. New York: Atheneum, 1969.

Medieval Jewish Life. Ed. R. Chazan. New York: Ktav Publishing, 1976.

Perlmann, M. "Eleventh-Century Andalusian Authors on the Jews of Granada", *Proceedings of the American Academy for Jewush Research* XVIII(1948–9) New York: Bloch Publishing, 1949.

Perlmann, M. "The Medieval Polemics between Islam and Judaism". *Religion in a Religious Age*. Ed. S. Goitein. Cambridge,MA: Association for Jewish Studies, 1974.

Stillman, N. *The Jews of Arab Lands*. Philadelphia: Jewish Publication Society, 1979.

The Illustrated History of the Jewish People. Ed. N. de Lange. New York: Harcourt Brace, 1997.

Three Jewish Philosophers. New York: Harper Torchbooks, 1965.

Weinberger, L. *Jewish Princes in Moslem Spain: Selected Poems of Samuel Ibn Nagrela*. University, Ala.: University of Alabama Press, 1973.

With Perfect Faith. Ed. J.D. Bleich. New York: Ktav Publishing, 1983.

Zolty, S. *And All Your Children Shall Be Learned*. Northvale, NJ: Jason Aronson, Inc., 1993.

Introduction

This book is entitled *The Jewish World in the Middle Ages*. I intend it to be a textbook appropriate for the high school student. Although there are certainly a number of texts available, Solomon Grayzel's *History of the Jews*, for example, they tend to be superficial in their treatment of the Middle Ages or written at a level of discourse which makes them simply unreadable for the typical high school student, as is the case with H.H. Ben-Sasson's *A History of the Jewish People*.

But why should the overburdened high school student devote time and extend effort to the study of the Jewish Middle Ages? Aren't there more useful ways for them to spend their time? Perhaps there are, but students who do not acquaint themselves with the Jewish past cannot pretend to understand the Jewish present. Antisemitism, for example, cannot be fully understood without an examination of its roots in history, its development over time, the myths about Jews and Judaism it has promoted. The concepts of *galut* (exile) and *ge'ulah* (redemption), which have always helped believing Jews to interpret their historical experience, are understood better when seen through the lens of history.

Beyond these benefits lies the chance to strengthen the Jewish identity of the student by acquainting them with the many significant accomplishments and contributions of Jews throughout history. Students who come to know the Jewish past will take pride in it and identify with it so that it becomes part of their own being. They will be sensitive to the continuities in the history of the Jews as well as to the changes. They will see how many of today's issues, problems, and challenges were confronted in the past.

My goals in this book are to provide students with a readable narrative, expose them to some of the classic texts of Jewish literature in translation, stimulate them to address some of the questions raised by the presented texts, and motivate them to want to study the history of the Jews in greater depth.

The book is divided into four parts. The first of these deals with the geonic period, which extends from approximately 600 to 1000. In the second, the subject matter is the Jews of Ashkenaz (France and Germany); this section takes in the period between 600 and 1400, although the Middle Ages of the Jews lasts somewhat longer than this. The third part deals with the Jews of Muslim Spain from the Muslim invasion of 711 to the Almohad invasion of 1148, while the fourth part deals with the Jews of Christian Spain from 1148 to their expulsion in 1492.

I have included a separate concluding chapter devoted exclusively to the Jewish woman in the Middle Ages. Women are certainly not prominent in our source material. I have made an attempt, nevertheless, to bring them to life.

Each chapter of the book is made up of several units. Each unit begins with an introductory essay on the subject at hand (e.g., the community or Jewish-Christian relations or Jewish culture). The introductory essay is followed by a selection of texts with questions relating to them. Suggestions are made as to possible paper topics on the subject being discussed, and the section concludes by noting some reference works on the topic being examined.

Teachers of the history of the Jews in the Middle Ages should feel free to use other texts of their own selection, to provide their own comments and insights, and to suggest other appropriate texts, themes, and topics. I hope that you will share your own wisdom with me. My intention is to prepare at some later date a teacher's guide to accompany this book.

I am most grateful to all who have been helpful to me in the preparation of this book. First and foremost are Dr. Robert Shapiro of the Ramaz School, Dr. Moshe Sokolow of Yeshiva University and Rabbi Abraham Lieberman of the Shulamit School, each of whom read this work, critiqued it and submitted suggestions to me for refinements and improvements. Mr. Robert Milch, copy editor for this book, did an outstanding job for which I am most grateful. I have benefited as well from the thinking and insights of a colleague and friend, Mr. Sam Kapustin.

Mr. Bernard Scharfstein, of KTAV Publishing House, welcomed my proposal of preparing a textbook on the Jews in the Middle Ages. He has been enormously supportive and his ongoing efforts in this direction are much appreciated.

Last, but certainly by no means least, are my children Adina, Mordechai, and Zehava, and my wife, Miriam, of whose love and support I am most undeserving.

1

The Geonim

THIS UNIT DEALS with the era between 600 and 1000, known as the geonic period. Although, as we will see, Jews lived in the Arabian Peninsula at this time, the main centers of Jewish life were Palestine and Babylonia. As the new religion of Islam spread through the Middle East and established the capital of its caliphate in Baghdad, Babylonia became the most important center of Jewish life.

Jews have always taken great pride in their culture, and the achievements in this sphere during the geonic period were enormous. Grammatical works, liturgical works, a Bible translation, works in halakhah, historical works, and a major work of Jewish philosophy were all produced. Of particular note, as we will see, are the contributions of R. Saadiah Gaon.

We will also examine Jewish political and social life in Babylonia. Of major importance here were two unique institutions. The first of these was the semi-autonomous secular administration of the Babylonian Jewish community. It was headed by a figure called the *rosh golah*, or exilarch, who was the representative of Babylonian Jewry to the Muslim government and, as such, its chief secular official. Jews saw him as their *nasi* (prince) and treated him as royalty. The second major institution comprised the two great yeshivot of Babylonia, Sura and Pumpedita, headed by scholars known as geonim. We will consider how these two institutions cooperated, and how sometimes they found themselves in conflict because the authority of the geonim was based on their scholarship, while that of the rosh golah was based on his family tree, his descent from King David. In addition, we will treat the challenge of Anan and the Karaites to the leadership of the rosh golah and the geonim.

It was during this period, in the year 622, that a new religion appears, the religion of Islam ("submission"). The prophet of Islam, Muhammad, had been exposed to monotheism by his many contacts with Jews and Christians in Arabia and Syria. In time this drew him away from the paganism in which he had been raised and which had become so disappointing to him and to many of his fellow Arabs. Muslim tradition teaches that Muhammad began spending his nights in meditation in the mountains outside the city of Mecca. During his hours of solitary contemplation he received a series of revelations through the agency of the angel Gabriel. When set down in writing, these became the Muslim holy book, or Qur'an.

In this section we will consider the emergence of this new religion, its sacred literature, and its doctrines. We will look at Muhammad and his expectation of acceptance by the Jews as well as his relations with the Jewish tribes in the area of Medina and elsewhere in the Arabian Peninsula. We will examine, finally, how Muslims related to Jews after the death of Muhammad.

POLITICS AND COMMUNITY

Babylonia was the most important center of Jewish life during the geonic period. Most of the world's Jews lived there, as had been the case long before the Muslim conquest in the 7th century. The two great yeshivot, Sura and Pumpedita, were located there, close to the city of Baghdad, which became the Muslim capital in 750. Communal leadership was in the hands of the rosh golah and the geonim; the great challenge to the community was presented by the Karaites.

The Rosh Golah

The *rosh golah*, or exilarch, was the representative of the Jewish community to the Muslim government. The Jewish self-governing institution known as the exilarchate actually dates from an earlier time, when the Persians ruled Babylonia. The Muslims took over the Persian system and made the *rosh golah* the representative of the Jews living in Iran and Iraq. Once Baghdad was established as the Muslim capital, however, he came to represent Jews living throughout the Muslim Empire.

The Muslim ruler, or caliph, appointed the *rosh golah*, but in accordance with long-established tradition, he always selected a member of the House of David, the ancient king of Israel. The *rosh golah* headed his own court and was responsible for collecting the poll tax imposed by the Muslim government. In addition, he was expected to supervise the implementation of the Pact of 'Umar, the series of rules that governed relations between Muslims and non-Muslims.

The territory directly ruled by the *rosh golah* was called a *reshut*. The surviving sources are unclear about the extent and precise location of the *rosh golah's reshut*. We do know, nevertheless, that the Jews living in the reshut were subject to taxes imposed by the *rosh golah*, and that he appointed judges for each community who were answerable to him alone. A judge who did not meet his responsibilities would be deposed.

The *rosh golah* had great symbolic importance to the Jews of Babylonia. They saw him as their own *nasi*, or prince.

The Geonim

The *geonim* were the heads of the yeshivot of Sura and Pumpedita. The title gaon is most probably an abbreviation of the phrase *rosh yeshivat gaon Ya'akov* ("the pride of Jacob"; Psalms 47:4). The institution of the geonate also predated Islam. When the Muslims took power, all the Jewish communities under Muslim rule turned to the *geonim* for religious guidance.

Just as the *rosh golah* was the head of a reshut, so too the geonim headed their own *reshuyot*. As noted earlier, our information regarding the extent and precise locations of the *reshuyot* is minimal. Still we know that the Jewish populace of each reshut was subject to various taxes that served as a primary source of income for the yeshivot. We know as well that, like the *rosh golah*, the *gaon* governing a *reshut* was empowered to appoint judges for each of its com-

8

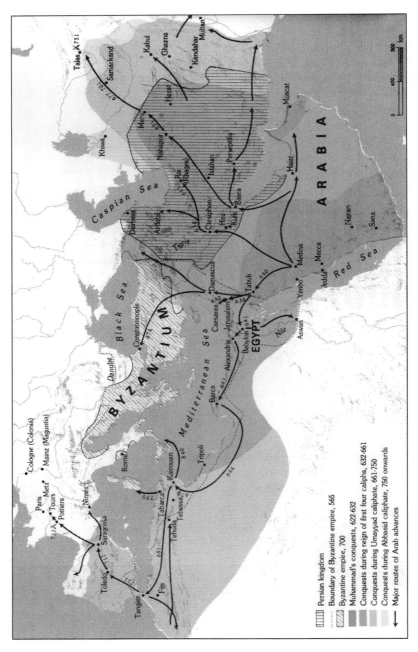

Arabian Conquest and the Rise of Islam (622–721)

munities. The judges he appointed were answerable to him, and thus the gaon was able to exercise control over the courts by deposing any judge whose performance was unsatisfactory.

The geonim exerted their greatest influence through their responsa. No body of law, even if written down, can possibly cover every conceivable situation and circumstance, and in such instances there must be a legal authority of some sort to search the law and issue a ruling. In Jewish communities wherever they were located, when cases arose on which the law was unclear, the presiding judge or rabbi sent a question, or *she'elah*, to one or the other of the geonim in Babylonia. The *gaon*'s answer, which cited all the relevant legal sources and provided a closely reasoned analysis of the case, is known as a *teshuvah*, or responsum.

The responsa dealt with many matters: marriage and divorce, business dealings of all kinds, civil law, kashrut, liturgy, interpretations of biblical texts. Of the vast number of responsa that must have been written in this period, around 10,000 have been preserved.

Beyond providing guidance in halakhah, the responsa had another important function. Because they came from a universally recognized central authority and provided precedents that were binding on all Jewish communities, they helped to unify the Jews of the far-flung Muslim Empire.

Jewish unity was further enhanced by the *yarhei kallah* (months of the kallah). On these yearly occasions, during Adar (the month before Pesah) and Elul (the month before Rosh Hashanah), there were massive gatherings at the yeshivot in Sura and Pumpedita. Those who attended would review the talmudic tractate that had been "assigned" to them at the previous *kallah* and the higher-level scholars would review and discuss questions that had been sent to the geonim since the previous *kallah*.

The Karaites

In the 8th century there arose a new Jewish group headed by a man named Anan ben David. Although his followers were at first called Ananites, within a century they came to be called Karaites, a term which reflects their reliance on the written text of the Bible as opposed to the rabbinic oral tradition embodied in the Talmud,

10

the *Torah she-b'al-peh*. Beyond this, little more can be said about
Anan, for the sources disagree about his character and his motives
for establishing a new sect. Some treat him as a sincere exponent
of the views he espoused, others as a disappointed and cynical
contender for the post of rosh golah.

In any event, Karaism spread rapidly for some decades, making
serious inroads in Jewish communities through the Middle East. It
was the great scholar Saadiah Gaon who finally turned the tide,
composing a work entitled *Refutation of Anan*. Saadiah made abundant use of his rhetorical gifts. He had an enormous sense of mission and of responsibility to the Jewish people beyond the borders
of Babylonia, viewing himself as the defender of Rabbinic Judaism;
thus he broadened and redefined the role of the geonate. One won-
ders what might have been the fate of the geonim and of the rabbinic tradition had Saadiah not stood ready to take on the Karaites.

Texts

Rabbi Natan ha-Bavli (1)

And from then on [i.e., after the new *rosh golah* is officially appointed by the caliph], he does not leave his house (to attend the
synagogue), and the people congregate and pray with him at all
times—whether on weekdays, Sabbaths, or festivals. And if he
wants to go out and pursue his needs, he rides in a viceregal carriage like the carriage of the king's ministers, in splendid clothes,
with up to fifteen people walking after him . . . and when he passes
a Jew they run up to him and seize him by the hand and implore
him, . . . until there are fifty or sixty gathered about him, until (he
reaches) his destination. . . . And he never goes out until he is
followed by his entire cohort, and his progress resembles that of
one of the king's ministers.

Brody, *The Geonim of Babylonia*, 74–75

Rabbi Natan ha-Bavli (2)

When the entire congregation is seated, the Exilarch emerges: . . .
the Gaon of Sura emerges after him and sits on the dais, after he
makes him a low obeisance, which he (the Exilarch) returns. After

him the *Gaon* of Pumpedita emerges and likewise bows to him and sits on his left, . . . the Exilarch in the middle, the *Gaon* of Sura sitting on his right and the *Gaon* of Pumpedita on his left. . . . Then the Exilarch delivers a sermon on the Torah portion of the day or permits the *Gaon* of Sura to deliver the sermon. And the *Gaon* of Sura offers permission to the *Gaon* of Pumpedita (to speak in his stead), and they honor each other, until the *Gaon* of Sura speaks.

Brody, The Geonim of Babylonia, 76

RABBI NATAN HA-BAVLI (3)

And when the head of the academy wants to examine them concerning their study texts (*girsa*), they gather around him in the four Sabbaths (i.e., weeks) of the month of Adar, and he sits and the first row recites before him, and the other rows sit silently. And when they reach a point which is obscure to them, they discuss it between themselves and the head of the academy listens to them and understands their words. Then he reads (?) and they are silent, and they know that he has understood their dispute. And when he finishes his reading, he recites and expounds the tractate which each of them recited at home during the winter and explains in the course of his exposition the point which the students have debated. And sometimes he asks them the explanation of laws . . . and expatiates to them on the meaning of each law, until all are clear to them. . . . Thus they did all the days of the month.

And on the fourth Sabbath, they call all the Sanhedrin and all the students, and the head of the academy examines each of them and investigates them until he sees which one is of quicker intelligence than his fellow. And when he sees one of them whose Talmud is not well ordered in his mouth, he deals harshly with him and reduces his stipend and rebukes and reprimands him, and informs him of the places where he has been lazy and negligent and warns him that if he does so again and fails to pay attention to his Talmud, he will be given nothing.

And this was their custom regarding responsa to questions: on each day of Adar he brings out to them all the questions which have arrived and gives them permission to respond. . . . Then each one speaks according to his understanding and wisdom, and they raise difficulties and resolve them and discuss each matter and analyze it thoroughly. And the head of the academy hears their words . . . and analyzes their words until the truth is clear to him and immediately orders the scribe to write in response. . . . And at the end of the month they read the responsa and questions in the presence of the entire fellowship and the head of the academy signs them, and then they are sent to their addressees. And then he divides the money among them.

Brody, The Geonim of Babylonia, 46

Saadiah Gaon, Refutation of Anan

Anan had a younger brother whose name was Hananiah. Now Anan was greater than his brother in knowledge of the Torah and older in years, but the scholars of that generation were not willing to set him up as exilarch because of the unmitigated unruliness and irreverence which characterized him. The sages, therefore, turned to Hananiah his brother because of his modesty, shyness, and fear of God, and made him exilarch. Then Anan became incensed, he and every scoundrel that was left of the Sadducean and Boethusian breed [sectaries of the latter days of the Second Temple], and he secretly determined to make a schism because he feared the government of that day. These heretics appointed Anan as their exilarch.

This matter was made known to the [Muslim] authorities on a Sunday and it was ordered that he be put into jail until Friday, when he was to be hanged, for he had rebelled against the government [in not accepting Hananiah, the caliph's appointee]. There, in the prison, he met a certain Muslim scholar [probably Abu Hanifa, d. 767], who was imprisoned, and was to be hanged also on that very Friday, for he had rebelled against the religion of Mohammed. The Moslem gave him a piece of advice, and this is what he said to him: "Are there not in the Torah commands which may permit of two interpretations?" Anan answered: "There certainly are." Then he said to him: "Take some point and interpret it differently from those who follow your brother Hananiah; only be sure your partisans agree to it, and don't fail also to give a bribe to the vizier. Perhaps he'll give you permission to speak. Then prostrate yourself and say: 'My lord King, have you appointed my brother over one religion or two?' And when he will answer you: 'Over one religion,' then say to him: 'But I and my brother rule over two different religions!' Then you'll surely be saved, if you'll only make clear to him the religious differences between your faith and the faith of your brother, and if your followers agree with you. Talk like this and when the king [al-Mansur, 754–775] hears these things, he'll keep quiet."

Through his sharp sophistry he taught them these things, and in order to save himself from violent death and to win a victory he spent a lot of money bribing his way until the king gave him permission to speak. Then he began saying: "The religion of my brother is dependent, in making the calendar, on astronomical calculation of the months and year, but my religion is dependent on the actual observation of the new moon and the signs of the ripening grain." Now since that king made his calculation, too, through actual observation of the new moon and the signs of the ripening grain, he was pacified and reconciled to Anan.

Marcus, *The Jew in the Medieval World*, 234–35

SAHL BEN MAZLIAH, *Tokhahat Megullah* ("An Open Rebuke")

This is to tell us that we are not bound to follow in the ways of our fathers in every respect, but we must reflect on their ways and compare their actions and their laws to the words of the Torah. If we see that the teachings of our fathers are exactly like the words of the Bible, then we must accept them and pay attention to them. We must follow them and dare not change them. But if the teachings of our fathers are different from the Bible, we must cast them out, and must ourselves seek and investigate and think about the commands of the Torah. That which is written in the Torah of Moses—peace be unto him—about the commandments and other things does not require any sign or witness to show us whether or not it is true; but that which our fathers have told us requires proof and a responsible witness so that one may determine if it is true or not, and only that law which is proved to us will we perform, for thus it is written: "Sow to yourselves according to righteousness, reap according to mercy" (Hosea 10:11).

14

And you, O House of Israel, have mercy on yourselves, and have compassion on your children. Behold the sun is rising and the light is shining! Choose the good way in which is found the living waters and walk therein. Do not walk in a dry and weary land where there is no water!

Do not say, how shall we do this? How can we follow the commandments if the Karaites themselves disagree? Which one of them shall we follow? [The answer is that] the Karaites do not say that they are leaders. They have made no arbitrary innovations to lead the people as they might like, but they investigate and examine the Torah of Moses and the books of the prophets—of blessed memory—and even look into the works of the sages of old.

Therefore they merely say to their Jewish brothers: "Learn, investigate, search, and inquire and do that which has been demonstrated to you through valid proof and which agrees with your reason." Do not say: "How is this possible?"; for this is what our Rock desires and wishes of us, and it is incumbent upon us to perform that commandment which becomes valid only through our understanding by proof and testimony, and not by arbitrary will.

Marcus, *The Jew in the Medieval World*, 234–35

Questions on the Texts

RABBI NATAN HA-BAVLI (1)

1. How does the day-to-day conduct of the newly appointed *rosh golah* reflect his status?
2. The exilarch conducts himself as if he were a member of the caliph's court. Why does he do this?

RABBI NATAN HA-BAVLI (2)

1. A public ceremony occurring on Shabbat marks the investiture of the *rosh golah*. Why do you think a public ceremony was used?
2. Both the *gaon* of Sura and the *gaon* of Pumpedita bow before the *rosh golah*. What is to be concluded from this part of the ceremony?

Rabbi Natan ha-Bavli (3)

1. During the fourth week of the *yarhei kallah*, the *gaon* would examine each student. What purpose was served by such examina-
tions?
2. Describe the procedure by which responses were formulated to
questions submitted to the *geonim*.

Saadiah Gaon, *Refutation of Anan*

1. How were Anan and Hananiah different? What led Anan to decide to form a new sect and to do so in secret?
2. What was Abu Hanifa's jailhouse advice to Anan?

Sahl ben Mazliah, *Tokhahat Megullah*

1. What is the fundamental principle of Karaism?
2. How might this principle be challenged? What is the response
offered in this selection? How would you respond to this challenge?

Paper Topics

Saadiah Gaon and the Challenge of Karaism
Karaite Halakhah
Anan and the Origins of Karaism
Saadiah Gaon and David ben Zakkai: a 10th-Century Power
    Struggle
The Exilarch and the Pact of 'Umar

Reference Works

R. Brody, *The Geonim of Babylonia and the Shaping of Medieval Jewish
    Culture*
Encyclopaedia Judaica, s.v. "Exilarch," "Gaon"
L. Nemoy, *Karaite Anthology*
N. Stillman, *The Jews of Arab Lands*

CULTURE

The geonim engaged in a variety of cultural pursuits. They were interested in grammar, in liturgy, in biblical study, in history, in philosophy. As we will see, the outstanding figure of this period in every area of culture was R. Saadiah Gaon, but others also made contributions.

Grammatical Study

Saadiah's contributions in the study of Hebrew grammar were numerous. He authored two major grammatical works. His *Sefer ha-Egron* was both a dictionary of Hebrew, important for those whose first language was Arabic, and a collection of rhymed word endings, a useful tool for poets writing in Hebrew. This book contains as well a history of the Hebrew language.

His other work in this area was the *Sefer Tzakhut ha-Lashon ha-Ivrit*. It is divided into 12 sections, each of which is devoted to one grammatical topic. Saadiah was the first to lay the foundations for the systematic study of Hebrew grammar.

Liturgy

In the domain of liturgy the trailblazer was R. Amram ben Sheshna, gaon of Sura from 846 to 861. R. Amram compiled the first *siddur tefillah* (prayer book). The Jews of Babylonia and of Palestine felt no urgent need for a siddur, as they had an uninterrupted continuous tradition which had kept alive the memory of the text and order of the prayers. The Jews of Western Europe had no such continuous tradition, however, and thus began to look to Sura and Pumpedita for liturgical guidance. R. Amram, who had been receiving many questions about tefillah from R. Isaac bar Shimon, head of the Barcelona community in Spain, decided that the time had come to answer all of R. Isaac's questions at once by compiling a siddur. This siddur would be accompanied by an outline of liturgical rules for the entire year.

Saadiah, who was gaon of Sura until his death in 942, also compiled a siddur, improving upon the efforts of R. Amram. He included his own piyyutim (liturgical poems), which were innova-

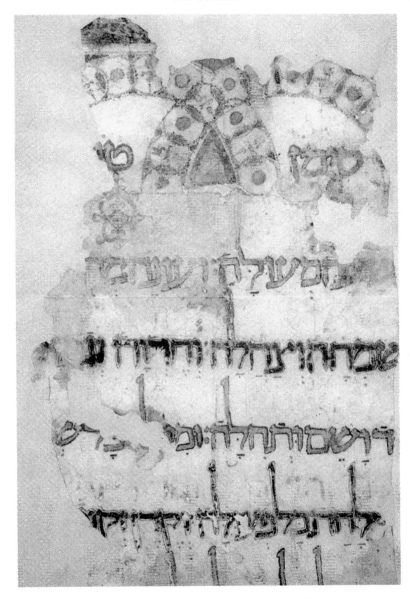

Ketubbah Fostat, Egypt 10–11th Centuries

tive in language, form, and content. These were so highly regarded that Maimonides was asked whether it was required to stand when reciting Saadiah's piyyutim. Saadiah's siddur became so valued that it is still used today by Yemenite Jews!

Bible Study

In Bible study Saadiah contributed the *Tafsir* ("Translation"), an Arabic rendering of the entire Tanakh, accompanied by a partial commentary. Saadiah's translation has had a very long life, for it is still the accepted Bible translation used by Arabic speakers.

Halakhah

The *She'iltot* ("Questions") is a collection of homilies authored by R. Ahai (680–752) of Shabha, which was located near the city of Basra in what is now southern Iraq. To be sure, it may seem odd to consider this work in a discussion of halakhah, but it includes much halakhah; its halakhic part is actually larger than its aggadic (non-halakhic) part. Moreover, those medieval rabbis who refer to it do so largely because of its halakhic content. It is also noteworthy that this book was the first post-Talmud work whose author is actually named.

The *She'iltot* consists of sermons delivered every Shabbat in the synagogues. Each *she'ilta* is divided into four parts. The first introduces the subject, speaks of the value of the commandments, and prepares for the question to be discussed. The second part is always introduced with the phrase "but it is necessary that you learn . . . ," followed by the question. The third part is the homily, which begins: "Praised be the Lord, who has given us the Torah and the commandments through our teacher Moses to instruct the people of Israel," with the preacher then proceeding from subject to subject. The fourth part is introduced by the formula "With respect to the question I have set before you . . . ," and then addresses the question posed in the second part.

Although the identity of its author or authors is uncertain, the late 8th or early 9th century produced a work known as the *Halakhot Pesukot*. Included in it are those areas of halakhah that were of practical import in its author(s)'s time: laws of prayer, Sabbath and festivals, family and commercial law. An attempt is made to identify the most important parts of the laws without entering into talmudic discussion and dialectic. In all likelihood, the text served as an early code of law.

The latter half of the 9th century saw the emergence of a second law code, the *Halakhot Gedolot*. Geonic and medieval rabbinic sources identify its author as R. Simeon Kayyara. We know little about him, however, beyond his being born in the city of Basra.

The *Halakhot Gedolot* provides a systematic, comprehensive summary of talmudic law. The halakhic positions it takes are based firmly on talmudic sources and on the principles of halakhah laid down by the rabbis. The Babylonian Talmud is the major source text, but use is made as well of the Jerusalem Talmud.

The *Halakhot Gedolot* is primarily a law code, but unlike the *Halakhot Pesukot*, it includes much more than this. It contains a significant amount of nonlegal material and halakhic material without practical importance in the geonic period. Among other things, for instance, it provides lists of prophets and of days on which voluntary fasts were undertaken. Other chapters deal with the Temple service and other matters that had no practical application after the destruction of the Second Temple.

Saadiah authored a number of short treatises on halakhic topics. One deals with inheritance law, another with buying and selling, another with the laws governing legal documents. He also wrote responsa. What is notable about them is that they are written in Arabic; Saadiah was the first to write responsa in Arabic.

History

The geonim also produced works of history. The most famous of these is *Iggeret Rav Sherira Gaon*, written in 986–87. Its author was Sherira Gaon, who headed the yeshiva at Pumpedita from 968 to 1106.

R. Jacob b. Nissim ibn Shahin, representing the North African community of Kairouan, had submitted a series of questions to R. Sherira, seeking some understanding of the evolution of the Mishnah and corpus of talmudic literature. He asked when and how the Mishnah, Tosefta, and the Talmud had been compiled, and also about the post-talmudic work of the geonim. These questions led Sherira to compose one of the classics of Jewish historical writing, an essay of almost 15,000 words that became a central source for the history of the geonim.

A second important historical work was authored by R. Natan ha-Bavli (10th cent.), a chronicler who probably lived in Baghdad; it is called *Akhbar Baghdad* ("History of Baghdad"). R. Natan's history is divided into two sections. The first deals with conflicts within the Babylonian leadership. He recounts, for example, the conflict, lasting from 909 to 916, between the exilarch Uqba and the gaon of Pumpedita, Kohen Zedeq. Likewise, he tells about the clash, sometime around 930, between the exilarch David ben Zakkai and the gaon of Sura, Saadiah Gaon.

The second section is itself divided in two. The first deals with the institution of the exilarch, and the second with the geonim and their academies. Our discussion of these subjects in the preceding units relied upon R. Natan ha-Bavli as a major source.

Philosophy

Saadiah Gaon wrote the first Jewish philosophical work, *Sefer Emunot ve-Deot* ("The Book of Beliefs and Opinions"). In the 10th century, Jews were confronted by two major challenges. The first of these was Karaism; Saadiah battled it in speech and in writing. The second was Greek philosophy; *Sefer Emunot ve-Deot* was directed toward this threat.

In the book's introduction Saadiah says that the Jews of his time have concluded that it is necessary to choose between Jewish tradition and Greek philosophy. Confused and misguided, they feel that they are facing an either-or situation: those who opt for Jewish tradition must reject the philosophical worldview, and those who opt for philosophy must reject Jewish tradition. As his book will show, however, says Saadiah, the two views can be reconciled.

Sefer Emunot ve-Deot deals with the key issues of Jewish philosophy: reason and revelation, divine providence, miracles, prophecy, evil, and the existence, unity, and incorporeality of God. It remains one of the classics of Jewish thought.

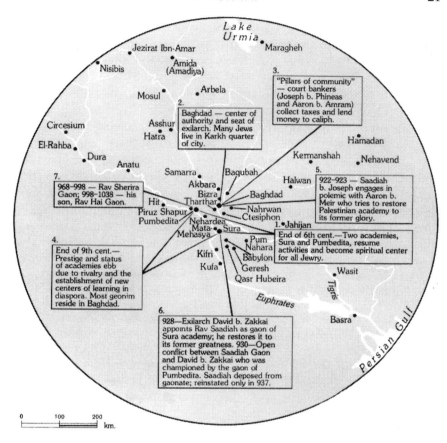

Map labels:

Lake Urmia

Jezirat Ibn-Amar
Amida (Amadiya)
Maragheh
Nisibis
Arbela
Mosul

2.
Baghdad — center of authority and seat of exilarch. Many Jews live in Karkh quarter of city.

3.
"Pillars of community" — court bankers (Joseph b. Phineas and Aaron b. Amram) collect taxes and lend money to caliph.

Circesium
Asshur
Hatra
El-Rahba
Dura
Anatu
Hamadan
Kermanshah
Nehavend

Samarra
Baqubah
Akbara
Bizra
Tharthar
Halwan
Baghdad

5.
922–923 — Saadiah b. Joseph engages in polemic with Aaron b. Meir who tries to restore Palestinian academy to its former glory.

7.
968–998 — Rav Sherira Gaon; 998–1038 — his son, Rav Hai Gaon.

Hit
Piruz Shapur
Pumbedita
Nehardea
Mata-Mehasya
Sura
Nahrwan
Ctesiphon
Jahijan

1.
End of 6th cent.—Two academies, Sura and Pumbedita, resume activities and become spiritual center for all Jewry.

4.
End of 9th cent.— Prestige and status of academies ebb due to rivalry and the establishment of new centers of learning in diaspora. Most geonim reside in Baghdad.

Kifri
Kufa
Pum Nahara
Babylon
Geresh
Qasr Hubeira
Wasit

Euphrates
Tigris

Basra
Persian Gulf

6.
928—Exilarch David b. Zakkai appoints Rav Saadiah as gaon of Sura academy; he restores it to its former greatness. 930—Open conflict between Saadiah Gaon and David b. Zakkai who was championed by the gaon of Pumbedita. Saadiah deposed from gaonate; reinstated only in 937.

0   100   200
km.

The Geonate in Babylonia

Texts

RESPONSUM OF AMRAM GAON

Amram ben Sheshna, head of the Academy in the city of Sura, to Rabbi Isaac, son of the Master and Rabbi Simeon, who is beloved and esteemed by our whole school . . .

R. Jacob son of R. Isaac, sent us the ten ducats which you have offered to the Academy; five for us, and five for the treasury of the Academy. We have ordered a blessing to be said for you; may it be fulfilled upon you and upon your children and posterity. As regards the arrangement of the prayers and blessings you have asked for, we have composed it according to the extant tradition, on the authority of the Tannaim and Amoraim, as Heaven has enlightened us. For the Talmud says: "R. Meir declares that we are obliged to utter a hundred blessings daily." David was the first who prescribed them: when he was informed that a hundred people died in Jerusalem daily, he ordered these prayers. It seems, however, that they were forgotten in the course of time and that the Tannaim and Amoraim were obliged to renew them. R. Natronai bar Hilai, head of Sura, sent the following responsum concerning them to the community of Lucena through R. Joseph: Each of these blessings cannot be said [in the morning when we get up] at the proper moment because our hands are also busy with impure matters. We have, therefore, to wash our face, hands, and feet first, as it is said: "Prepare to meet thy God, O Israel" (Amos 4:12). Afterwards every Israelite is bound to recite them simultaneously. In Spain a custom is established for the reader to recite these blessings in order to represent thus the ignorant people at the same time.

Kobler, *Letters of Jews Through the Ages*, 1:75–77

SHALOM BAR BOAZ GAON TO AN INQUIRER

You ask: what is the rule concerning the robbery of non-Jewish property? Is such a robbery prohibited exclusively as a profanation of the Holy Name?

This is our decision: The prohibition of robbery has no reference to the profanation of the Holy Name. For it is a halakhah that all robbery whatsoever of non-Jewish property is forbidden. The profanation of the Holy Name is discussed only with respect to lost property. R. Pinhas ben Jair said: It is not permitted to appropriate even the lost property of non-Jews, since it leads to a profanation of the Holy Name. In the story related of R. Ashi that once, when traveling, he sent for a grape grown in the garden of a non-Jew, this is certainly to be understood for payment and in the certain assurance that the grapes were offered for sale. Far be the idea that such a man as Rabbi Ashi committed any falsehood or fraud, he who declared it as a principle that one must not cause an untrue opinion in anybody, Jew or non-Jew.

Kobler, *Letters of Jews Through the Ages*, 1:72

SAADIAH GAON, FOREWORD TO HIS TRANSLATION OF THE TANAKH

I only composed this book because a petitioner asked me to isolate the simple meaning of the Torah text in a separate work, containing nothing of the discussions of language . . . [or] of the questions of the heretics, or of their refutations; or of the "branches" of the rational commandments or the mode of performance of the revealed ones; but extracting the matters of the Torah text alone. And I saw that what he had requested [that I do] concerning this would be advantageous, in order that the audience might hear the matters of the Torah regarding narrative and command concisely, and the labor of someone seeking a particular story would not be protracted because of the admixture of demonstrations of every aspect which would be burdensome. [And if] he later wants to investigate the legislation of the rational commandments and the mode of performance of the revealed ones, and the refutation of the claims of those who attack the biblical stories, let him seek it in the other book [i.e., the commentary]. . . . And when I saw this I composed this book, the *tafsir* of the simple meaning of the Torah text alone, clarified by knowledge of the intellect and the tradition; and when I was able to add a word or a letter which would make the desired intention clear . . . I did so.

Brody, *The Geonim of Babylonia*, 302–3

SAADIAH GAON, *Sefer Emunot ve-Deot* (1)

Having completed the inquiry with which we were first concerned, it is desirable that we should now mention the sources of truth and certainty, which are the origin of all knowledge and the fountain of all cognition. We shall discuss the matter so far as it has a bearing on the subject of this book. We affirm then that there exist three sources of knowledge: the knowledge given by sense perception; the knowledge given by reason; inferential knowledge. We proceed now to give an explanation of each of these Roots.

By the knowledge of sense perception we understand that which a man perceives by one of the five senses, i.e., sight, hearing, smell, taste, and touch. By the knowledge of reason we understand that which is derived purely from the mind, such as the approval of truth and the disapproval of falsehood. By inferential knowledge we understand a proposition obtained from reason or sense perception. Where there is no way of denying these propositions, the previous proposition must of necessity be accepted. For example, we are compelled to admit that man possesses a soul, although we do not perceive it by our senses, so as not to deny its obvious functions. Similarly, we are compelled to admit that the soul is endowed with reason, although we do not perceive it by our senses, so as not to deny its [reason's] obvious function.

. . . but we, the Congregation of the Believers in the Unity of God, accept the truth of all the three sources of knowledge, and we add a fourth source, which we derive from the three preceding ones, and which has become a Root of Knowledge for us, namely, the truth of reliable Tradition. . . .

Scripture already declares that reliable tradition is as true as the things perceived by sight. Thus it says, "For pass over the isles of the Kittites, and see, and send unto Kedar, and consider diligently" (Jeremiah 2:10). Why does it add the words "and consider diligently" in connection with the matter of report? The answer is: because a report [tradition] is, unlike sense perception, liable to be falsified in two ways, either through a wrong idea or through willful distortion. For this reason Scripture warns, "and consider diligently." Having considered deeply how we can have faith in tradition, seeing that there are these two ways [of possible falsification] I found, by way of reason, that wrong idea and willful distortion can only occur and remain unnoticed if they emanate from individuals, whereas, in a large collective group, the underlying ideas of the individuals who compose it will never be in agreement with one another, and if they willfully decide and agree on inventing a story, this will not remain unnoticed among their people, but whenever their story is put out, there will be related, at the same time, the story of how they came to agree upon it. And when a tradition is safe against these two possibilities [of falsification], there is no third way in which it could possibly be falsified. And if the Tradition of our Fathers is viewed from the aspect of these principles, it will appear sound and safe against any attack, and true, and firmly established.

Altmann, *Three Jewish Philosophers*, 36–37, 110–11

SAADIAH GAON, *Sefer Emunot ve-Deot* (2)

I must further explain that man does not perform any action unless he chooses to do it, since it is impossible for one to act if he has no free will or fails to exercise his free will. The fact that the Law does not prescribe punishment for one who commits an illicit act unintentionally is not because he has no free will, but because of his ignorance of the cause and effect of his particular action. Thus, we say of one who killed a person unintentionally that, for instance, the hewing of the wood was done intentionally and with his free will, whereas his failure to prevent the accident was unintentional. Or to quote the case of one who has desecrated the Sabbath, the gathering of the sticks may have been intentional, but the person forgot that particular day was the Sabbath.

Having dealt with all these points, I maintain further that the Creator (be he exalted) does not allow His power to interfere in the least with the actions of men, nor does He compel them to be either obedient or disobedient. I have proofs for this doctrine founded on sense perception, reason, Scripture and tradition.

In regard to sense perception, I have found that a man observes from his own experience that he has the power to speak and be silent, the power to seize a thing and to abandon it; he does not notice any other force that would hinder him in any way from exercising his willpower. The simple truth is that he directs the impulses of his nature by his reason, and if he follows the bidding of reason, he is prudent; if he does not, he is a fool.

As to the proof based on reason, our previous arguments have already shown how untenable is the idea that one action can be attributed to two agents. Now one who thinks that the Creator (be He exalted and glorified) interferes with the actions of men, does in fact ascribe one single action to God and man together. Furthermore, if God used compulsion against man, there would be no sense in His giving him commandments and prohibitions. Moreover, if he compelled him to do a certain action, it would be inadmissible to punish him for it. In addition, if men acted under compulsion, it would be necessary to mete out reward to believers and infidels alike, since each of them did only what he was ordered to do. If a wise man employs two workmen, the one that he may build, the other that he may destroy, it is his duty to pay wages to both. Moreover, it is impossible to assume that man acts under compulsion, for if this were the case, he would have to be excused, since one knows that man is unable to prevail against the power of God, and if the infidel offered the excuse that it was not within his power to believe in God, it would be necessary to consider him as justified and to accept his excuse.

As to the proofs based on Scripture, we have already mentioned the verse, "Therefore choose life" (Deuteronomy 30:19). . . .

As to the proofs based on tradition, our ancient teachers have told us, "Everything lies in the hands of God except the fear of God." . . .

Perhaps someone will ask further: "If God knows that which is going to be before it comes into being, He knows in advance if a certain person will disobey him; now that person must by necessity disobey God, for otherwise God's foreknowledge would not prove to be correct." The fallacy underlying this question is even more evident than that underlying the previous one. It is this: He who makes this assertion has no proof that the knowledge of the Creator concerning things is the cause of their existence. He merely imagines this to be so, or he chooses to believe it. The fallacy of this assumption becomes quite clear when we consider that if God's knowledge of things were the cause of their existence, they would have existed from eternity, since God's knowledge of them is eternal. We do, however, believe that God knows things as they exist in reality, i.e., of those things which He creates, He knows in advance that He is going to create them, and of those things which are subject to man's free will He knows in advance that man is going to choose them. Should one object, "If God knows that a certain person will speak, is it possible for that person to be silent," we answer quite simply that if that person was to keep silent instead of speaking we should have said in our original statement that God knew that this man would be silent, and we were not entitled to state that God knew that this person would speak. For God knows man's ultimate action such as it will be whether sooner or later after all his planning; it is exactly the thing that God knows, as it is said, "The Lord knoweth the thoughts of man" (Psalms 94:11), and furthermore, "For I know their inclination how they do even now" (Deuteronomy 31:21).

Altmann, *Three Jewish Philosophers*, 119–21, 122–23

Babylonia, Eretz Yisrael and the Diaspora

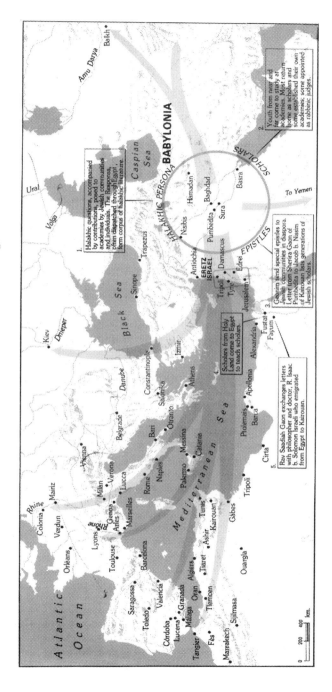

1. Halakhic questions, accompanied by contributions, posed to academies by Jewish communities and individuals. The Responsa, often dispatched through Egypt, form corpus of halakhic literature.

2. Youth from near and far come to study of academies. Most return home as scholars and some established their own academies; some appointed as rabbinic judges.

3. Geonim send special epistles to Jewish communities in diaspora. Letter from Sherira Gaon of Pumbedita to Jacob b. Nissim of Kairouan lists generations of Jewish scholars.

4. Scholars from Holy Land come to Egypt to teach scholars.

5. Rav Saadiah Gaon exchanges letters with philosopher and doctor, R. Isaac b. Solomon Israeli who emigrated from Egypt to Kairouan.

SCHOLARS

EPISTLES

HALAKHIC PERSONA

BABYLONIA

ERETZ ISRAEL

To Yemen

Atlantic Ocean

Mediterranean Sea

Black Sea

Caspian Sea

Amu Darya

Ural

Volga

Dnieper

Danube

Rhine

Rhône

0 200 400 km.

Questions on the Texts

RESPONSUM OF AMRAM GAON

1. On what basis does Amram draw his conclusions? Didn't Jews engage in tefillah (prayer) before the time of the tannaim (1st— 3rd cent. C.E.) and amoraim (3rd—6th cent.)?
2. How did the custom of Lucena, Italy, differ from that of Spain?
3. What conclusions may be drawn from this responsum regarding the sources of religious authority for the Jews during the geonic period?

RESPONSUM OF SHALOM BAR BOAZ GAON

1. How are the halakhot governing robbery and lost property different? The same?
2. What lesson can be derived from the story of R. Ashi?
3. How does the question posed here shed some light on the Jews' everyday life in the Muslim world?

SAADIAH GAON, foreword to Tanakh translation

1. Saadiah writes here that he is responding to a request that he focus on the Torah text alone. What would be the goal of this effort?
2. What was the purpose of the commentary?
3. Saadiah wrote both a siddur (prayer book) and a Tanakh translation with commentary (which is still in use today). What does this tell you about Jewish cultural literacy during the geonic period?

SAADIAH GAON, *Sefer Emunot ve-Deot* (1)

1. What does Saadiah mean by "inferential knowledge"? How does our belief in the soul clarify the meaning of this concept?
2. How does Saadiah think traditions should be evaluated and thereby established as reliable or unreliable?

SAADIAH GAON, *Sefer Emunot ve-Deot* (2)

1. Saadiah argues for free will on the basis of reason. What arguments does he use?

2. "If God knows what I will do, how can it be assumed that I actually have free will?" How would Saadiah respond to this question?

Paper Topics

Iggeret Rav Sherira Gaon: A History of the Oral Law
Sefer Emunot ve-Deot : Some Themes/Topics of this Work
The Siddur of Saadiah Gaon and the Siddur of Today: Similarities and Differences
The Cairo Genizah as Source on the Geonim
Saadiah and Freedom of the Will
Babylonian Talmud or Jerusalem Talmud: Which Became More Authoritative and Why?

Reference Works

J. D. Bleich, *With Perfect Faith*
R. Brody, *The Geonim of Babylonia and the Shaping of Medieval Jewish Culture*
Encyclopaedia Judaica, s.v. "Aha," "Amram Gaon," "Saadiah Gaon"
C. Sirat, *A History of Jewish Philosophy in the Middle Ages*

MUHAMMAD, ISLAM, AND THE JEWS

A New Religion

The 7th century presented the Jews of the Arabian Peninsula with a new challenge: the Muslim religion. Jews had lived in Arabia for centuries before the appearance of Muhammad—perhaps even as early as the biblical period. By the time of Muhammad's birth in 571, the Jews of Arabia were numerous and integrated fully into the life and culture of the peninsula. They supported themselves by date-growing, caravan commerce, and crafts. They spoke Arabic, were organized into clans and tribes, and had absorbed many of the values of desert society.

Nonetheless, the Jews of Arabia were a separate group with their own distinctive customs and characteristics. Arab poets of the pre-Islam period described the curious Jewish customs they had observed, and the holy book of the Muslims, the Qur'an, makes frequent mention of such Jewish practices as Shabbat and kashrut (the dietary laws). Many pagan Arabs seem to have been acquainted with some of the religious ideas and ethical notions of Judaism. The Jews, then, held fast to their own identity.

Then came Muhammad ibn 'Abd Allah, a member of the Hashemite clan of the tribe of Quraysh. Muhammad was born in Mecca, which was a major center of commerce and trade. As a merchant, he encountered Jews and Christians in his travels through Syria in the north, through northeastern Arabia, through Yemen in the south. The merchants with whom Muhammad had contact preached the moral and ethical essentials of monotheism. They spoke of what the One God expected of men. They spoke of God rewarding the righteous and punishing the sinner. They spoke of the sins of thievery, of murder, of adultery, of oppressing the widow and the orphan. They spoke of the obligation to maintain fair weights and measures, to be honest in business.

The world of the Arabs was very receptive to such messages. Paganism was no longer satisfying. Although the Arabs were interested in the message of monotheism, they were not inclined to become Jews or Christians. Muhammad, too, heard the message of monotheism. He came to believe that there was only one God, but became convinced that the one God had revealed His message to different cultures at different times in their own languages. This led him to wonder why God, in His infinite mercy, had never revealed His teachings to the Arab people, thus leaving them in ignorance. How might the Arab people gain access to God's teachings in their own language?

Muhammad spent much time in meditation and in night vigils. According to Muslim tradition, one such vigil, on a lonely mountainside outside Mecca, brought a revelation from God: he, Muhammad, had been chosen to bring God's teachings to his people. Although somewhat taken aback, Muhammad eventually became convinced that God—Allah—had spoken to him through the angel Gabriel and was revealing His message in clear Arabic. Historians believe that it was Muhammad's dissatisfaction with pagan idolatry combined with his contacts with Jews and Christians that brought him to monotheism.

Muhammad began to reach out to others. He began with the

members of his family. His wife, Khadija, his adopted son, Zayd ibn Haritha, and his cousin 'Ali were the first converts to Islam. He then began to preach to the people of Mecca. Although he met with some success, most of the Meccans rejected and ridiculed Muhammad; some simply ignored him, while others persecuted him.

In September 622, Muhammad and some 200 followers left Mecca and went to the city of Yathrib, also called Medina, located about 250 miles to the north. This event, known as the Hijra (Emigration), is regarded as a major moment in the history of Islam, so significant that it became the opening date of the Muslim calendar.

Muhammad was warmly received in Medina. Several residents had already accepted his teachings and began to urge others to do so as well. Soon after his arrival, seventy-five accepted Islam and swore allegiance to its prophet, Muhammad. They committed themselves to defend him as one of their own. The new religion now began to spread, and within two years time, the Meccans, who had rejected Muhammad earlier, embraced him instead.

Qur'an, Hadith, Sunna

The Qur'an ("Recital") is the Holy Scripture of Islam. Muslims believe that it was revealed to Muhammad, part by part, between 610 and his death in 632. It consists of 114 suras, or chapters, arranged in order of length.

The Qur'an is the source of Islamic belief and a guide for the life of the believer. It includes commandments about prayer, charity, marriage and divorce, children and inheritance, lawful foods, spoils of war, and many other matters; thus it contains the Islamic religious, social, civil, commercial, military, and legal code. The Qur'an teaches that there is only one God and one true religion; that all humans will undergo a final judgment in which the just will be rewarded with eternal bliss and the sinners punished; and that when men turned from truth, God sent prophets to lead the way back. Among these were Moses and Jesus, but Muhammad is the last and greatest of God's true prophets. Thus, by giving primary status to Moses or Jesus, respectively, and refusing to accept Muhammad, Jews and Christians misread their holy books and are misguided. Allah provided the Qur'an to communicate correct teachings.

The Hadith ("Story, Narration") is a body of oral tradition providing information about what Muhammad said, did, and approved or disapproved. These stories, which supplement the Qur'an with information about matters that it does not deal with or does not deal with at length, make their first appearance between 680 and 700. So many of these traditions existed by the middle of the 9th century that it became necessary to collect, sift, and systematize them. This task was left for eminent scholars to carry out, based in part on their judgment as to the reliability of the members of the chain of transmission that handed down the hadith and of the person with whom each story originated. Their efforts produced six approved collections, which came to be known as The Six Genuine Ones.

The Sunna, or "trodden path," of Muhammad—the way he conducted himself in life, as learned from the Hadith—serves as a model for Muslim believers. It establishes a religious norm of practice and right living which they strive to use as a model. After the death of Muhammad, the Sunna came to encompass both the living tradition of the first Muslim generation after Muhammad and the deductions drawn after them from their conduct; these three elements came together as the Sunna of the Prophet.

The Five Pillars

The duties of the Muslim are known as the Five Pillars. The first of these is the profession of faith. A Muslim is obligated to say once in his life the following: "There is no God except Allah; Muhammad is the messenger of Allah." The prevailing conception is that this profession of faith suffices on its own, but Muslim scholars have concluded that six conditions must be met for this to be the case: (1) it must be said aloud; (2) it must be perfectly understood; (3) it must be believed in the heart; (4) it must be professed until death; (5) it must be recited correctly; and (6) it must be professed and declared without hesitation. This profession of faith is also used in the call to prayer.

The second of the Muslim's duties is prayer. The formal, ritualized prayer is the *salat*, while the less formal, more extemporaneous prayer, the spontaneous outpouring of the soul, is the *du'a*. Five prayer times are prescribed: dawn, midday, afternoon, evening, and night. Each prayer may be said privately or in a congregation; if in a congregation, there is a prayer leader who directs. Prayer on Fridays, the Sabbath day of Muslims, takes place in the mosque.

Prayer must be preceded by ritual purification of both person and place. After this preparation a standard ritual is followed: ascriptions of praise and glory to Allah, recitations of passages from the Qur'an, formulas of prayer, bowing and prostration. Once this ritual has been completed, the individual is permitted to make spontaneous personal petitions, followed by more ritual formulas and actions. The prayer service is then complete.

The third Muslim duty is charity. Muslims are obligated to set aside 2.5 percent of their income for charity. These monies are used primarily to support the poor. They serve other needs as well, such as the supply of funds needed to redeem captives or to maintain public facilities.

The fourth duty is fasting. Muslims fast during Ramadan, the ninth month of the year, the month during which they believe the Qur'an was revealed. (The Muslim calendar is a lunar one, so Ramadan rotates through the various seasons of the solar year.) On each day of Ramadan, Muslims may not eat, drink, or have marital relations; each night, when the daily fast obligation is complete, eating and drinking may be resumed and Muslim communities engage in celebration.

The fifth pillar is pilgrimage (*Hajj*). The pilgrimage is to Mecca and takes place at the beginning of the twelfth month of the Muslim calendar. Every Muslim who is able to do so is required to make the pilgrimage at least once in his lifetime. The pilgrims who go to Mecca at this time begin by visiting the central shrine and then move around to other holy places inside and outside the city. At the central shrine they walk around the Ka'aba (cube), located at its center, and kiss the black stone, located at one corner of the Ka'aba. Only a small number of Muslims actually go on the pilgrimage, since the majority cannot meet the fourth of the four requirements of being free, Muslim, of age, and able; they are excused from the pilgrimage for this reason. He who goes on a pilgrimage to Mecca earns thereby the right to be called *Hajji*.

Some groups of Muslims add a sixth pillar, jihad (holy war), although most see this as mandatory without being a pillar. Muslims believe that the world has two parts. The first of these is the House of Islam; the second is the House of Warfare. Muslims are obligated to fight until those in the second part choose conversion or submit to Muslim rule. This battle is a holy war, in which all are obligated to participate; those who fall are assured a place in Paradise.

Muhammad and the Jews

Muhammad expected that the Jews would accept him as a prophet even greater than Moses. He was certainly a monotheist. His new religion had strong similarities to Judaism. It emphasized prayer rather than sacrifices; it stressed the desirability of a moral and ethical life similar to that of Jews and Christians; it was other-worldly, interested in the afterlife; it had a generally positive atti-tude toward the Bible and asserted that the Jewish prophets were indeed true prophets.

The Jews, though, did not accept Islam. They were simply un-convinced by Muhammad's claims to prophecy. They saw Islam as far too different from Judaism. Moreover, Muhammad was not sufficiently knowledgeable about the Bible and Jewish religious thought; indeed he was illiterate! Learned Jews made mincemeat of him and of his ignorance. In addition, although he preached morality, his own personal life was severely lacking in this area.

Muhammad's failure to draw the Jews to him led him to a new approach: coercion. Utterly convinced that his teachings were true, he felt that whatever the Jews were using to contradict them must of necessity be false.

Three tribes of Jews lived in the vicinity of Medina: the Banu Qaynuqa', the Banu 'l-Nadir, and the Banu Qurayza. The Banu Qaynuqa', who were mainly craftsmen and artisans, were the weakest of the three militarily; they surrendered to the Muslims unconditionally. Their property was seized and they were forced to flee, ending up in Syria. The mercies of the Muslims spared their lives.

The Banu 'l-Nadir were next. They were wealthy and occupied some of the finest property in Medina; the Muslims, by contrast, were experiencing severe financial stress. Looking for a pretext, Muhammad accused the Banu 'l-Nadir of plotting to kill him; they were told to leave Medina if they valued their lives. At first they were inclined to resist the decree of eviction and were ready to do battle, but instead they surrendered on condition that they could take all movable goods with them except weapons. Leaving Medina, they traveled to the Jewish oasis of Khaybar and settled there.

The only tribe that remained was the Banu Qurayza. The battle between Mecca and Medina in 627 demanded a show of loyalty to Medina; accordingly the Banu Qurayza provided spades, picks, and baskets for the construction of a defensive trench. While the battle was going on, however, they remained in their forts in a state of armed neutrality. Meanwhile they were approached by the Meccans, who sought to win them over. Although they did not join the Meccans, the loyalty of Banu Qurayza to Medina became suspect, and thus Muhammad turned his attention to them.

Banu Qurayza held firm for 25 days, but soon it became apparent that there was no hope. They offered to surrender on the same terms as Banu 'l-Nadir, but Muhammad felt the need to make an example of them. The adult males were condemned to death, and the women and children to slavery. Between 600 and 900 males were beheaded in the central marketplace of Medina.

There were still Jews living in Khaybar, most of them Banu 'l-Nadir. Muhammad turned his attention to them in May 628, engaging them in all-out war. The Jews fiercely resisted their Muslim opponents, forcing the latter to fight from fortress to fortress, but the Muslims prevailed. Some of the Khaybar Jews were able to settle with the Muslims; their personal safety and their homes and property were to be spared, in exchange for one-half of their annual date harvest. The Banu 'l-Nadir, however, were given no chance to make such a deal.

Islam and the Jews after Muhammad

Within one century virtually the entire Near East came under Muslim rule. Just fifteen years after Muhammad's death, the two great powers of the time, the Byzantine and Sassanian empires, were defeated by the Muslim armies, overrunning the Sassanian territories in Mesopotamia and Persia and the Byzantine territories in Asia Minor, Syria, Egypt, and Palestine. By 711 the Muslims had conquered North Africa and reached as far west as Spain, taking it from the Christian Visigoths, with much assistance from the Jews. They were on the verge of conquering France but were defeated in battle at Tours by Charles Martel, prince of the Franks. In the east the Islamic world extended as far as Pakistan, India, and Indonesia; it also included the huge area, until recently part of the Soviet Union, from the Caspian Sea to Afghanistan and China.

The enormous military successes of the Muslims made them a minority in the territories they had conquered, at least temporarily, and presented them with the problem of how to deal with their non-Muslim Jewish subjects. Their answer was the famous Pact of 'Umar.

The Qur'an had spoken about Jews and Christians as the People of the Book:

> Fight against those to whom the Scriptures were given, who believe not in Allah nor the Last Day, who forbid not what Allah and His Apostle have forbidden and follow not the true faith, until they pay the tribute out of hand and are humbled.

Jews (and Christians), it was concluded on the basis of this and similar texts, should be required to pay a poll tax and a land tax. They were, as well, to be humbled, treated as second-class citizens.

The Pact of 'Umar, attributed to Caliph 'Umar ibn al-Khattab (ruled 634–44), demanded more than this. 'Umar had defeated a community of Christians in Syria and had extended to them the terms of surrender. The Christians were promised protection of life and property, as well as the right to worship freely, in return for their payment of the poll and land taxes.

Christians were to conduct themselves as a subject population. They were never to strike a Muslim, nor were they to carry arms, ride horses, or use normal saddles on their mounts. They were not to build new houses of worship nor repair old ones. They were not to hold public religious processions (including funeral processions), nor pray too loudly. They were not to proselytize. They had to wear clothing that differentiated them from Muslims. As Muslims began to dress in accord with the fashion trends of the time, Jews and Christians had to wear special identifying badges.

The Pact of 'Umar became the prototype for Muslim relations with Jews and Christians, who were called dhimmis ("protected people"). As Muslims began to settle permanently in conquered regions, new provisions were added to the Pact. Jews and Christians were forbidden to build homes higher than Muslim homes, to have Arab names, to teach the Qur'an to their children, and to sell fermented beverages.

Texts

THE QUR'AN ON THE JEWS

O you who believe! Take not the Jews and the Christians as friends. They are friends to one another. Whoever of you befriends them is one of them. Allah does not guide the people who do evil.

Qur'an, Sura 5:51

There is to be no compulsion in religion. Rectitude has been clearly distinguished from error. So whoever disbelieves in idols and believes in Allah has taken hold of the firmest handle. It cannot split. Allah is All-hearing and All-knowing.

Qur'an, Sura 2:256

Have you not seen those who have received a portion of the Scripture? They purchase error and they want you to go astray from the path. But Allah knows best who your enemies are and it is sufficient to have Allah as a helper.

Some of the Jews pervert words from their meanings and say, "We hear and we disobey," and "Heed us!" twisting with their tongues and slandering religion. If they had said, "We have heard and obey," or "Hear and observe us," it would have been better for them and more upright. But Allah had cursed them for their disbelief, so they believe not, except for a few.

Qur'an, Sura 4:44–46

And for the evildoing of the Jews, We have forbidden them some good things that were previously permitted them, and because of their barring many from Allah's way, and for their taking usury which was prohibited for them, and because of their consuming people's wealth under false pretense. We have prepared for the unbelievers among them a painful punishment.

Qur'an, Sura 4:160–61

The Jews say, "Ezra is the son of Allah," and the Christians say, "The Messiah [Jesus] is the son of Allah." Those are the words of their mouths, conforming to the words of the unbelievers before them. Allah attack them! How perverse they are!

They have taken their rabbis and their monks as lords besides Allah, and so to the Messiah son of Mary, though they were commanded to serve but one God. There is no God but He. Allah is exalted above that which they deify beside Him.

Qur'an, Sura 9:30–31

Indeed you will surely find that the most vehement of men in enmity to those who believe are the Jews and the polytheists. But you will also surely find that the closest of them in love to those who believe are those who say, "We are Christians." That is because there are among them priests and monks, and because they are not arrogant.

Qur'an, Sura 5:82

THE PACT OF 'UMAR

'Abd al-Rahman b. Ghanam related the following: When 'Umar b. al-Khattab—may Allah be pleased with him—made peace with the Christian inhabitants of Syria, we wrote him the following.

In the name of Allah, the Merciful, the Beneficent.

This letter is addressed to Allah's servant 'Umar, the Commander of the Faithful, by the Christians of such-and-such a city. When you advanced against us, we asked you for a guarantee of protection for our persons, our offspring, our property, and the people of our sect, and we have taken upon ourselves the following obligations toward you, namely:

We shall not build in our cities or in their vicinity any new monasteries, churches, hermitages, or monks' cells. We shall not restore, by night or by day, any of them that have fallen into ruin or which are located in the Muslims' quarters.

We shall keep our gates wide open for passersby and travelers. We shall provide three days' food and lodging to any Muslims who pass our way.

We shall not shelter any spy in our churches or in our homes, nor shall we hide him from the Muslims.

We shall not teach our children the Qur'an.

We shall not hold public religious ceremonies. We shall not seek to proselytize anyone. We shall not prevent any of our kin from embracing Islam if they so desire.

We shall show deference to the Muslims and shall rise from our seats when they wish to sit down.

We shall not attempt to resemble the Muslims in any way with regard to their dress, as for example, with the *qalansuwa* (conical cap), the turban, sandals, or parting the hair (in the Arab fashion). We shall not speak as they do, nor shall we adopt their *kunyas* (special name form used by Muslims).

We shall not ride on saddles.

We shall not wear swords or bear weapons of any kind, or ever carry them with us.

We shall not engrave our signets in Arabic.

We shall not sell wines.

We shall clip the forelocks of our head.

We shall always adorn ourselves in our traditional fashion. We shall bind the *zunnar* (a type of belt) around our waists.

We shall not display our crosses or our books anywhere in the Muslims' thoroughfares or in their marketplaces. We shall only beat our clappers in our churches very quietly. We shall not raise our voices when reciting the service in our churches, nor when in the presence of Muslims. Neither shall we raise our voices in our funeral processions.

We shall not display lights in any of the Muslim thoroughfares or in their marketplaces.

We shall not come near them with our funeral processions.

We shall not take any of the slaves that have been allotted to the Muslims.

We shall not build our homes higher than theirs.

(When I brought the letter to 'Umar—may Allah be pleased with him—he added the clause "We shall not strike any Muslim.")

We accept these conditions for ourselves and for the members of our sect, in return for which we are to be given a guarantee of security. Should we violate in any way these conditions which we have accepted and for which we stand, then there shall be no covenant of protection for us, and we shall be liable to the penalties for rebelliousness and sedition.

Then 'Umar—may Allah be pleased with him—wrote: "Sign what they have requested, but add two clauses that will also be binding upon them: namely, they shall not buy anyone who has been taken prisoner by the Muslims, and that anyone who deliberately strikes a Muslim will forfeit the protection of this pact."

Stillman, *The Jews of Arab Lands*, 157–58

THE AFFAIR OF THE BANU QAYNUQA'

Meanwhile the affair of the Banu Qaynuqa' took place. It is considered one of the military exploits of the Apostle of Allah—may Allah bless him and grant him peace. This is the story.

The Apostle of Allah—may Allah bless him and grant him peace—assembled them in the market of Qaynuqa'. Then he said to them, "O Jews, beware lest Allah bring down upon you vengeance like that which has descended upon the Quraysh. Accept Islam, for you know that I am a prophet who has been sent. You will find that in your scriptures and Allah's covenant with you."

"O Muhammad," they replied, "you seem to think that we are your people. Do not delude yourself because you have till now encountered people with no knowledge of war and thus have gained advantage over them. By Allah, if we should go to war with you, you will surely learn that we are men!"

Ibn Ishaq continued: "Asim b. 'Umar b. Qatada informed me that the Banu Qaynuqa' were the first Jews who violated the agreement between them and the Apostle of Allah—may Allah bless him and grant him peace, and they went to war with him between Badr and Uhud.

Ibn Hisham adds: 'Abd Allah b. Jafar b. al-Miswar b. Makhrima mentioned on the authority of Abu 'Awn that the cause of the Qaynuqa' affair was that an Arab woman had come with some merchandise to the market of the Banu Qaynuqa'. She sat down next to a goldsmith there. Then they began urging her to unveil her

face, which she refused. The goldsmith moved close to the hem of
her garment and tied it behind her back. When she got up her
privities were exposed. They laughed at her and she screamed.
Then a Muslim jumped upon the goldsmith who was Jewish and
killed him. Then the Jews overwhelmed the Muslim and killed
him. The family of the slain Muslim called upon their co-religion-
ists for help against the Jews. The Muslims were furious and thus
there was bad blood created between them and the Banu Qaynuqa'.

(Ibn Izhaq's narrative now continues:) So the Apostle of Allah—
may Allah bless him and grant him peace—besieged them until
they surrendered unconditionally.

'Abd Allah b. Ubayy b. Salul stood up for them with him after
Allah had delivered them into his power, and said, "O Muham-
mad, deal kindly with my clients." (For they were allies of the
Khazraj.)

But the Apostle of Allah—may Allah bless him and grant him
peace—was slow to respond, so he said again, "Muhammad, deal
kindly with my clients." At this he turned away from him, so 'Abd
Allah stuck his hand into the collar of the Apostle's coat of mail.

"Unhand me!" the Apostle said to him. His face became dark
with rage. "Woe unto you, unhand me!"

"No, by Allah," came the answer, "I will not let you go until
you deal kindly with my clients. Four hundred men without coats
of mail, and three hundred with, protected me from all manner of
men. Are you going to cut them down in a single morning? By
Allah, I am a man who fears the changes of circumstances."

"They are yours," replied the Apostle of Allah—may Allah bless
him and grant him peace.

During the time that the Apostle had besieged them, he placed
Bashir b. Abd al-Mundhir in charge of Medina. The entire siege
lasted fifteen days.

Stillman, *The Jews of Arab Lands*, 122–23

CALIPH AL-MUTAWAKKIL AND THE AHL AL-DHIMMA

In that year (235/850), al-Mutawakkil ordered that the Christians
and all the rest of the *ahl al-dhimma* (protected people) be made to

wear honey-colored *taylasans* (hoods, cowls) and the *zunnar* belts. They were to ride on saddles with wooden stirrups, and two balls were to be attached to the rear of their saddles. He required them to attach two buttons on their *qalansuwas*—those of them that wore this cap. And it was to be of a different color from the *qalansuwa* worn by Muslims. He further required them to affix two patches on the exterior of their slaves' garments. The color of these patches had to be different from that of the garment. One of the patches was to be worn in front on the breast and the other on the back. Each of the patches should measure four fingers in diameter. They too were to be honey-colored. Whosoever of them wears a turban, its color was likewise to be honey-colored. If any of their women went out veiled, they had to be enveloped in a honey-colored *izar* (a large outer wrap). He further commanded that their slaves be made to wear the *zunnar* and be forbidden to wear the *mintaqa* (a gold/silver belt).

He gave orders that any of their houses of worship built after the advent of Islam were to be destroyed and that one-tenth of their homes be confiscated. If the place was spacious enough, it was to be converted into a mosque. If it was not suitable for a mosque, it was to be made an open space. He commanded that wooden images of devils be nailed to the doors of their homes to distinguish them from the homes of Muslims.

He forbade their being employed in the government offices or in any official business whereby they might have authority over Muslims. He prohibited their children studying in Muslim schools. Nor was any Muslim permitted to teach them. He forbade them to display crosses on their Palm Sundays, and he prohibited any Jewish chanting in the streets. He gave orders that their graves should be made level with the ground so as not to resemble the graves of Muslims. And he wrote to all his governors regarding this.

Stillman, *The Jews of Arab Lands*, 167–68

Questions on the Texts

THE QUR'AN ON THE JEWS

1. Muhammad expected Jews and Christians to follow him and accept his prophecy. Was this not against the Qur'an's own instructions in Suras 5:51 and 2:256? Explain the discrepancy.

2. What accusations are being made here (Sura 4:160–61) against the Jews?
3. Which groups are seen as most distant from Muslim teachings? as closest?
4. How is this explained by the Qur'an?

The Pact of 'Umar

1. Who is/are the author/s of this document? Support your answer.
2. Why must there be a commitment not to teach the Qur'an? not to sell wines?

The Affair of the Banu Qaynuqa'

1. Muhammad confronts the Banu Qaynuqa' in the marketplace. On what basis does his claim to prophethood rest?
2. What event created hostility between the Banu Qaynuqa' and the Muslims? Who came to the defense of the Jews after the defeat of Banu Qaynuqa'? Why?

Caliph al-Mutawakkil and the *Ahl al-Dhimma*

1. How was the dress of Christians and Jews to differ from that of Muslims? What do you think the caliph intended by insisting upon such differences?
2. What other restrictions were to be placed on Christians and Jews? Can we conclude that such restrictions are typical of lands under Muslim control in the 9th century? Why/Why not?

Paper Topics

The Pact of 'Umar
The Doctrine of Jihad
Muhammad and the Jewish Tribes of Medina
Shi'ites and Sunnis: Differences and Similarities
Prayer in Islam
Charity in Islam
Dhimmis (Protected People) under Muslim Rule

Reference Works

M. Cohen, *The Cross and the Crescent*
Encyclopedia of Islam
B. Lewis, *The Jews of Islam*
A. Jeffrey, *Islam, Muhammad and His Religion*
F. Rahman, *Islam*
N. Stillman, *The Jews of Arab Lands*

THE GEONIC PERIOD (600–1000)

622	Qur'an revealed to Muhammad; hijra from Mecca to Medina. Jews join Arab tribes in supporting Muhammad
624	Jewish tribes driven out of Arabia
651	Muslim conquest of Mesopotamia
691	'Abd al-Malik builds Dome of the Rock
700	Pact of 'Umar
717	'Umar II oppresses Jews and other minorities
750	Ahai writes *She'iltot*
765	Anan founds Karaism
786	Harun al-Rashid imposes heavy taxes and other restrictions on Babylonian Jews
825	Simeon Kayyara writes *Halakhot Gedolot*
850	Babylonian Jews required to wear yellow head covering or patch
860	Amram Gaon prepares first Siddur and sends it to Spain
900	Babylonian Jewish bankers finance Muslim caliphs
928	Saadiah appointed gaon of Sura
930	Saadiah removed by exilarch
932	Saadiah writes *Sefer Emunot ve-Deot*, first book of Jewish philosophy
968	Sherira becomes gaon of Pumpedita; authors numerous responsa, many with his son, Hai
987	Sherira writes *Iggeret*, discussing evolution of Talmud
998	Hai becomes last gaon of Pumpedita

2

The Jews of France and Germany

THIS UNIT DEALS with the Jews of France and Germany—the region known in Hebrew as Ashkenaz. Their history began as early as the 8th century, when Charlemagne and his sons ruled this area, and has lasted into the 20th century.

We will begin by considering the political life of the self-governing Jewish communities of Ashkenaz. The Jews sought to govern themselves in accordance with halakhic law and confronted important issues in this regard. For example, it had to be decided who would govern and what powers they would have. Such questions were settled at periodic rabbinic conferences attended by representatives from all the communities of Ashkenaz. We will look at several of these conferences, profiling some of the important rabbinic authorities and communal leaders who were present.

Some historians contend that the Crusades—a series of Christian military expeditions against the Muslims, beginning in the 11th century—represent a major turning point in the history of Ashkenaz. They argue that pre-Crusade Ashkenaz cannot be compared with post-Crusade Ashkenaz because the lives of Jews changed dramatically in this era. The violence to which they were subjected made them feel vulnerable and dependent on government protection; at the same time they found themselves forced to engage in moneylending, as it was no longer safe for them to travel the roads of Europe, a necessary part of commercial activity. Other historians reject this contention. They point out that Jews had been dependent on charters granted by rulers like Charlemagne (8th century) long before the Crusades. The First Crusade had a tragic impact on several communities in Ashkenaz; we will take a closer look at this unfortunate part of our history.

The medieval period brought special challenges to Jewish-Christian relations. The Paris Disputation was one such challenge. Blood libels and libels of Host desecration were another, as was required attendance at conversionist sermons. The Fourth Lateran Council, convened by Pope Innocent III, formulated five decrees that would affect the Jews enormously, especially the decree mandating special dress for them.

A major issue for Jews was their move into moneylending. A brief section of this unit will examine this major economic change in Jewish life, examining the factors that bought it about. Some of the texts presented will relate to the acceptability of moneylending in halakhah.

Although one might have expected otherwise, Jewish culture flourished during the period of the Crusades. There were outstanding Bible commentators, especially Rashi; there were outstanding students of Talmud and halakhah, the tosafists; and there were the pietists known as Hasidei Ashkenaz.

Our look at medieval Ashkenaz will, of necessity, be an abbreviated one, but perhaps it will be enough to whet the reader's appetite to taste more.

POLITICS AND COMMUNITY

The communities of Northern France and Germany, the region customarily referred to as Ashkenaz, are an important part of the Jewish history of the Middle Ages. The Jews of Ashkenaz governed themselves. The power of self-government brought with it important benefits, but also significant responsibilities. In this section we will consider the legal status of the Jews in medieval Europe, the important issues faced by them as a self-governing community, and the responsibilities assumed by their communal leaders.

The origins of Jewish self-government in medieval Europe are a matter of dispute among scholars. In the view of S. W. Baron (1895–1989), a distinguished historian, self-government was con-

48

1. End 10th cent.—Emperors Otto I and Otto II issue edicts subordinating Jews to bishops. They are to reside in separate neighborhoods and enjoy certain privileges.

3. Rabbenu Gershom, c.960-1030, head of *yeshiva* and known as *Me'or ha-Golah* (Light of the Exile). Among his important *takkanot* (regulations) are a ban on bigamy and an order forbidding amending Talmudic texts.

4. Henry II expels Jews who refuse to convert. Among forcibly baptized is son of Rabbenu Gershom.

8. Prince Vratislav II (1061-1092) grants autonomy to Jews.

7. 1090 — Henry IV confirms privileges granted by Ruediger and grants additional ones.

6. 1084—Bishop Ruediger allocates special neighborhood to Jews; encloses it with wall; grants privileges. Group of Jews arrive from Mainz.

5. Rashi (R. Solomon b. Isaac) studies at *yeshivoth* of Worms and Mainz. 1068—Returns to Troyes and establishes *yeshiva*. Composes commentary on Bible and Talmud.

2. 982—Kalonymus, a Jew whose family moved to Mainz in 917, saves life of Otto II.

POLAND
GERMANY
Magdeburg
Merseburg
Xanten
Neuss
Cologne
Aachen Bonn
LORRAINE (LOTHRINGEN)
Mainz Bamberg
Worms
Trier
Speyer
Metz
Regensburg
Prague
Paris
FRANCE
Troyes
London
Rhine
Danube
HUNGARY
Lyons
BURGUNDY
Milan
ITALY
CROATIA
PAPAL
Lucca
Marseilles
SERBIA
Adriatic Sea
STATES
CORSICA
Rome
SARDINIA
Mediterranean Sea
0   200   400
km.

Jewish Communities in Ashkenaz up to 1096

nected to the emergence of cities in the 11th century. The development of a middle class and a merchant class, and the creation of municipal institutions, led to an embryonic strain of representative government. These advances, in turn, led to the emergence of quasi-independent and semi-autonomous Jewish communities.

In the view of another distinguished historian, Y. Baer (1888–1980), Jewish self-government was based upon precedents originating in ancient Israel and Babylonia, rather than on patterns adopted from the governmental systems of the feudal states of medieval Europe. Thus the roots of Jewish communal organization may be found in the Mishnah and Talmud. While localized adaptations and alterations would evolve political structures pointedly divergent from the talmudic paradigm, the precedent was never wholly abandoned. The majority of scholars side with Baer, noting that self-rule and autonomy characterized Jewish communities far away from Western Europe. In this connection, one naturally thinks of the exilarchate in Persian and Muslim Babylonia, described in the preceding chapter.

The Jews of Europe were denied feudal tenure because obviously they could not pledge troth to Christianity. Since their status had to be regularized in some way, they were eventually awarded the dubious distinction of *servi camerae*, or "Serfs of the [Royal] Chamber," a legal notion that first surfaced in the 1230s in the laws of Frederick II of Hohenstaufen, the Holy Roman Emperor, whose domains included the extensive Jewries of Sicily and Germany. This designation had two important effects: (1) by making them, in a technical sense, the property of the ruling sovereign, so that hostile actions against them were actions against the crown, it provided a certain degree of protection, at least in legal theory; but (2), since they were his property, the sovereign could appropriate their wealth to whatever extent he wished, whether in taxes or by confiscation. The monetary demands of the sovereigns were generally quite harsh, but they tended not to take everything, because this would have left the Jews destitute and unable to provide further revenue.

The religio-legal definition of the Jew was a major point of contention between medieval popes and emperors. The 13th century saw renewed interest in the factitious civil law code of ancient Rome and the broadly philosophical teachings of Aristotle. Both these influences tended to obscure the bifurcation between the strictly spiritual and temporal. Popes increasingly exercised direct control in both realms, asserting the "plenitude of apostolic powers." This was especially true of Innocent III, Gregory IV, and Innocent IV.

The emperors, particularly Frederick II, rejected ecclesiastical claims to political authority. This vigorous challenge eventually caused Frederick to be excommunicated twice, once in 1227 and again in 1239. Pope Gregory IV and Frederick engaged in a heated dispute over the management, religious and social implications, and foundations of collective polities and the presumed relationship to the nature of their direction and oversight. The battle continued through the 13th century, with the status of the Jew a recurrent focus of the ongoing debate.

Jewish Population Figures

Before looking at Jewish self-government in Ashkenaz, it is important to consider the size of the French and German communities. In his *Sefer ha-Massa'ot* ("Book of Travels"), the famous medieval Jewish traveler, Benjamin of Tudela, writes that at the end of the 12th century there were 6,000 Jews in the six major communities of France. By the end of the 13th century, some 150 places boasted Jewish settlements, although 100,000 Jews were expelled from France in 1306, and the year 1348 brought the Black Death, which reduced the Jewish population further. The 14th century saw some increase, but 1394–95 brought another expulsion, so that only about 25,000 Jews remained.

With regard to Germany, the Jewish populace can be estimated by using what is known about the First Crusade in 1096 as a demographic resource. The Hebrew Chronicle of Solomon bar Shimshon and the Christian chronicles of Albert of Aix and Ekkehard of Aura are useful for this purpose. There were about 20 Jewish communities in Germany at the time of the First Crusade, some in the Rhine area (Speyer, Worms, Mainz [also known as Mayence], and Cologne), others in the northeast (Magdeburg, Halle). Of particular importance was Regensburg, a community in southern Germany that was notable for its many synagogues. On the basis of the Crusade chronicles it would appear that Mainz had no more than 1,300 Jews, while Cologne had roughly 2,000. The total number of Jews in Germany was no more than 20,000.

Communal Organization and Administration

Let us now consider the form of communal organization in Ashkenaz. An issue of great importance in the communities of Ashkenaz was whether community decisions required unanimity or, instead, the agreement of the majority. It was the view of Rabbenu Tam (R. Yaakov b. Meir, 1100–1171), a grandson of Rashi and the leading rabbinic figure of the 12th century, that the critical passage in Bava Batra 8b empowered the leaders of a community, once they had determined weights, measures, prices, and wages, to act upon and penalize any violations of the community's practice; violations of the rules, however, required the unanimous agreement of the

community. Another 12th-century scholar, R. Eliezer b. Yoel ha-
Levi (Rabiah), however, held that communal decisions only
needed majority consent—not unanimous agreement. He saw this
principle expressed in the talmudic statement that "a decree is not
to be imposed upon the community unless the majority can endure
it." R. Meir of Rothenburg (ca. 1215–1293), the great leader of
German Jewry in the 13th century, accepted the view of Rabbenu
Tam.

The communities in France and in Germany were administered
by elected officials, usually selected from among the wealthy, with
the community at large showing its support for them by making
financial contributions to meet communal needs. The officials of
the community were responsible for maintaining the principles of
justice as set forth in Jewish law; this responsibility was usually
given to the most scholarly of the elected leaders.

Takkanot

The communal leadership was empowered to enact new legislation (called *takkanot*) to compel individuals to obey the communal
regulations and to guide their lives, but this power was sometimes
limited in order to protect the rights of the individual under Jewish
law. Taxation was an especially important area of concern for the
communal leaders, and one of the instruments they used to enforce
their decisions was the power of *herem* (excommunication). One
on whom this power was exercised would be excluded from the
religious life of the community and ostracized socially; he could
not be counted for a *minyan*, his male children would be denied
circumcision, he would be denied burial in the Jewish cemetery,
and business dealings with him were forbidden. (The question of
who had the authority to declare a *herem* was considered at the
1250 synod at Mayence, as will be explained below.)

In Germany a significant development of communal institutions
took place in the wake of the First Crusade. The communal leaders
begin to gather on market days and issue *takkanot* in many areas of
life, *takkanot* that would be binding on individual communities or
groups of communities. The main purpose of such *takkanot* was to
strengthen religious life and provide opportunities for increased
Torah study. There were also *takkanot* aimed at enhancing commu-

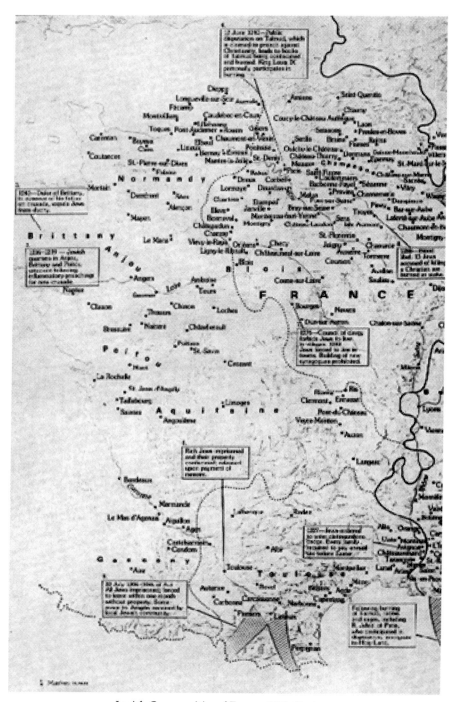

Jewish Communities of France: 13th Century

Jewish Communities of France: 13th Century

nal life; for example, everyone was obligated to pay taxes and prohibited from making false statements, and the officials had the right to shift funds around when the good of the community required this. The authority of the local leaders was strengthened by making it unacceptable for anyone to seek tax exemptions from non-Jewish officials, to take disputes into non-Jewish courts, or to pursue divorce rulings or excommunication rulings outside the local community.

Synods

In post-Crusade France and Germany, the many local Jewish communities began to work together. It was in this period that the first synods, or gatherings of representatives from different communities, were held to discuss the issues of the time. Under the leadership of Rabbenu Tam, synods were convened and *takkanot* were enacted. Among other things, the synods ruled that prayer services could be interrupted at any point by someone who felt that he had been humiliated and defamed before a non-Jew by a fellow Jew, that anyone who had lived in a community for a month could be required by that community to pay taxes, and that it was forbidden to remove a *tallit* (prayer shawl) or *mahzor* (festival prayer book) from a synagogue without the owner's permission. Later synods considered other issues of importance; in 1215, for instance, a meeting was held to discuss how to deal with the important rulings of the Fourth Lateran Council regarding Jews.

Rabbinic gatherings were also held in Germany during the 13th century and thereafter. Among the major leaders involved were R. David of Muenzberg, R. Eliezer b. Joel ha-Levi (Rabiah), and R. Meir of Rothenburg. A major issue confronted by the 1196 synod was that of *yibbum*, which requires a widow to marry her late husband's brother, and *halitzah*, a ceremony that frees the widow from this obligation. The German rabbis favored the use of halitzah because otherwise widows would be unable to remarry.

Three more synods were convened between 1200 and 1223. At the first of these it was declared that Jews were not permitted to cut their hair or shave their beards in the style of non-Jews, to gamble, to divorce their wives without the consent of the community, or to refuse to perform *halitzah*, and that every community member was required to pay taxes to support the communal institutions. The second synod confirmed the above measures and added that one could not use the utensils of non-Jews for Jewish wine or eat food cooked by non-Jews, that every Jew was to set aside a fixed time for study, and that synagogue services were to be carried on with decorum. The third synod reenacted and confirmed the decisions of the previous two.

The synod of Mayence in 1250 focused on the issue of herem. The delegates, among them R. David ben Shealtiel and R. Yehudah ben Moshe ha-Kohen, prohibited any rabbi from declaring a herem without communal consent and prohibited any community from declaring a herem without the consent of its rabbi.

The 1280s saw a synod in Nuremberg led by the great R. Meir of Rothenburg. The major issue was that of a woman who leaves her husband with the persuasion and encouragement of family members. The synod decided that such a woman lost all her property and all right to the support her husband was required to provide as guaranteed in her *ketubbah* (marriage contract), i.e., food, clothing, and housing. In addition, her husband was permitted to divorce her even against her will.

Communal Functions and Services

The communities of Ashkenaz were governed internally by a community board known as a *kahal*. Smaller communities were administered by only one official, while larger ones had several officials, including *parnassim* (aldermen), *gabbaim* (supervisors), and so forth. There were also representatives whose primary task was to represent a community, a region, or even the entire country in dealing with the king, the nobles, or church officials. The title rav was in use by the 12th century, although the authority of a rav took a bit more time to be fully defined. Large communities had rabbanim who functioned as *dayyanim* (judges) administering civil law, *roshei yeshiva* (heads of yeshivot), or religious guides. Other paid community officials included *hazzanim* (prayer leaders), *shammashim* (sextons), and *shohetim* (meat slaughterers).

The communities of Ashkenaz provided religious, educational, judicial, financial, and social welfare services. Religious needs focused on the *shuls*, which served as places for tefillah but also functioned as community centers. Religious leaders were expected to oversee the cemetery, supervise kosher meat slaughter, and maintain the town's *mikveh* (ritualarium). Community schools were supervised, with taxes imposed when deemed necessary and libraries provided.

In northern France in the 12th century the principle of *herem bet din* was first established. This principle meant that any local court could compel a resident of any other community to litigate before it; thus no appeals to outside authorities could be made and each individual community would hold final authority. As was mentioned above, an additional power was that of *herem* (excommunication)—religious, social, and economic, and it was used widely. The finances of Jewish towns were under the control of their leaders, who served as the fiscal agents of the local ruler and were thus responsible for collecting the taxes imposed on the Jews.

Finally, social-economic services were provided to Jews by the communities. Polygamy became subject to Jewish communal regulation until Christian societies forbade it; ordinances were passed against mixed dancing, gambling, and any violations of *taharat ha-mishpahah* (laws governing family purity). Charity was made available to those who needed it for food, clothing, and shelter, especially orphans and widows. The sick were supplied with medical care and any necessary medications; visiting the sick was regarded as an important tzedakah (charity) obligation.

Prominent Rabbinic Figures

Among the leading rabbanim of the first half of the 11th century in France was R. Yosef Bonfils of Limoges. In his view, communal authority had two bases. The first of these was the principle of *hefker bet-din hefker*, which gave Jewish courts the power to expropriate property. The second was the principle of *bet-din makkin ve-onshin she-lo min ha-din*, which permitted the community to enforce criminal law and use the punishment flogging when deemed necessary. It is most significant that the community is here characterized as a bet-din, although the subject of discussion is a rule of the community.

In his teshuvot R. Yosef deals with a number of the main issues of 11th-century communal life. Among these is the issue of a community majority imposing its will on a resisting minority, a matter that would be considered again in the 12th century, as seen above. He deals as well with the rights of one community to involve itself in the communal issues of another and the permissibility of turning to non-Jewish courts in the absence of a bet-din able to impose its will.

Rabbenu Gershom

Without question the outstanding rav in pre-Crusade Germany was Rabbenu Gershom (ca. 950–1028), who later came to be called *Me'or ha-Golah* ("Light of the Exile"). His leadership role found expression both in literary works and in contributions to communal organization. His prominence cannot be understated.

Although he is most famous for having instituted a prohibition on polygamy among Jews and for forbidding divorces to which the wife does not consent, some of his responsa deal with communal issues. He was asked, for example, whether a *kohen* (priest) who converted and then returned to Judaism regained the halakhic status of being allowed to recite the *Birkhat Kohanim* (Priestly Blessing recited on festivals) or receive the first *aliyah* to the Torah. He also dealt with issues pertaining to moneylending and to dealing with Christians at the time of their holidays. Of particular importance is a *teshuvah* in which Rabbenu Gershom sees the community functioning as a *bet-din,* using the power of *hefker bet-din hefker* (see above); other *teshuvot* reiterate this conception of the community's function.

Rabbenu Tam

The leading rav in 12th-century northern France was Rabbenu Tam. He was held in high regard throughout the Jewish world because of his unquestionable mastery of the Talmud, and people everywhere turned to him for religious guidance. Questions were received by him from northern France, southern France (Provence), Germany, and even from southern Italy. Many of these related to the halakhot governing moneylending, wine made by non-Jews, and the tax responsibilities of Jews.

Rabbenu Tam was a major figure for many reasons. He maintained close relationships with nobles and rulers, largely due to his business as a wine-maker. Many of his *teshuvot* show this to have been the case. Moreover, he was strong-minded, willing to respond to challenges offered by others. An example of this can be seen in his major controversy with R. Meshullam of Melun, who had adopted certain *minhagim* (customary practices) that had been rejected by Rashi and most other French scholars. Rabbenu Tam passionately condemned R. Meshulam's position.

R. Meir of Rothenburg

As indicated earlier, the dominant leadership figure in 13th-century Germany was R. Meir of Rothenburg (ca. 1215–1293). His authority was based on his vast knowledge of halakhah, and not on any official post. A major thinker on political and communal organization, he had a great deal to say regarding human freedom, government by consent, legal assumption of agreement, limitation of power of authority, and group responsibility.

R. Meir believed that the innate, unbounded freedom of the individual may be limited only by voluntary consent, for in his view it was voluntary consent that led Jews to agree to be bound by talmudic law and by the minhagim of their community and country. Talmudic law, he argued, permitted the residents of a town to organize themselves into a political body or community, and provided that body with certain rights so long as the principle of "the majority rules" obtained. In matters of religion or matters serving the public interest or matters without religious purpose or public benefit, custom and *takkanot* are acceptable if there is a majority vote in favor; where there is no local custom, the vote must be unanimous. R. Meir, then, combined the freedom of the individual with the sanctity of contract; as was noted above, he endorsed here the view of R. Tam on the issue of majority vs. unanimity.

An abundance of R. Meir's *teshuvot* have survived, most of them relating to Jewish civil law. They deal with business transactions, real estate, inheritance, marriage contracts, partnerships, agents, sureties, trustees, employers, informers, community government, community property, settling rights, and taxation. Many relate to the latter, a major concern of the medieval communities.

Self-government was an important part of Jewish life in Ashkenaz, but it brought along certain responsibilities. We have considered in this section the way in which the legal status of Jews was defined in medieval Europe, some of the issues confronted by Jews as self-governing communities, and the responsibilities assumed by the leadership figures in the communities in Ashkenaz.

Texts

RABBENU TAM

Therefore we have taken counsel together: the elders of Troyes and its sages and those in its surrounding environs; the sages of Dijon and its environs; the leaders of Auxerre and Sens and its adjacent communities; the elders of Orleans and its surrounding territories; our brethren the inhabitants of Chalons; the sages of the area of Rheims; our masters in Paris and their neighbors; the scholars of Melun and Etampes; the inhabitants of Normandy and Brittany and Anjou and Poitou; the greatest of our generation, the inhabitants of Lotharingia. Of those listed here, some have assented, but the reaction of others we have not heard—for the matter was urgent. Therefore we have depended on the fact that we know them to be great authorities who accede to their inferiors. For the law is a just one, and, were it not so stipulated, it would be worthy of stipulation.

Chazan, "The Blois Incident of 1171"

RASHBAM, RABBENU TAM, SAMUEL B. JACOB, ISAAC B. SOLOMON OF TROYES

We have voted, decreed, ordained and declared under the herem [the threat of excommunication], that no man or woman may bring a fellow Jew before Gentile courts or exert compulsion on him through Gentiles, whether by a prince or a common man, a ruler or an inferior official, except by mutual agreement made in the presence of proper witnesses.

No man shall try to gain control over his neighbor through a king, prince, or judge, in order to punish or fine or coerce him, either in secular or religious matters, for there are some who play the part of saints and do not live up to ordinary standards.

He who transgresses these decrees of ours shall be excommunicated, all Israel shall keep apart from him, those who sign this decree as well as those who do not sign, their pupils, and the pupils of their pupils, their comrades, great and small.

As for him who transgresses our decree, his bread is that of a Samaritan [i.e., is not kosher], his wine is that of libations [i.e., may not be used for ordinary purposes], his books are as those of the magicians [i.e., may not be read], and who converses with him is like unto him; and he shall be in excommunication like him. But he who takes these matters to heart, and is apprehensive of the words of our Creator and our words, will find our words good and upright. There is an old ordinance against informers, *malshinim*, and those who tell tales in secret.

Finkelstein, *Jewish Self-Government in the Middle Ages*, 155–58

RABBI MEIR OF ROTHENBURG

Whether regarding the election of officers, appointment of cantors, or the creation of a charity chest and appointment of its officers; whether to build or destroy anything in the synagogue, or to buy a community wedding hall or bakery, or to provide all other community needs—all such matters shall be decided by a vote of the majority. Should the minority refuse to heed the decision of the majority, this majority, or its appointed officers, shall use coercive force, whether through Jewish law or the law of the land, to compel the minority to abide by its rulings. Should an expense of money be involved therein, the minority shall have to defray its part of the expenses.

Agus, *Rabbi Meir of Rothenburg*, 114–15

RABBENU GERSHOM

Even though Reuven has given up any hope of recovering the object, since the community has decreed that anyone to whom there comes a lost object must return it to its owners, Shimon must follow this decree of the community, even though the Torah has declared that it is now his, that which the bet-din declares to be ownerless is ownerless (*hefker bet-din hefker*).

Should it be asked: when it is said that a bet-din has the power to declare ownership, that applies only to a bet-din like that of Shammai and Hillel; this power, however, is not held by today's batei-din. This is not the case, for even persons of little distinction and learning chosen as communal leaders now hold the power of declaring ownership.

Grossman, *Hakhme Ashkenaz ha-Rishonim*, 131
(trans. J. Bloomberg)

Charter of Speyer, September 13, 1084

In the name of the Holy and Undivided Trinity.

When I wished to make a city out of the village of Speyer, I Rudiger, surnamed Huozmann, bishop of Speyer, thought that the glory of our town would be augmented a thousandfold if I were to bring Jews.

1. Those Jews whom I have gathered I placed outside the neighborhood and residential area of the other burghers. In order that they not be easily disrupted by the insolence of the mob, I have encircled them with a wall.

2. The site of their residential area I have acquired properly—first the hill partially by purchase and partially by exchange; then the valley I received by gift of the heirs. I have given them that area on the condition that they pay annually three and one-half pounds in Speyer currency for the shared use of the monks.

3. I have accorded them the free right of exchanging gold and silver and of buying and selling everything they use—both within their residential area and outside, beyond the gate down to the wharf and on the wharf itself. I have given them the same right throughout the entire city.

4. I have, moreover, given them out of the land of the Church burial ground to be held in perpetuity.

5. I have also added that, if a Jew from elsewhere has quartered with them, he shall pay no toll.

6. Just as the mayor of the city serves among the burghers, so too shall the Jewish leader adjudicate any quarrel which might arise among them or against them. If he be unable to determine the issue, then the case shall come before the bishop of the city or his chamberlain.

7. They must discharge the responsibility of watch, guard, and fortification only in their own area. The responsibility of guarding they may discharge along with their servants.

8. They may legally have nurses and servants from among our people.

9. They may legally sell to Christians slaughtered meats which they consider unfit for themselves according to the sanctity of their law. Christians may legally buy such meats.

In short, in order to achieve the height of kindness, I have granted them a legal status more generous than any which the Jewish people have in any city of the German kingdom.

Lest one of my successors dare to deny this grant and concession and force them to a greater tax, claiming that the Jews themselves usurped this status and did not receive it from the bishop, I have given them this charter of the aforesaid grant as proper testimony. In order that the meaning of this matter remains throughout the generations, I have strengthened it by signing it and by the imposition of my seal; as may be seen below, I have caused it to be sealed.

Chazan, *Church, State and Jew in the Middle Ages,* 58–59

EMPEROR FREDERICK II OF HOHENSTAUFEN (1236)

In the name of the Holy and Undivided Trinity, Frederick II, through the favor of divine mercy august emperor of the Romans and king of Jerusalem and Sicily:

It is by the contents of the present letter that present and future generations shall know that all the serfs of our court in Germany have beseeched our majesty that we deign by our grace to confirm for all the Jews of Germany the privilege of our divine grandfather Frederick, granted to the Jews of Worms and their associates. These are the contents of that privilege:

. . . We confirm for the Jews by our natural mercy the above privilege and those stipulations contained in it, in the same manner as our divine and august grandfather granted to the Jews of Worms and their associates.

Moreover, we wish that all present and future know the following. When a serious crime was imputed to the Jews of Fulda concerning the death of certain boys of the town, because of that terrible incident the harsh opinion of the neighboring populace, spawned by recent misfortune, was projected against the rest of the Jews of Germany, although covert attacks were not yet in evidence. In order to clarify the truth concerning the aforesaid crime, we had many of princes and magnates and nobles of the empire, along with abbots and clerics, convened to provide counsel.

When diverse views on the matter had been expressed, not adequate to provide clear counsel, as is fitting, we concluded that one could not proceed more properly against the Jews accused of the aforesaid crime than through those who had been Jews and had converted to the cult of the Christian faith. They, since opposed to Judaism, would not withhold whatever they might know against the Jews, whether through the Mosaic books or through the contents of the Old Testament.

Although through the authority of many books, which our majesty distributed, our conscience had the innocence of the aforesaid Jews reasonably proven, in order to provide satisfaction for both the populace and the law, by our counsel and that of our princes, magnates, nobles, abbots and clerics, with unanimous agreement, we sent special messengers to all kings of the West, through whom we had many experienced experts in Jewish law sent from their kingdoms to our presence. When they had tarried in our court for some time, we commanded, in order to ascertain the truth of this matter, that they diligently conduct a study and instruct our conscience whether there survives any belief leading to the perpetrating of any act regarding human blood, which might impel the Jews to commit the aforesaid crime.

When their findings were published on this matter, then it was clear that it was not indicated in the Old Testament or in the New that Jews lust for the drinking of human blood. Rather, precisely the opposite, they guard against the intake of all blood, as we find expressly in the biblical book which is called in Hebrew *Bereshit*, in the laws given by Moses, and in the Jewish decrees which are called in Hebrew *Talmud*. We can surely assume that for those to whom even the blood of permitted animals is forbidden, the desire for human blood cannot exist, as a result of the horror of the matter, the prohibition of nature, and the common bond of the human species in which they also join Christians . . .

Therefore, we decree by the authority of the present privilege that no one, whether cleric or layman, proud or humble, whether under the pretext of preaching or otherwise, judges, lawyers, citizens, or others, shall attack the aforesaid Jews individually or as a group as a result of the aforesaid charge. . . . Whoever presumes to contravene the edict of this present confirmation and of our absolution bears the offense of our majesty.

Chazan, *Church, State and Jew in the Middle Ages*, 124–26

POPE INNOCENT III

The two crowns, of royalty and the priesthood, were given to the people of God, but with this difference, that the priesthood was created at God's command, while royalty was established at man's request [compare Exodus 28:1 with I Samuel 8:7]. It is also true that the period of the Judges extended from Moses to Samuel and from the first high priest, Aaron, to the first king, Saul—a very long period.

Feldman, *Ancient and Medieval Jewish History*, 304

General Questions

1. Why were popes and emperors at odds during this period? How and why did Jews and their status become involved?
2. What were some of the takkanot (ordinances) issued by the synods in France and Germany? What does this show us regarding the concerns of these communities?
3. What services were provided by the communities of France and Germany?
4. Upon what principles did R. Meir of Rothenburg base his views on political and communal organization? Explain each briefly.
5. With what matters did R. Meir deal in his responsa?

Questions on the Texts

RABBENU TAM

1. Did the Jewish communities of 12th-century Northern France tend to work together or function separately? What leads you to this conclusion? Why might this have been the case?

RASHBAM, RABBENU TAM, SAMUEL B. JACOB, ISAAC B. SOLOMON OF TROYES

1. Why might informers have been a particular problem in 12th-century Ashkenaz? Was it inconceivable for communities to handle such situations independently?

R. MEIR OF ROTHENBURG

1. What was R. Meir's view on the issue of unanimity vs. majority?
2. What decisions were in the hands of the communal leaders? How did they compel obedience to their rulings?

RABBENU GERSHOM

1. What does *hefker bet-din hefker* mean? Does it confer too much power on the community's leaders?

THE CHARTER OF SPEYER

1. What privileges did the bishop extend to the Jews of Speyer? Why did he do so?
2. What conclusions can be drawn from this document about the situation of the Jews of Ashkenaz in 1084, twelve years before the First Crusade?

FREDERICK II

1. On the basis of what argument does Frederick II affirm his authority over Jews?
2. Of what were the Jews of Fulda accused? How did Frederick deal with this accusation?

POPE INNOCENT III

1. On the basis of what argument does Pope Innocent III affirm his authority over Jews?

66

Paper Topics

THE SYNODS OF MEDIEVAL FRANCE/MEDIEVAL GERMANY

Rabbenu Gershom, Rashi, Rabbenu Tam, R. Meir of Rothenburg (or any other prominent rabbinic figure): Choose one of these and discuss his role in communal leadership.

FRENCH/GERMAN JEWS AS *Servi Camerae*

Can the French/German Jews be seen as governing themselves? (Consider the pros and cons.)

Majority Opinion vs. Unanimous Opinion: How Can Each Position Be Supported?

Reference Works

I. Agus, *Rabbi Meir of Rothenburg*
————, *The Heroic Age of Franco-German Jewry*
S. W. Baron, *A Social and Religious History of the Jews*
R. Chazan, *Church, State and Jew in the Middle Ages*
————, *Medieval Jewry in Northern France*
L. Finkelstein, *Jewish Self-Government in the Middle Ages*

CULTURE

The Jews of Ashkenaz placed a high valuation on books and learning. They were devoted to the study of Tanakh, the study of Talmud, the study of halakhah, and the study of midrash. But the Jews of Ashkenaz were dramatically different from the Jews of Spain, for whom poetry, mysticism, the Hebrew language, history, and philosophy were also major interests. We will have the opportunity to consider these differences when the picture has been filled out a bit more.

Ashkenaz produced major contributions in Bible commentary, most especially the commentary of Rashi to the Torah. It also produced major commentaries on the Talmud, again including one by Rashi, as well as those of the tosafists. Ashkenaz was the home of

R. Meir of Rothenburg, the dominant figure in the halakhah of the 13th century. In Ashkenaz, too, there emerged the group known as Hasidei Ashkenaz, a pietist group which enriched the spiritual life of medieval Jewry. Let us consider each of these groups or figures on their own.

Rashi as Bible Commentator

The commentary on the Torah, Nevi'im (Prophets), and Ketuvim (Writings) by Rashi (R. Shlomo Yitzhaki, 1040–1105) was a major contribution to the study of these texts. It is difficult to imagine studying the Torah without the assistance of Rashi, so much so that the halakhic imperative of *shnayim mikra ve-ehad targum* (two readings of the weekly Torah portion accompanied by a translation) may be fulfilled by studying the Torah with Rashi's comments.

"Rashi's Chapel," Built in the 17th Century.

In his commentary to the Torah, Rashi attempts to combine literal interpretation, which was characteristic of the French approach to the Tanakh, with midrashic interpretation. He is not, however, wedded to the midrash, sometimes choosing to recast it, abridging or supplementing the text so that it will be more readable to the ordinary reader. On occasion he departs from the midrash, asserting that it does not conform to the literal meaning of the scriptural text.

Among the other figures who engaged in biblical commentary, the most notable was Rashi's grandson, Rashbam (Rabbi Samuel b. Meir, 1080–1158). In addition, there were R. Menahem b. Helbo (11th cent.), R. Joseph Kara (ca. 1060–1070), R. Shemaya (11th cent.), and R. Yosef b. Yitzhak Bekhor Shor (12th cent.). As important as each of these was, however, Rashi remained the one who made the Torah accessible to everyone, whether scholars or just ordinary Jews.

Rashi as Commentator on the Talmud

Rashi's commentary to the Talmud is a work of major significance, one whose value cannot be underestimated. Without Rashi the Talmud would have remained a closed book to all but scholars. Rashi's commentary made the Talmud accessible to everyone. It is a central tool even today, some 1,000 years after its composition.

To be sure, Rashi was only transmitting tradition, but the excellence of his commentary lies in his ability to simplify complicated material, anticipating the learner's difficulties, and with just a word or two setting aside some objection that the learner might raise; in short, Rashi was an accomplished pedagogue. The goal of Rashi's commentary is to link the student with the text. To accomplish this, Rashi determines the exact reading of the text, rejecting all other options; he explains difficult words, phrases, and technical terms; he helps the student understand passages by explaining technical processes, e.g., how certain tools are used, methods of manufacture, etc.; he provides information regarding the authors of certain statements, e.g., whether they were tannaim or amoraim, from which generation, masters or disciples; he supplies punctuation, indicating the equivalents of today's question marks, exclamation points, italics; and he foresees problems and questions that a student might see in the text. In short, Rashi made it possible to study Talmud with little assistance.

Ba'alei ha-Tosafot

This was also the period in which the Tosafot were composed. There were hundreds of tosafists, but the dominant figure in the 12th century was Rabbenu Tam, although his nephew and student, R. Isaac b. Samuel, achieved prominence as well. In the 13th century it is unquestionably R. Meir of Rothenburg whose authority dominates. The approach of Tosafot to the text of the Talmud is, at the same time, analytic in character and decisive regarding halakhic practice. The texts of Tosafot draw a picture of the discussions in the yeshivot of medieval France and Germany: the text is commented upon, the student's questions on it are addressed, the final halakhah is presented. The starting point is the commentary of Rashi; his comments are presented more fully or comments are added where Rashi has not commented at all. On occasion Rashi's interpretations are rejected and other possibilities are suggested.

This evaluation and criticism of Rashi is essential to the work of the tosafists, but they go beyond the limits of a specific Talmud passage, broadening its scope. They bring parallel texts; they search out arguments, distinctions to be drawn, inner logic to be seen in a passage. They also raise issues not even considered in relation to the text. Thus they are not just commenting on the Talmud text or adding to Rashi; they are creating a major cultural product that will make them the dominant force in the Torah study of the 12th and 13th centuries.

R. Jacob b. Meir, known as Rabbenu Tam, was recognized, both in Ashkenaz and beyond, as the greatest scholar of his generation. A grandson of Rashi, Rabbenu Tam lived in Ramerupt, France, and engaged in occupations typical of medieval Jews, moneylending and viticulture. His major work was the *Sefer ha-Yashar*, which includes both responsa and commentary on the Talmud. The main trend of the latter is to confirm the accuracy of the Talmud texts; nothing is to be emended by deletions or addenda, even if these are supported by logical argument or parallel sources. In addition, as noted, Rabbenu Tam was prominent among the tosafists; many

70

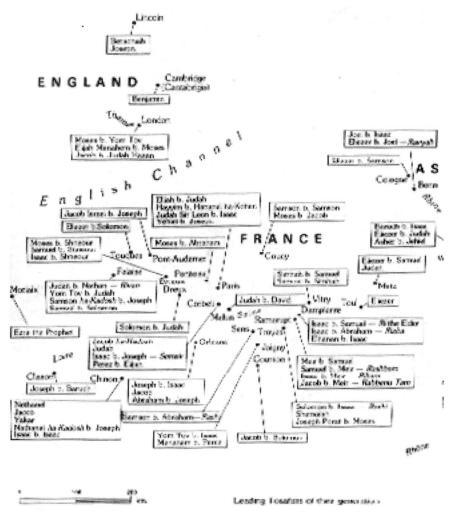

The Tosafists

of his explanations, glosses, and decisions are found among the comments of the Tosafot on the Talmud.

R. Isaac (Ri), who lived in the second half of the century, was one of the most important tosafists. Almost no page in the Talmud can be found without a comment by Ri. He too authored responsa,

Spiritual Creativity

The Tosafists

although they certainly lack the polemic, controversy, and vehemence that characterize those of his uncle, Rabbenu Tam.

In the 13th century, the most outstanding figure was R. Meir of Rothenburg. R. Meir was a teacher and a scholar, but he was also one of the authors of the Tosafot and was regarded as the final authority in Germany on ritual, legal, and communal matters. In his youth, R. Meir studied with R. Isaac b. Moshe, author of the *Or Zarua*; later he studied with two of the great tosafists, R. Solomon of Falaise and R. Yehiel of Paris, both of whom participated in the Paris Disputation, which brought about the tragic burning of the Talmud in 1242. After this event, R. Meir moved back to Rothenburg, remaining there until 1286.

By the time he was only 35, R. Meir was regarded as the *gedol hador*, the greatest scholar of his generation. His opinions on halakhic questions were solicited by rabbis throughout Germany, Austria, and France. R. Meir's influence on the Jews of Ashkenaz took on three forms: many of his students became leaders of major communities in Germany, Bohemia, and Austria; two of them, in particular, were major figures in their own right, Rabbenu Asher (Rosh) and R. Yaakov (author of the *Arba'ah Turim*); and the works of his students were studied by subsequent generations of scholars, becoming authoritative sources for R. Moshe Isserles (Rema), who drew upon them as he put together his *Mappah* for the *Shulhan Arukh* of R. Yosef Karo.

Hasidei Ashkenaz

The 12th and 13th centuries also saw the emergence of Hasidei Ashkenaz. This was a pietist movement that originated in the communities of Speyer, Worms, and Mayence. The most prominent figures among the Hasidei Ashkenaz were R. Judah b. Samuel he-Hasid (ca. 1150–1217) and his student, R. Eleazar b. Judah (ca. 1165–ca. 1230). R. Judah was the principal author of the classic "manual" of medieval German pietism, *Sefer Hasidim*, while R. Eleazar wrote a work of halakhah, *Sefer ha-Roke'ah* ("Balsam"), and a theological work, *Sodei Razayya* ("Secrets of Secrets").

Let us consider their theology and then the themes in the teachings that emerge from it. In their theology the Hasidim of Ashkenaz addressed the essential problems of a religious worldview: the nature of creation, miracles, cosmology and divine providence, anthropology and psychology, angelology and demonology. They showed particular interest in divine revelation, prayer, and divine providence, asking: what did the prophets see in their visions? to whom does one pray? what is the relationship between man's deeds and the way God provides for the world?

This theology produced several important doctrines, most notably the idea of *Rezon ha-Boreh* ("the will of the Creator"). The Hasidei Ashkenaz saw the will of God as taking in more than the divine will of earlier Jewish thought; in their view, Judaism includes both hasidut (pietism) and halakhah, which may be pictured as one circle within another circle of religious meaning. In addition to fulfilling the traditional religious obligations, the hasid was expected to go beyond, setting up safeguards around the forbidden, and exhibiting unmatched and unprecedented intensity and fervor in his religious practice.

The desire of the Hasidei Ashkenaz to uncover the will of the Creator led them to seek it out, to discover ways to fulfill it that would bring them beyond the minimal demands of halakhah into the area of hasidut. But this was not without its challenges. A central theme of the German hasidim was the effort to do the will of the Creator in a world that presents ongoing trials that make it almost impossible to fulfill God's will; these trials, however, were designed to provide opportunities to earn reward in the next world—in the words of the rabbis, "reward is proportional to pain" (*le-fum za'ara agra*). For the pietists of Ashkenaz, teshuvah (repentance) was an especially prominent theme; because their lives were full of great challenges, impossible challenges, this was quite natural. Asceticism, although not sexual asceticism, was advocated; to enjoy too much pleasure in this world was to give in to the evil impulse, the yetzer ha-ra. Some of the hasidic leaders engaged in social criticism, supporting a system of graduated taxation, for example, in which the wealthy would pay more than the poor; it was regarded as praiseworthy to bring benefit to society, but blameworthy to lead Jews into sin.

Thus the culture of Ashkenaz was enormously rich. It yielded the majestic commentaries of Rashi on the Torah and the Talmud. It produced the insights and analyses of the Ba'alei ha-Tosafot, who became and remain a central part of Talmud study in today's study halls. It provided the enormous contributions of R. Meir to halakhah, contributions upon which Rama drew as he prepared his *Mappah* to the *Shulhan Arukh*. It also generated the pietist movement of Hasidei Ashkenaz, with all that they advocated.

74

Texts

RASHI ON GENESIS 3:7

There are many midrashic explanations, and our rabbis have already collected them in their appropriate places in Bereshit Rabbah and other midrashim. I am only concerned with the plain sense of Scripture and with such midrashim that explain the words of Scripture in a manner that fits with them.

RASHBAM ON VAYESHEV (GENESIS 37:2)

Let those who love reason know and understand that which our sages taught us (Shabbat 63a): "A verse never departs from its plain meaning." It is still true that in essence the Torah's purpose is to teach us and relate to us, teachings, rules of conduct and laws, which we derive from hints [hidden] in the plain meaning of Scripture, through superfluous wording, through the 32 principles of R. Eliezer, the son of R. Yosi the Galilean, or the 13 principles of R. Yishmael. . . .

Similarly, Rabbi Solomon [Rashi], my mother's father, who illumined the eyes of all the Diaspora, who wrote commentaries on the Torah, Prophets and Hagiographa [Ketuvim], set out to explain the plain meaning of Scripture. However I, Samuel, son of his son-in-law, Meir—may the memory of the righteous be a blessing—[often] disputed [his interpretations] with him to his face. He admitted to me that if only he had had the time, he would have written new [revised] commentaries, based on the insights into the plain meaning of Scripture that are newly thought of day by day.

RABBENU TAM, *Sefer ha-Yashar*

. . . for you certainly know that it is my way to raise questions and to cite texts which appear to be in conflict. I do not propose forced answers, as questions can be addressed without proposing such forced answers. . . . Within the course of the Talmud discussion I interpret and my questions serve a useful purpose in presenting my own interpretation, for even when the Talmud says "obligated" in one place and "free of obligation" in another, I provide explanation.

Urbach, *Baalei ha-Tosafot*, (trans. J. Bloomberg)

R. Eleazar of Worms

For each person who has the wisdom of God in his heart joyfully considers the desire of fulfilling the will of his Creator and of performing His commandments with all his heart. One who loves God is not concerned with the pleasure of this world, and is not desirous of leisure enjoyment with his wife and children. Everything mundane is unimportant to him; nothing matters except performing the will of his Creator, leading others to virtue, sanctifying His name, and even making sacrifices of himself out of love for Him.

Sefer ha-Rokeach: *Hilkhot Hasidut — Shoresh Avodat ha-Shem*, 5–6

R. Judah b. Samuel

Draw out every word, so as to concentrate in your heart on whatsoever is uttered by your lips . . . with rhythm and the sound of the melody and in a loud voice. . . . And when you pray, add whatever is relevant to the specific blessing. . . . And if you cannot add, seek ye out melodies. Pray in the chant which you find sweet and pleasant . . . for words of entreaty and request, let it be a melody that makes the heart weep . . . for words of praise, one that makes the heart rejoice, in order that your mouth be full . . . of love and joy for the One who sees your heart and blesses it with bounteous affection and jubilation.

If somebody comes to you who does not understand Hebrew, but is God-fearing, or a woman, tell them that they should acquire the prayers in a language they understand. For prayer consists only of comprehension by the heart, and if the heart does not understand what comes from the mouth, what value has it? Therefore it is better to pray in the language that one understands.

Wistinetski and Freimann, *Sefer Hasidim*, 7–9

R. Judah b. Samuel

The robber has to think about the distress he has caused [to his victim] and all dependent on him and the deprivations which he has caused them; and he should pay them back both according to the full damage he has caused, secondary results included, as well as according to the character and status of those robbed. . . . And he should add from his own money in return for the pleasures he derived from the stolen property, and he should take on penitence in measure to counterbalance these pleasures. . . . The depth of this repentance . . . can be imparted only to the one who feels true remorse and wishes to be clear before the Holy and Blessed One.

Wistinetski and Freimann, *Sefer Hasidim*, 26

Questions on Texts

RASHI ON GENESIS 3:8

1. What is Rashi's "plan of action" for the study of Humash (Bible) as reflected in this text? (You may want to look at Rashi on Genesis 3:22, 24.)
2. Where might there be room to criticize this approach? Explain.

RASHBAM ON VAYESHEV (GENESIS 37:2)

1. *Ein Mikra yotzei midei peshuto*: How does Rashbam understand this principle as applied to biblical interpretation?
2. What was Rashi's concession to Rashbam's observations about his commentary?

RABBENU TAM, *Sefer ha-Yashar*

1. How does Rabbenu Tam describe his method of Talmud study?
2. How do you think his method differs from that of Rashi?

R. ELEAZAR OF WORMS, *Sefer ha-Roke'ah*

1. What should be the main concern of the true hasid?
2. How should this concern affect his life?

R. JUDAH B. SAMUEL, *Sefer Hasidim*, par. 11

1. What role is played by rhythm? A loud voice? Melody?
2. Should it always be the same *type* of melody? Explain.

3. Compare paragraphs 1 and 2. How do they differ regarding tefillah (prayer)?

R. JUDAH B. SAMUEL, *Sefer Hasidim*, par. 22

1. What does the Torah require of a robber as compensation?
2. What does this passage require?
3. What do the Hasidei Ashkenaz add by being more stringent?

Paper Topics

Biblical Exegesis in Ashkenaz
R. Meir of Rothenburg: Contributions to Jewish Life and Culture in
    Ashkenaz
Rabbenu Tam: Contributions to the Culture of Ashkenaz
Piety and Society: Major Teachings of Hasidei Ashkenaz
Sefer Hasidim: The Theology of Hasidei Ashkenaz

Reference Works

J. Dan, *Jewish Mysticism and Jewish Ethics*
E. Kanarfogel, *Jewish Education and Society in the Middle Ages*
G. Scholem, *Major Trends in Jewish Mysticism*
K. Stow, *Alienated Minority: The Jews of Medieval Latin Europe*
I. Marcus, *Piety and Society: The Jewish Pietists of Medieval Germany*

JEWS AND CHRISTIANS

The history of Jewish-Christian relations in Ashkenaz begins with the 6th century papacy of Gregory I, who came to be known as Gregory the Great. It was Gregory who formulated the official policy of the church toward Jews, rejecting forced conversion brought about by violence and economic persecution, and endorsing, instead, conversion through persuasion and the offering of enticements. Moreover, Gregory ruled that any already existing rights of Jews were to be protected.

A second major figure in Jewish-Christian relations was Bishop Agobard of Lyons, France, who lived in the 9th century during the reign of Louis the Pious, son of Charlemagne. Agobard's letters reveal much about Jewish-Christian relations. He complains that Jews have too much influence at the court of Louis. Important people seek their blessings and prayers. The Jews show official documents of privilege, sealed in gold. Louis permits them to build new synagogues. Simple Christians have expressed a preference for Jewish preachers. The market days have been switched from Saturdays so that Jews need not be inconvenienced. In brief, the official attitude of antisemitism, as crystallized by Gregory I, has not yet worked its way down to ordinary Christians. Louis the Pious is giving the Jews free rein.

Another of Agobard's letters criticizes the Jews' view of God. Their picture of God is anthropomorphic. They speak of God as though He had hands, a body, and so forth. They attach great importance to the letters of the Hebrew alphabet, affirming that these holy letters have magical powers. Magic is important to the Jews, he says, and Christians are likely to be attracted to such beliefs should they be permitted to interact with Jews. The Jews in Agobard's time were acquainted with books like the *Sefer Yezirah* ("Book of Creation"), the earliest Hebrew work of speculative mystical thought, and *Shiur Komah*, expounding a mystical doctrine about God's appearance, dating from the time of the Talmud; Agobard spoke with Jews about these books but quotes from them with little respect and much ridicule. Despite his powerful criticism of Louis the Pious, however, the Jews continued to be treated well; the antisemitic views of the church leaders had not yet taken root among the Christians of France.

Lateran IV

Innocent III, who was pope from 1198 to 1216, brought the institution of the papacy to the peak of its influence both within and outside the church. In November of 1215, he convened an international conference of church leaders, known as the Fourth Lateran Council because it was held in Rome's Lateran basilica.

The council addressed a number of challenges facing the Catholic Church. The first of these was Muslim control of the Middle East and much of Spain; the second was heresy, especially the heresy of the Cathari in southern France; and the third was the spread of apocalyptic movements and ideas, a major figure being Joachim of Flora. Regarding the first issue, a crusade was called to recapture Jerusalem from the Muslims. Regarding the second, a crusade was launched against the Cathari, a heretical Christian sect based in southern France. Further efforts to suppress heresy included the use of the inquisition. As for the third issue, the council prohibited the establishment of new rules for religious orders, with the exception of Dominicans and Franciscans. In general the church proposed to take aggressive action against anyone outside truly orthodox Catholicism.

The Fourth Lateran Council concerned itself as well with the Jews, issuing a number of important decrees. Jews were forbidden to leave their homes during the three days preceding Easter because at this time Christians were in mourning over the crucifixion, but the Jews were not ashamed to wear festive clothes. Jews were not to hold public offices, for it was inappropriate to have Jews governing Christians. Should the interest rates of Jewish moneylenders be "excessive," a social and economic boycott would be imposed upon them. Finally, Jews must be differentiated from non-Jews in dress, although the precise character of the distinctive dress was not specified.

Of particular interest is the last decree, the Jewish badge. It requires a closer look. In the fifty to sixty years subsequent to Lateran IV, church councils all over Europe issued decrees regarding distinctive dress for Jews. For example, a 1222 decree of the council of Oxford, England, provided a rationale: Jews and Christians should not intermingle lest they be tempted sexually; distinctive dress for Jews would be helpful in this regard. The Oxford decree also gave specific form to the required special dress. Similar rationales were offered by other conciliar decrees, although the specific forms of dress varied.

The Lateran Council's decrees encountered some resistance from Jews and from local authorities. The archbishop of Besançon received a letter from Pope Innocent IV in 1245, indicating that the Jews must be compelled to adhere to the decree regarding their dress; if not, Christians would be forbidden to do business with them. Similarly, the Jews of Breslau were refusing to wear the conical hats that would distinguish them from Christians.

Local authorities resisted as well. The church council of Valencia,

Spain, declared in 1248 that if this resistance continued, the church would compel the Jews to put on the badge. The church council of Albi, France, urged local officials to follow its dictates and threaten Christians with excommunication should they do business with Jews who refused to wear the badge.

What might have led local authorities to ignore the decrees of church councils? A letter from Pope Honorius III to the bishop of Toledo in 1219 is most revealing. The bishop reports that the Jews of Castile are so upset by the decree of Lateran IV regarding their dress that they are threatening to leave Christian Spain for the part of Spain controlled by Muslims. Such a population shift would have a disastrous impact on Christian Spain, he warns, because of the fundamental role in its economy played by Jews. The pope responded by canceling the dress decree for the Jews of Castile.

The Disputation of Paris

One of the low points in the history of medieval Ashkenaz was the Disputation of Paris, conducted in 1240. The instigator was one Nicholas Donin, a convert from Judaism, who called the attention of Pope Gregory IX to the centrality of the Talmud in Judaism and Jewish life, and the resulting "stubbornness" of the Jews. The result was that the Talmud was placed "on trial."

The "prosecutor" was Donin, and the "defense attorney" was R. Yehiel of Paris, one of the great scholars of his time. The judges were three bishops.

Two major charges were leveled against the Talmud: (1) the Jews have weakened the authority of the Bible by setting up a rival "Scripture," the Talmud; no such rival authority has a right to exist; and (2) the Talmud blasphemes Christianity, especially Jesus. The accusation also alleged that the Talmud contained anti-Christian statements as well as foolishness and obscenity.

The assertion that Judaism had created a "competitor" for the Bible was disputable, but the assertion that the Talmud attacks Jesus had some basis. In one passage (Sanhedrin 107b) the Talmud indicates that Jesus was a student of R. Joshua ben Perahiah who lapsed into idolatry and was therefore pushed aside by R. Joshua. Elsewhere (Sanhedrin 43a) the Talmud tells us that Jesus was stoned on the day before Passover, accused of seducing the Jews

Jews at the Bottom of the Medieval Social Hierarchy

to idolatry. In another passage (Gittin 56b), Jesus is described as suffering in hell, immersed in boiling excrement.

As for anti-Christian statements, the Mishnah (Avodah Zarah 2:1) says: "Cattle may not be left in the inns of the idol-worshippers (*'akum*), since they are suspected of bestiality; nor may a woman be left alone with them, since they are suspected of lewdness." The term *'akum* was taken to refer to Christians.

The accusations of foolishness and obscenity relate to the talmudic story that Og, king of Bashan, sought to eliminate the Israelites by crushing them with a stone; he lifted a mountain in order to carry this out, but God intervened and prevented it from happening (Berakhot 54b). They also relate to the talmudic assertions that Adam copulated with animals before Eve and that Ham castrated Noah.

R. Yehiel found it difficult to respond to the first charge, but regarding the second he affirmed that the Jesus of the Talmud was not the Jesus of Christianity. As for the accusation that there were anti-Christian statements in the Talmud, he said that these really referred to the pagans and idolaters of the ancient world. As for the charge of foolishness and obscenity, he pointed out that aggadic passages in the Talmud do not have the same authority as halakhic passages and need not be understood literally, though they can be.

The results of this "debate" were a foregone conclusion. Twenty-four wagonloads of Talmud volumes were condemned and burned in Paris in 1242. R. Yehiel tried to rise to the defense of the Talmud, but the judges were bishops and he was not permitted to attack the Christian scriptures, only to defend the Talmud.

Libels

The growing popular suspicion and hatred of the Jews in 12th- and 13th-century Northern Europe found expression in the blood libel and the libel of host desecration. The first instance of the blood libel was in Norwich, England, in 1144. In 1171, the entire Jewish community of Blois, France, some 30 people, was killed over a blood libel; this was the first instance of the accusation in continental Europe. By the end of the 13th century, however, there were blood libels in Germany almost every year. The second libel was that of host desecration. The Jews were accused of attempting to reenact the crucifixion by stabbing the eucharist, or host. This was a remarkable allegation, for in order to reenact the crucifixion by desecrating the host, the Jews had to believe that Jesus was actually present in it—otherwise what was the point? Still, many Christians listened to this libel beginning with the 13th century, when the Fourth Lateran Council adopted the doctrine of literal transubstantiation (Jesus actually being present in the wafer and wine of the eucharist) as official church teaching.

Texts

LETTER OF POPE GREGORY THE GREAT (590–604)

Very many, though indeed of the Jewish religion, resident in this province [Rome], and from time to time traveling for various matters of business to the regions of Marseilles, have apprised us that many of the Jews settled in those parts have been brought to the font of baptism more by force than by preaching. . . .

. . . when anyone is brought to the font of baptism, not by the sweetness of preaching but by compulsion, he returns to his former superstition, and dies the worse from having been born again.

Let, therefore, your Fraternity [the Dominican order] stir up such men by frequent preaching, to the end that through the sweetness of their teacher they may desire the more to change their old life.

Marcus, *The Jew in the Medieval World*, 22

LETTER OF BISHOP AGOBARD OF LYON TO LOUIS THE PIOUS (826–27)

[I wish to call] the attention of His Piety [to the fact that] it is extremely necessary to be aware of the damage which is being caused to the Christian faith by the Jews in several [ways]. They deceive the simple Christians and boast that they are beloved to him [Louis] in the merit of their ancestors, that they enter and leave his presence with honor, [and] that important people desire their [i.e., the Jews'] prayers and blessings and conceded that they would like to have had arise among them a lawgiver like the one who arose among the Jews. They say that his advisers are angry with us, because we prevent Christians from drinking their [the Jews'] wine,

Massacre of Jews, "Poisoners of Wells."

and, in attempting to prove this, they boast that they have received from them [Louis's advisers and other nobles] large amounts of silver in exchange for wine. And they [the Jews] say that in the canons of the Church there is no [requirement] that Christians distance themselves from Jews in regard to food and drink. They display documents of privilege in his name, sealed with a gold seal, whose content, in our opinion, is not in accord with the truth. They display women's garments, insinuating that these have been sent to their women from his relatives and from matrons of the court. They speak much about the glory of their ancestors, and they are permitted, contrary to the law, to build new synagogues. The matter has come to such a point that the fools among the Christians say that the Jewish preachers are better for them than our priests. And [the problem has become particularly acute] after the above-mentioned emissaries decided to move the market days, which had been on Saturdays, to other days, in order that the Sabbath of the Jews not be desecrated.

Dinur, *Yisrael be-Golah* 1:1, p. 138 (trans. J. Bloomberg)

FOURTH LATERAN COUNCIL DECREE (1215)

In some provinces a difference in dress distinguishes the Jews or Saracens [Muslims] from the Christians, but in certain others such a confusion has grown up that they cannot be distinguished by any difference. Thus it happens at times that through error Christians have relations with the women of Jews or Saracens, and Jews or Saracens with Christian women. Therefore, that they may not, under pretext of error of this sort, excuse themselves in the future for the excesses of such prohibited intercourse, we decree that such Jews and Saracens of both sexes in every Christian province at all times shall be marked off in the eyes of the public from other peoples through the character of their dress.

Marcus, *The Jew in the Medieval World*, 27

COUNCIL OF TARRAGONA DECREE (1239)

So also do we require that Jews and Saracens [Muslims] differ in dress from Christians and that they not employ Christian women. Christian women who live among Jews and Saracens, but fail to establish residence elsewhere within two months of the publication of this regulation, will have no penitence of theirs accepted and will have no privilege of Christian burial unless special permission is granted.

Dinur, *Yisrael be-Golah* 2:1 (trans. J. Bloomberg)

THE DISPUTATION OF PARIS (1240)

Donin: The Talmud contains many passages directed against Gentiles, saying a Gentile may be left to die, though not actually killed;

a Jew who kills a Gentile is not liable to the death penalty, whereas a Gentile who kills a Jew is liable; it is permitted to steal the money of a Gentile; a Jew must not drink wine touched by a Gentile; one may mock Gentile religion; Gentiles are presumed to be habituated to adultery, bestiality and homosexuality; it is forbidden to help a Gentile women to give birth or to suckle her child; it is forbidden to praise the beauty of a Gentile.

R. Yehiel: These Gentiles mentioned in the Talmud are not Christians. For proof, you may see that we Jews do much business with Christians, and the Talmud forbids this with Gentiles. Jews have undergone martyrdom countless times for their religion and would not disobey the Talmud if they really thought the people called "Gentiles" in the Talmud included Christians. Jews have much social intercourse with Christians and this is forbidden by the Talmud with Gentiles, by whom is meant the ancient Egyptians and Canaanites, who were steeped in immorality of every kind. Jews teach Hebrew to Christians, which is forbidden to "Gentiles."

Maccoby, *Judaism on Trial*, pp. 160–61

Questions on the Texts

LETTER OF POPE GREGORY THE GREAT

1. In this letter, Pope Gregory expresses his views regarding the conversion of the Jews. Do you think that the approach he prefers appealed to the ordinary Christians? Why? Why not? Did they practice what he preached?
2. Why was Gregory so protective of the Jews' existing rights? What might explain this?

LETTER OF BISHOP AGOBARD TO LOUIS THE PIOUS

1. Why might it have been in Louis's interest to be favorable toward the Jews?
2. Describe Jewish-Christian relations in 9th-century France as seen in this letter.

LATERAN IV DECREE

1. What were the concerns of the Fourth Lateran Council regarding Jewish-Christian relations? How were these concerns to be addressed?
2. What made Innocent III so confident that the council's decrees would be honored? Had the church's influence grown since the time of Agobard?

TARRAGONA COUNCIL DECREE

1. Why are Muslims included in an anti-Jewish decree?
2. What new requirement is here imposed on Christians who are neighbors of Jews?
3. With what are they threatened if they fail to comply?

DISPUTATION OF PARIS

1. Which of the supposed anti-Christian statements are more controversial? Less controversial?
2. Is R. Yehiel's response to Donin's charges regarding anti-Christian statements convincing? If not, why not?

Paper Topics

Pope Gregory the Great and the Jews
Bishop Agobard and the Jews
Pope Innocent III and the Jews: The Jewish Badge
The Disputation of Paris
The Blood Libels

Reference Works

R. Chazan, *Church, State and Jew in the Middle Ages*
M. Cohen, *Under Crescent and Cross*
H. Maccoby, *Judaism on Trial*

THE CRUSADES

Let us begin with a definition: a Crusade was an attempt by the Christians of Western Europe to take Palestine, the Holy Land, back from the Muslims, with particular attention paid to Jerusalem. We will consider three of the Crusades.

The First Crusade was called by Pope Urban II in 1096. Those who participated were promised that all their sins would be forgiven, while anyone who fell in battle was guaranteed entry to heaven. People joined the First Crusade for a variety of reasons. Most had religious motives: they desired to redeem the Holy City from the nonbelievers, the Muslims. The 11th century had reawakened the Christians of Europe to the message of the church; the frustration experienced by Agobard with the Christians of the 9th century had given way to a new religious enthusiasm among the masses. This change was due largely to the influence of the monks, especially those involved in the Cluny monasteries. It was clear, of course, that not every Christian could live the difficult life of a monk, but any Christian could go on a Crusade!

While most Crusade participants had religious motives, others had economic or political motives. The population of Europe was growing enormously. Farmers, most of whom were peasants, sought land elsewhere. Merchants and traders sought a share of the wealth found in the Eastern Christian Empire. Some had political motives; knights, dukes, and counts wanted land in the East, land that would bring with it power and influence.

Jerusalem was conquered by the Christians in 1099, with many Muslims and Jews killed in the process. Four Christian kingdoms were established in the Near East: Jerusalem, Antioch, Tripoli, and Edessa. On their way to the Holy Land, many Christians wondered why they ought to be traveling so far. Europe itself was full of infidels—the Jews! Some 10,000 Jews were killed by Christians "on the way" in the towns of Cologne, Speyer, Worms, and Mayence (Mainz).

The Second Crusade was called in 1144 by Pope Eugene III. The Muslims had captured Edessa, leading to a reawakening of the crusader spirit. The results of the Crusade were catastrophic, for it ended with a major military defeat of the Christians in Damascus. The Jews, however, suffered much less than in the First Crusade, although Rabbenu Tam was attacked by the crusaders but managed to escape. St. Bernard, the spiritual father of the Crusade, had argued in a letter that it was very much contrary to the spirit of

Christianity to attack Jews. Certainly Jews should be encouraged to convert, but never with violence.

The Third Crusade was called in response to the reconquest of Jerusalem by the great Muslim leader Saladin in 1187. The leaders of the Crusade were Frederick Barbarossa, emperor of Germany, Philip Augustus, king of France, and Richard the Lion-Hearted, king of England. The results were tragic. Barbarossa drowned on the way; Philip quarreled with Richard and went home; and Richard was unable to take Jerusalem back from Saladin. Meanwhile, the Jews endured attacks, especially in England. The best-known of these took place in York, where some 500 Jews committed suicide, including one of the authors of the Tosafot, R. Yom Tov of York.

Attacks on Jewish Communities

Three major Jewish communities in the region of Germany known as the Rhineland were attacked by crusaders on their way to the Holy Land during the First Crusade. The first community attacked was Cologne, where some 1,500 Jews lived. Cologne was the principal economic center of the Rhineland; major fairs were held there three times a year. Rabbinic synods were also held there to discuss issues of the community. When the crusaders came, the bishop of Cologne attempted to protect the Jews, but he was unsuccessful. Most of Cologne's Jews were killed, among them R. Moses Kohen Zedek, a highly regarded rabbi and scholar.

Speyer was the next community attacked. Here the bishop was able to rescue the Jews. Ten of them lost their lives at the hands of the crusaders, but the rest survived. Some were hidden by the bishop himself, while others were sent to fortified villages that were under his protection.

In Worms the story was quite different. As they became aware of the coming of the crusaders, the Jews divided themselves into two groups. Some remained in their homes, having been assured of protection by the townspeople; others went to the bishop's palace, confident that he would protect them. The crusaders struck first at those who had remained in their homes, killing them and taking their property. After this the crusaders moved to the bishop's palace; there many Jews took their own lives before the crusaders

The Church Triumphant   *and The Synagogue Blindfolded*

could. Some 800 Jews died, with no really serious effort by the bishop to protect them, as had been the case in Speyer.

In the town of Mayence, the Jews were victims of a group of some 12,000 crusaders led by a German noble, Emicho, who saw himself as having come to avenge the death of Jesus on the cross. The people of Mayence welcomed the crusaders, opening the gates of the city before them. The bishop had taken money from the Jews in exchange for inviting them into his palace, but once the battle began, he and his men fled. The Jews had bribed the bishop, thinking he would protect them; when this failed, though, they tried to defend themselves. When it became clear that there was no hope, they chose the path of *kiddush ha-Shem* (martyrdom), killing family members and then taking their own lives. The martyrs of Mayence numbered 1,100.

Texts

THE CRUSADERS IN MAYENCE

It was on the third of Sivan . . . at noon [May 17, 1096] that Emicho the wicked, the enemy of the Jews, came with his whole army against the city gate, and the citizens opened it up for him. Then the enemies of the Lord said to each other: "Look! They have opened up the gate for us. Now let us avenge the blood of the hanged one [Jesus]."

The children of the holy covenant who were there [i.e., the Jews], martyrs who feared the Most High, although they saw the great multitude, an army numerous as the sand on the shore of the sea, still clung to their Creator. Then young and old donned their armor and girded on their weapons and at their head was Rabbi Kalonymus ben Meshullam, the chief of the community. Yet because of the many troubles and the fasts which they had observed they had no strength to stand up against the enemy. Then came gangs and bands, sweeping through like a flood, until Mayence was filled from end to end.

. . . Each Jew in the inner court of the Bishop girded on his weapons, and all moved towards the palace gate to fight the crusaders and the citizens. They fought each other up to the very gate, but the sins of the Jews brought it about that the enemy overcame them and took the gate.

. . . The Bishop's men, who had promised to help them, were the very first to flee, thus delivering the Jews into the hands of the enemy. They were indeed a poor support; even the Bishop himself fled from his church for it was thought to kill him also because he had spoken good things of the Jews.

When the children of the holy covenant saw that the heavenly decree of death had been issued and that the enemy had conquered them and had entered the courtyard, then all of them—old men and young, virgins and children, servants and maids—cried out together to their Father in heaven and, weeping for themselves and for their lives, accepted as just the sentence of God. . . .

With a whole heart and with a willing soul they then spoke: "After all it is not right to criticize the acts of God—blessed be His name—who has given to us His Torah and a command to put ourselves to death, to kill ourselves for the unity of His holy name. Happy are we if we do His will. Happy is anyone who is killed or slaughtered, who dies for the unity of His name, so that he is ready to enter the World to Come, to dwell in the heavenly camp with the righteous—with Rabbi Akiba and his companions, who were killed for His name's sake."

As soon as the enemy came into the courtyard they found some of the very pious there with our brilliant master, Isaac ben Moses. He stretched out his neck and his head they cut off first. . . .

The women there girded their loins with strength and slew their sons and daughters and then themselves. Many men, too, plucked up courage and killed their wives, their sons, their infants. . . . The maidens and the young brides and grooms looked out of the windows and in a loud voice cried: "Look and see, O our God, what we do for the sanctification of Thy great name in order not to exchange you for a hanged and crucified one."

Thus were the precious children of Zion, the Jews of Mayence, tried with ten trials like Abraham, our father, and like Hananiah, Mishael, and Azariah. They tied their sons as Abraham tied Isaac his son, and they received upon themselves with a willing soul the yoke of the fear of God. . . .

The ears of him who hears these things will tingle, for who has ever heard anything like this? Inquire now and look about, was there ever such an abundant sacrifice as this since the days of the primeval Adam? Were there ever 1,100 offerings on one day, each one of them like the sacrifice of Isaac, the son of Abraham?

Marcus, *The Jew in the Medieval World*, 115–18

LETTER OF ST. BERNARD OF CLAIRVAUX

To the venerable Lord and most dear father Henry, archbishop of Mainz [Mayence], that he may find favor before God, from Bernard, abbot of Clairvaux:

. . . The fellow you mention in your letter has received no authority from men or through men, nor has he been sent by God. If he makes himself out to be a monk or a hermit and on that score claims liberty to preach and the duty of doing so, he can and should know that the duty of a monk is not to preach but to pray. He ought to be a man for whom towns are a prison and the wilderness a paradise, but instead of that he finds towns a paradise and the wilderness a prison. . . .

I find three things most reprehensible in him: unauthorized preaching, contempt for episcopal authority, and incitation to murder. A new power forsooth! Does he consider himself greater than our father Abraham who laid down his sword at the bidding of Him by Whose command he took it up? Does he consider himself greater than the Prince of the Apostles [Peter] who asked the Lord [Jesus]: "Shall we strike with our swords?" He is a fellow full of the wisdom of Egypt which is, as we know, foolishness in the sight of God. He is a fellow who answers Peter's question differently to the Lord who said: "Put back thy sword into its place; all those who take up the sword will perish by the sword." Is it not a far better triumph for the Church to convince and convert the Jews than to put them all to the sword? Has that prayer which the Church offers for the Jews, from the rising up of the sun to the going down thereof, that the veil may be taken from their hearts so that they may be led from the darkness of error into the light of truth, been instituted in vain? If she did not hope that they would believe and be converted, it would seem useless and vain for her to pray for them.

Chazan, *Church, State and Jew in the Middle Ages*, 104–5

R. Moses Kohen Zedek's Speech to the Martyrs of Cologne

Then the pious and faithful one—the priest who stood above his brethren—said to the congregation seated around him at the table: "Let us recite the grace to the living God and to our Father in Heaven. For the table is set before us in place of the altar. Now let us rise up and ascend to the house of the Lord and do speedily the will of our Creator. For the enemy has come upon us today. We must slaughter on the Sabbath sons, daughters, and brothers, so that He bestow upon us this day a blessing. Let no one have mercy—neither on himself nor on his companions. The last one remaining shall slaughter himself by the throat with his knife or pierce his belly with his sword, so that the impure and the hands of evil ones not sully us with their abominations. Let us offer ourselves up as a sacrifice to the Lord, like a whole burnt offering to the Most High offered on the altar of the Lord. We shall exist in a world that is entirely daylight, in paradise, in the shining light. . . . We shall eat as part of the society of the saintly in paradise. We shall be part of the company of R. Akiba and his associates. We shall be seated on a golden throne under the Tree of Life. Each of us shall point to him by finger and say: "This is our God; we trusted in Him [and He delivered us. This is the Lord in whom we trusted;] let us rejoice and exult in His deliverance." There we shall observe the Sabbath [properly], for here, in this world of darkness, we cannot rest and observe it properly." They all responded loudly, with one mouth and one heart: "Amen. So may it be, and so may it be His will." The pious Rabbi Moses began to recite the grace, for he was a priest of Almighty God. He intoned: "Let us bless our God of whose bounty we have eaten." They responded: "Blessed is our God of whose bounty we have eaten and through whose goodness we exist." He intoned: "May the Merciful avenge during the days of those who remain after us and in their sight the blood of your servants which has been spilled and which is yet to be spilled. May the Merciful save us from evil men and from conversion and from idolatry and from the impurity of the nations and from their abominations." He further intoned many benedictions related to the event at hand, because of the edict hanging over them.

Chazan, *European Jewry and the First Crusade,* 124–25

Questions on the Texts

THE CRUSADERS IN MAYENCE

1. Describe the strategy of the Mayence Jews as they confronted Emicho.
2. Which models did the Jews of Mayence choose for themselves?
3. Do the halakhot of *kiddush ha-Shem* permit the taking of one's own life?

LETTER OF ST. BERNARD OF CLAIRVAUX

1. Where has Rudolph, the offender, gone wrong? With whom is he to be contrasted?
2. What approach does St. Bernard prefer for the conversion of the Jews? Can he be seen as undercutting the spirit of the Crusades by defending the Jews? Explain.

R. MOSES KOHEN ZEDEK'S SPEECH

1. What imagery does R. Moses use in characterizing the martyrdom of Cologne's Jews?
2. How does R. Moses make use of the experiences of R. Akiba and his colleagues?
3. Does R. Moses "identify" with the concept of a suffering deity? Explain.

Paper Topics

St. Bernard of Clairvaux and the Jews
Chroniclers of the Crusades
Participants in the Crusades: Kings, Nobles, Knights, Commoners
Kinnot (Lamentations) from the Crusade Period

Reference Works

S. Baron, *A Social and Religious History of the Jews*
R. Chazan, *Church, State and Jew in the Middle Ages*
———, *European Jewry and the First Crusade*

————, *Medieval Jewry in Northern France*
K. Stow, *Alienated Minority: The Jews of Medieval Latin Europe*

MONEYLENDING

Feudalism was the economic and political system that characterized Christian Europe during much of the Middle Ages. Land was
divided among the most powerful nobles. Each noble had serfs,
who were bound to the land and obligated to work it. The noble
also had knights, whose job it was to protect him and his land. The
members of all of these classes, whether they were nobles, knights,
or serfs, were bound together by an oath of loyalty to Jesus and to
Christianity. This left the Jews outside feudalism, with no protection for their land.

Nonetheless Jews remained in agriculture. In the 9th century
Bishop Agobard of Lyons complained about their involvement in
selling wines and meat. As late as the 12th century many French
Jews, including both Rashi and Rabbenu Tam, owned vineyards
and produced wine. The Jews of England dealt in grain and wool.

The 12th century was a period of growth and of success. There
was major population growth, much of it the result of immigration.
The communities that had been destroyed during the First Cru-
sade were rebuilt; new urban centers developed and grew with the
Jews' help, and many Jews were involved largely in local trade.
Agriculture continued as well. As for relations between Christians
and Jews, things returned to the way they had been before the First
Crusade; there was virtually no anti-Jewish violence during the
Second Crusade, largely due to the appeals made by St. Bernard of
Clairvaux. There were exceptions, though; as noted earlier, Rab-
benu Tam was attacked by crusaders in Ramerupt in 1146, but
managed to escape.

Jewish culture flourished too, as we have seen. Remarkable accomplishments were made in the areas of Bible commentary, halakhah, and pietism.

The 13th century, however, saw a significant social and economic
decline. The vast majority of Jews became impoverished. They
were subjected to a spiritual onslaught, as reflected by the Disputation of Paris, and to humiliating restrictions, such as the Fourth

Lateran Council's demand that Jews wear an identifying badge. The physical existence of the Jew in Western Europe was in serious danger. This culminated in the expulsion from England in 1290 and the first expulsion from France in 1306. The year 1298 brought pogroms to Germany under the leadership of Rindfleisch.

The 12th and 13th centuries saw the Jews of Ashkenaz begin to move out of farming into moneylending. A number of factors contributed to this. The church began to have more influence on ordinary Christians, finally succeeding in establishing its authority and spiritual leadership. The monks were especially important here, particularly those of the Cluniac order. The 13th century also saw a reduced necessity to allow Jews to be involved in commerce, because more Christians, especially the Venetians, had now entered this field; the conquests of the crusaders had opened the way to the East (which had previously been closed by Muslim conquests). In addition to competition from Christian merchants, the post-Crusade roads were especially dangerous to Jewish travelers. Farming was no longer an option, as the church had forbidden Jews to own slaves because they might be influenced to convert to Judaism.

The only area that remained open to Jews was moneylending. Jewish involvement in moneylending, however, brought with it hostility. There is a natural antagonism between borrower and lender, for the lender symbolizes the weakness and vulnerability of the borrower. The church prohibited Christians from becoming moneylenders, since it held that lending at interest was immoral. The Jew who engaged in moneylending was looked upon with disdain even though he was performing a vital economic function. The Jews had to charge high interest rates; anywhere between 43% and 86% was seen by kings as an acceptable rate. In 1244 Frederick II of Austria fixed the maximum interest rate Jews could charge at 173 percent! The major reason for such high interest rates was the lack of security regarding repayment of loans.

As noted above, the Jew had no official place in feudal society. But feudal society demanded that everyone have a place, so Jews began to be defined as *servi camerae*, "Serfs of the Chamber"—i.e., the Royal Treasury. This legal concept, as was mentioned in an earlier section, came into use in the 12th century, and with increasing frequency in the 13th; it appears in documents from France,

Germany, and Spain. As a definition of the Jews' status, it had two major ramifications: (1) the Jews received protection from the king or emperor, and (2) their money and property belonged, at least in theory, to the lord, and he could demand however much he wanted. Generally the lords allowed the Jews to retain some of their property but instead imposed very high taxes on them. The status of *servi camerae* was extremely humiliating.

The Jews, then, were compelled by the forces of history to move into the practice of moneylending. Few real alternatives presented themselves, and the church's view of moneylending as immoral naturally resulted in the Jews being seen as immoral. Scholars of the halakhah, however, as we will see in some of the texts below, had to confront a different question: the permissibility of lending to non-Jews at interest.

Texts

RESPONSUM OF R. YOSEF TOV ELEM (11TH CENT.)

Townsmen have come to collect taxes for the king and have imposed a decree on each man and woman to pay a pound or its equivalent regarding any items put up for sale. . . . Leah has vineyards, and they [the townsmen] have decided that vineyards are property on their own and fruit is property on its own . . . for when they are harvested, one can sell them, even though one will have no benefit from them once they are sold, just as is the case with principal and interest—and principal and interest are taxed. Leah claims that she should not be taxed so heavily for her vineyard, for the vineyard demands much investment of time and hard work, whether in specific tasks or in collecting fruit, and every year the townsmen come to take their taxes . . . , so the farmer invests much sweat and eats little sometimes, for the vines are dried out (as the result of insufficient rainfall), so that nothing comes from all the hard work. By contrast, money ready for interest is more pleasant than vineyards, for a pledge is held by the lender (as security for the loan), and his money grows without any effort or expense. . . .

[Rav Yosef answers:] It appears to me that Leah argues justifiably that business and loans at interest cannot be compared to the holding of land [thus the tax obligations of each should be determined independently] . . . that the tax obligation of a pound of merchandise should not be imposed likewise on a landholding

Teshuvot Maharam of Rothenburg, no. 941 (trans. J. Bloomberg)

TOSAFOT TO BAVA METZIA 70B

Regarding the present custom to loan money to Christians, Rabbenu Tam explains that in a law of the rabbis, the rule is to follow the less stringent view, and thus the halakhah follows the view that R. Nahman and R. Huna never forbade loaning at interest to Christians. Even according to [the alternative view] loans at interest should be permitted, for we have had placed upon us the tax burden of kings and nobles, and our lives are dependent on permission to lend. In addition we are among the nations, and it is impossible for us to make a living in any way without doing business with Christians. Thus interest should not be forbidden "lest he learn from his deeds" any more than other forms of business.

(trans. J. Bloomberg)

R. DAVID KIMHI ON PSALMS 15:5

David [traditionally regarded as the author of Psalms] and Ezekiel forbade only that which the Torah had forbidden, but taking interest from a Christian is permitted, as the Torah states: "To the foreigner you may charge interest" (Deuteronomy 23:21), [for] interest, ordinarily taken from the foreigner willingly, is permitted. A Jew is obligated to act kindly [with hesed] toward other Jews, and loans offered without interest are kind and generous [tovah], regarded in some places as more generous than gifts, for many are embarrassed to take gifts but less embarrassed to accept a loan. This is not the case when a Jew deals with a Christian, for the Jew is not obligated to treat him with special kindness and loan him money without interest, for most of them hate Jews, although certainly if the Christian acts kindly toward the Jew, the Jew must act in a kindly manner in return. I have written at length on this matter, so that there will be found a response to those Christians who claim that David never permitted Jews to take interest on loans [to Christians]. This is inconceivable, for David never forbade that which Moses had permitted [in the Torah].

Kimhi, *Ha-Perush ha-Shalem al-Tehillim* (trans. J. Bloomberg)

Questions on the Texts

GENERAL

1. What factors led the Jews into moneylending?
2. How did the move into moneylending change Jewish-Christian relations?

R. YOSEF TOV ELEM

1. What problem is R. Yosef asked to address?
2. What conclusions can be drawn from this teshuvah regarding Jews' occupations in 11th-century France?
3. Did the movement of Jews into moneylending cause any tensions in the Jewish communities of France?

TOSAFOT BAVA METZIA 70B

1. One view in this text sees loans to non-Jews at interest as permitted. Explain the basis for this conclusion.
2. How does Rabbenu Tam support the other position on this question?
3. Do you think Jews were facing criticism from Christians for their involvement in moneylending? Why might this have been happening?

R. DAVID KIMHI ON PSALMS 15:5

1. Hesed (compassion) is a major theme in Kimhi's comments on this verse. How does he use this theme?
2. How did the Christians of Kimhi's time (12th cent.) use King David (i.e., the verse from Psalms) in connection with the issue under discussion? (Does their use of a psalm show some familiarity with the Bible?)
3. What conclusions can be drawn from Kimhi's comments as to Jewish-Christian relations in 12th-century Provence?

Paper Topics

The Catholic Church and Moneylending
Moneylending: Halakhah and the Realities of the Times

Business Relations with Christians: Permitted or Forbidden by Halakhah?

Yayn Nesekh (wine used for church services) and *Stam Yaynam* (any wine of a non-Jew): Do These Prohibitions Apply Today?

Moneylending in Ashkenaz and Sefarad: Comparison and Contrast

Reference Works

H. H. Ben-Sasson, *A History of the Jewish People*
Encyclopaedia Judaica, s.v. "Moneylending"
N. Gross, *Economic History of the Jews*

THE JEWS OF ASHKENAZ (800–1400)

800	Charlemagne becomes emperor of West and founds Holy Roman Empire
	Jews move up Rhine Valley, settling in nearby parts of France and Germany
820	Louis the Pious succeeds Charlemagne, but is deposed in 833
	Louis shields Jews from hostile churchmen like Agobard. Jews permitted to buy and sell pagan slaves
843	Empire divided among Louis's three sons: Gaul to Charles the Bald; Germany to Louis; Rhine Valley to Lothair
920	R. Moses of Lucca and son Kalonymus move from Italy to Mainz.
987	Capetians succeed Carolingians in France
1000	Rabbenu Gershom bans polygamy, reading another person's mail, and divorce without wife's consent
1066	Normans conquer Anglo-Saxon England
	Jews follow William, establishing a community in England
	Rashi composes commentaries on Torah and Talmud
1084	Bishop of Speyer gives charter to Jews

1096	First Crusade
	Jews attacked in Cologne, Speyer, Worms, Mainz
1135	Rashbam writes commentary on Torah
1140	Gratian's code of canon (church) law
1144	Second Crusade
	Tosafists create new conception of Talmud study
1160	R. Abraham ben David becomes major authority in Provence
1171	First blood libel case in Blois, France
1187	Third Crusade
	500 Jews martyred in York, England
1200	R. David Kimhi writes Bible commentary stressing scientific-philological analysis
1215	King John of England extends rights to nobles: Magna Carta
	Fourth Lateran Council
1232	Works of Rambam burned by Dominicans in Provence
1236	Frederick II extends *servi camerae* status from Sicily to entire Holy Roman Empire
1240	Disputation of Paris
1242	Talmud burned
1290	Edward I expels Jews from leave England
1298	Rindfleisch leads attacks against Jews in Germany
1306	Jews expelled from France
1309	Dead body of R. Meir of Rothenburg is ransomed
1315	Jews invited to return to France
1322	Charles IV expels Jews again
1335	R. Jacob ben Asher writes *Arba'ah Turim*
1348	Black Death: Jews accused of poisoning wells
1394	Final expulsion of Jews from France

3

The Jews in Muslim Spain

This unit deals with the experiences of the Jews in Spain during the period from 711 to 1148 when the country was almost entirely under Muslim control. Jews had lived in Spain for several centuries before the coming of the Muslims, but conditions had deteriorated with the conversion of the Visigoths to Christianity in the 6th century and the enactment of an ongoing series of anti-Jewish laws. For this reason they enthusiastically supported the Muslim invaders in the hope of being relieved of the burdens imposed on them by their Christian overlords.

As explained in the first part of this book, Islam categorized Jews (and Christians) as dhimmis, "protected people." While on the one hand this status made them second-class citizens in some respects, it also ensured certain fundamental rights: the unrestricted practice of their faith, and the freedom to settle wherever they chose, pursue a wide range of professions, and establish religious and communal institutions.

Under Muslim rule, the Jews of Spain flourished and prospered. A culture of poets and philosophers emerged who were able to draw upon Muslim poetic and philosophical sources as well as their own Jewish sources. In addition, a class of courtiers came into being who served the Muslim government, in some cases exercising great power and influence; the two most notable such figures were Hasdai ibn Shaprut and Shmuel Ha-Nagid. Economic opportunities were many and varied, and Jews pursued a wide range of occupations, including agriculture, commerce, finance, and crafts of every kind.

A major turning point occurred in 929, when the Muslim ruler of Spain, 'Abd-ar-Rahman III, took for himself the title of caliph. By this means, he declared his own independence from the Muslim center in Baghdad and set up his own separate center in Spain. This important change had a major impact on the life of Spanish Jewry, as will become apparent in the course of our studies.

POLITICAL LIFE

The political life of the Jews in Muslim Spain focuses on two major figures: Hasdai ibn Shaprut (915–970) and Shmuel ibn Nagrela

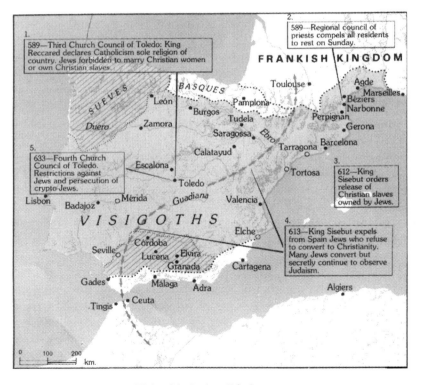

Visigothic Spain—7th Century

(993–1055). Ibn Shaprut, a doctor by profession, caught the attention of Caliph 'Abd-ar-Rahman III with his work on antidotes to poisons. This led to his appointment as court physician, carrying with it political power and influence. A man blessed with great linguistic skills, ibn Shaprut was asked to participate in the very important translation of a pharmacological work, *De Materia Medica*; while a monk translated it from Greek to Latin, ibn Shaprut translated from Latin to Arabic. This great achievement transformed the Spanish caliphate into an independent center of scientific study and research.

Ibn Shaprut also functioned in the role of diplomat. Thus, when the interests of 'Abd-ar-Rahman, the Muslim caliph, began to coincide with those of Constantine, the Christian emperor of Byzantium, they designated ibn Shaprut to become involved, since they needed a person who could work with both of them and conduct the necessary sensitive negotiations. Somewhat later on, 'Abd-ar-Rahman needed to deal with Christian kingdoms of the north and with the German Emperor Otto I. In each case the caliph called upon ibn Shaprut, who used his influence at court and his political connections to achieve his own goals for Spanish Jewry.

Ibn Shaprut's impact was felt especially through his stimulation of self-esteem among Spanish Jews. When he learned about the kingdom of the Khazars, a largely Jewish independent state located south of Russia, ibn Shaprut began to correspond with its ruler, Joseph. The Jews of Spain had been reminded for some time that they had no kingdom of their own, clear proof that they had been rejected by God; the existence of an independent Jewish kingship in Russia served to reestablish their feelings of national pride and self-esteem. Moreover, the actual presence of a Jewish kingdom led to messianic speculation, as ibn Shaprut and others wondered whether the king of the Khazars might have secret knowledge as to when the Jews would be gathered together by the Messiah and brought back to the land of Israel. The exchange of letters between ibn Shaprut and the Khazar king, reproduced below, reveals much about the concerns of the Jews of Spain.

Ibn Shaprut was also largely responsible for a major change in the orientation of the Jews of Muslim Spain. Prior to his time, the Jews had turned for religious guidance to the scholars of the East, the geonim of Sura and Pumpedita. Now, however, they began to look to their own scholars, men such as R. Moshe ben Hanoch. This represented the establishment of independence and autonomy for Spanish Jewry.

The second major figure in Jewish political life was Shmuel ibn Nagrela, also known as Shmuel ha-Nagid. A figure of real power in Muslim Spain, ibn Nagrela attained the highest governmental post, that of vizier, and thereby came to be recognized as the nagid, or prince, of the Jews. So great was his status that he became even more powerful than ibn Shaprut.

Ibn Nagrela's access to influence in Spain is tied to the fall of Cordoba in 1013. With this event Muslim Spain was broken up into thirty Muslim kingdoms. This was very important to the Jews of Spain, for it resulted in the fragmentation of power and ongoing internal warfare, both of which affected the special role they played as allies of this or that faction. Granada, in southern Spain, was held by the Zirids, and it was there that ibn Nagrela went. Although it is unclear how he gained influence, it might well have been through his saving the reigning king from conspirators seeking his death.

Ibn Nagrela was a multi-dimensional figure whose contributions to Jewish culture were many. He was an accomplished poet, counted as one of the four great poets of Muslim Spain. He was a master of halakhah, a student of his own father and of R. Hanoch ben Moshe, who eventually composed his own halakhic work. He was fluent in both Hebrew and Arabic and had been trained as well in the curriculum of the courtiers, which included ancient sciences and Arab poetics.

Beyond this, however, ibn Nagrela held real power in Muslim Spain, for he was the commander of the army—a remarkable position to be held by a Jew! The ongoing struggle of Granada with Seville, controlled by the Abbasids, meant that military leadership was a critical responsibility. Indeed, ibn Nagrela devoted much of his poetry to the trials of battle.

Texts

I. The Letter of Rabbi Hasdai, Son of Isaac Ibn Shaprut, to the King of the Chazars, about 960

I, Hasdai, son of Isaac, son of Ezra, belonging to the exiled Jews of Jerusalem in Spain, a servant of my lord the King, bow to the earth before him and prostrate myself towards the abode of your Majesty from a distant land. I rejoice in your tranquility and magnificence and stretch forth my hands to God in heaven that He may prolong your reign in Israel. . . .

Praise be to the beneficent God for His mercy towards me! Kings of the earth, to whom his [Abd-al-Rahman's] magnificence and power are known, bring gifts to him, conciliating his favor by costly presents, such as the King of Constantinople, and others. All their gifts pass through my hands, and I am charged with making gifts in return. [Ibn Shaprut, who knew several languages, received these embassies.] Let my lips express praise to the God of heaven, who so far extends His lovingkindness towards me, without any merit of my own, but in the fullness of His mercies!

I always ask the ambassadors of these monarchs who bring gifts, about our brethren the Israelites, the remnant of the captivity, whether they have heard anything concerning the deliverance of those who have languished in bondage and have found no rest. [He was anxious to know if the "lost ten tribes" existed as an independent Jewish state anywhere.]

At length mercantile emissaries of Khorasan [a land southeast of the Caspian Sea] told me that there is a kingdom of Jews which is called Al-Chazar. But I did not believe these words for I thought that they told me such things to procure my goodwill and favor. I was therefore wondering, till the ambassadors of Constantinople came [between 944 and 949] with presents and a letter from their king to our king, and I interrogated them concerning this matter.

They answered me: "It is quite true, and the name of that kingdom is Al-Chazar. It is a fifteen days' journey by sea from Constantinople, but by land many nations intervene between us; the name of the king now reigning is Joseph; ships sometimes come from their country to ours bringing fish, skins, and wares of every kind. [The Chazars, great traders, got their wares from the Russians to the north.] The men are our confederates and are honored by us; there is communication between us by embassies and mutual gifts; they are very powerful; they maintain numerous armies with which they occasionally engage in expeditions." When I heard this report I was encouraged, my hands were strengthened, and my hope was confirmed. Thereupon I bowed down and adored the God of heaven. [Hasdai was happy: Christians could no longer say the Jews were without a country as a punishment for their rejection of Jesus.]. . . .

I pray for the health of my lord the King, of his family, and of his house, and that his throne may be established for ever. Let his days and his sons' days be prolonged in the midst of Israel!

II. The Letter of Joseph the King, Son of Aaron the King, the Turk—May His Creator Preserve Him—to the Head of the Assembly, Hasdai, the Son of Isaac, Son of Ezra—about 960

. . . I wish to inform you that your beautifully phrased letter was given us by Isaac, son of Eliezer, a Jew of the land of Germany. [Isaac carried it through Germany, Hungary, and Russia to Chazaria.] You made us happy and we are delighted with your understanding and wisdom. . . . Let us, therefore, renew the diplomatic relations that once obtained between our fathers, and let us transmit this heritage to our children. [Joseph believed the Chazars had once had diplomatic relations with the Spanish Arabs.]

You ask us also in your epistle: "Of what people, of what family, and of what tribe are you?" Know that we are descended from Jophet, through his son Togarmah. [In Jewish literature Togarmah is the father of all the Turks.] I have found in the genealogical books of my ancestors that Togarmah had ten sons. These are their names: the eldest was Ujur, the second Tauris, the third Avar, the fourth Uguz, the fifth Bizal, the sixth Tarna, the seventh Chazar, the eighth Janur, the ninth Bulgar, the tenth Sawir. [These are the mythical founders of tribes that once lived in the neighborhood of the Black and Caspian Seas.] I am a descendant of Chazar, the seventh son.

I have a record that although our fathers were few in number, the Holy One blessed be He, gave them strength, power, and might so that they were able to carry on war after war with many nations who were more powerful and numerous than they. By the help of God they drove them out and took possession of their country. Upon some of them they have imposed forced labor even to this very day. The land [along the Volga] in which I now live was formerly occupied by the Bulgarians. Our ancestors, the Chazars, came and fought with them, and, although these Bulgarians were as numerous as the sand on the shores of the sea, they could not withstand the Chazars. So they left their country and fled while the Chazars pursued them as far as the Danube River. Up to this very day the Bulgars camp along the Danube and are close to Constantinople. The Chazars have occupied their land up till now. [The Chazars, known since the second century, dominated southern Russia during the early Middle Ages.]

After this, several generations passed until a certain King arose whose name was Bulan. He was a wise and God-fearing man, trusting in his Creator with all his heart. He expelled the wizards and idolators from the land and took refuge in the shadow of His wings. . . . After this his fame was spread broadcast. [Bulan probably ruled about 740. He was the first Jewish Chazar ruler.] The kings of the Byzantines and the Arabs who had heard of him sent their envoys and ambassadors with great riches and many great presents to the King as well as some of their wise men with the object of converting him to their own religion. [The Byzantines and Arabs hoped to stop the raids of the Chazars by converting them.]

But the King—may his soul be bound up in the bundle of life with the Lord his God—being wise, sent for a learned Israelite. The King searched, inquired, and investigated carefully and brought the sages together that they might argue about their respective religions. Each of them refuted, however, the arguments of his opponent so that they could not agree. When the King saw this he said to them: "Go home, but return to me on the third day. . . ."

On the third day he called all the sages together and said to them: "Speak and argue with one another and make clear to me which is the best religion." They began to dispute with one another without arriving at any results until the King said to the Christian priests "What do you think? Of the religion of the Jews and the Moslems which is to be preferred?" The priest answered: "The religion of the Israelites is better than that of the Moslems."

The King then asked the kadi [a Moslem judge and scholar]: "What do you say? Is the religion of the Israelites, or that of the Christians preferable?" The kadi answered: "The religion of the Israelites is preferable."

Upon this the King said: "If this is so, you both have admitted with your own mouths that the religion of the Israelites is better.

Wherefore, trusting in the mercies of God and the power of the Almighty, I choose the religion of Israel, that is, the religion of Abraham. If that God in whom I trust, and in the shadow of whose wings I find refuge, will aid me, He can give me without labor the money, the gold, and the silver which you have promised me. As for you all, go now in peace to your land." [This account of Bulan's conversion is apparently legendary. Another Hebrew source tells us that Judaism was adopted by the Chazars when a Jewish general was made king. Jewish fugitives from Constantinople also made many converts in Chazaria.]

From that time on the Almighty helped Bulan, fortified him, and strengthened him. He circumcised himself, his servants, attendants, and all his people. [Arabic sources say the royal family and nobility became Jews, but only a part of the people.] Then Bulan sent for and brought from all places wise men of Israel who interpreted the Torah for him and arranged the precepts in order, and up to this very day we have been subject to this religion. May God's name be blessed and may His remembrance be exalted for ever!

Since that day [about 740] when my fathers entered into this religion, the God of Israel has humbled all of their enemies, subjecting every folk and tongue round about them, whether Christian, Moslem, or pagan. No one has been able to stand before them to this day [about 960]. All of them are tributary. [But only about ten years later Joseph was defeated by the Russians, 969.]

After the days of Bulan there arose one of his descendants, a king, Obadiah by name, who reorganized the kingdom and established the Jewish religion properly and correctly. He built synagogues and schools, brought in Jewish scholars, and rewarded them with gold and silver. [The Jewish scholars could have come from Bagdad and Constantinople.] They explained to him the Bible, Mishnah, Talmud, and the order of divine services. The King was a man who revered and loved the Torah. He was one of the true servants of God. May the Divine Spirit give him rest!

He was succeeded by Hezekiah, his son; next to him was Manasseh, his son; next to him was Hanukkah, the brother of Obadiah; next Isaac, his son; afterwards, his son Zebulun; then his son Moses; then his son Nissi; then his son Aaron; then his son Menahem; then his son Benjamin; then his son Aaron II; and I, Joseph, the son of Aaron the King, am King, the son of a King, and the descendant of kings. [These kings probably had Turkish names besides their Hebrew ones.] No stranger can occupy the throne of my ancestors: the son succeeds the father. This has been our custom and the custom of our forefathers since they have come into existence. May it be the gracious will of Him who appoints all kings that the throne of my kingdom shall endure to all eternity.

You have also asked me about the affairs of my country and the extent of my empire. I wish to inform you that I dwell by the banks of the river known as the Itil [Volga]. At the mouth of the river lies the Caspian Sea. The headwaters of the river turn eastward, a journey of four months distance.

Alongside the river dwell many tribes in cities and towns, in open as well as fortified places. . . . Bear in mind that I dwell at the delta of the Itil and, by God's help, I guard the mouth of the river and do not permit the Russians who come in ships to enter into the Caspian so as to get at the Moslems. Nor do I allow any of their [the Moslems'] enemies who come by land to penetrate as far as Derbend. [Derbend, an Arab city, was the gate through which the nomads in Russia hoped to rush through and raid the rich towns of Asia Minor.] I have to wage war with them, for if I would give them any chance at all they would lay waste the whole land of the Moslems as far as Bagdad. . . .

You have also asked me about the place where I live. I wish to inform you that, by the grace of God, I dwell alongside this river on which there are situated three capital cities. The queen dwells in one of them; it is my birthplace. It is quite large, built round like a circle, the diameter of which is fifty parasangs. [The King lived on an island in the Volga; there were also towns on both banks.]

Jews, Christians, and Moslems live in the second city. Besides these there are many slaves of all nations in it. It is of medium size, eight square parasangs in length and breadth.

In the third I reside with my princes, officers, servants, cupbearers, and those who are close to me. It is round in shape and its diameter is three parasangs. The river flows within its walls. This is my residence during the winter. From the month of Nisan [March–April] on we leave the city and each one goes forth to his vineyards, fields, and to his work. . . .

You mention in your letter that you yearn to see my face. I also would very much like to see your pleasant countenance and the rare beauty of your wisdom and greatness. Would that it were according to your word. If it were granted me to be associated with you and to behold your honored, charming, and pleasant countenance, then you would be my father and I your son. According to your command would all my people be ruled, and according to your word and discreet counsel would I conduct all my affairs. Farewell.

Kobler, *Letters of Jews Through the Ages*, 97–119

Battle of Alfuente

The day was obscure and misty, and the sun like my heart was dark.
And the voice of the multitudes was like the voice of the Almighty like
    the sound of the sea and its breakers at the time of its raging tempest.
When the sun came out, the earth was dissolving at its pillars as if drunk,
And the horses sped and then turned back like vipers drawn from their
    caves.
The flying spears like lightning filled the air with light.
And the arrows were like drops of rain and the bucklers as sieves,
The bows were used like serpents and each spit out a bee with his mouth.
The sword upon their heads was like a torch whose light was dimmed as
    it fell.
And the blood of men upon the earth ran like the blood of rams at the
    side of the Temple court.

The Night in the Fortress

A mighty force I posted for the night in the fortress
Which sovereigns had long since destroyed.
We slept within it and by its side
Even as its owners slumbered below.

And to myself I said: "Where are the multitudes
And the nations who dwelt here before us?
And where those who built and laid waste;
The princes and paupers, the slaves and masters?

Where are the parents and those who mourn and where fathers
And sons and the bereaved and the bridegrooms?

Great nations follow one another
In the days and years that pass.

They were once neighbors upon the earth,
Even as now they lie within its bosom
Exchanging their palaces for the tomb;
For delightful gardens, the dust of earth.

Were they to raise their heads and come forth
They would make us lose our lives and property.
Indeed, O my soul, indeed like them will I be
On the morrow, myself and this huge force!

War the Maiden

War at the outset is like a beautiful maid
With whom every one wishes to flirt.
At the end it is like a despised hag
Bringing tears and sadness to whomever she meets.

L. Weinberger, *Jewish Princes in Moslem Spain: Selected Poems of Samuel Ibn Nagrela*

Questions on the Texts

1. Although a man of much influence in Spain, Hasdai is greatly interested in the Khazars. Why?
2. How might Hasdai's correspondence with Joseph, the Khazar king, be relevant to the world of today?
3. How does ibn Nagrela view his responsibilities as a military leader? Bring evidence from poem 1.
4. What questions does ibn Nagrela pose to those who have shared the experience of war? What conclusions does he draw? (poem 2)

Paper Topics

Hasdai as a Diplomatic Figure
Hasdai's Influence in the Jewish Community

Shmuel ibn Nagrela: Successes and Failures in Granada's Political
Life
Joseph ibn Nagrela: The Challenges and Dangers of Political Power

Reference Works

E. Ashtor, *The Jews of Muslim Spain*
G. Cohen, *Sefer ha-Qabbalah (The Book of Tradition)*
J. Gerber, *The Jews of Spain*
R. Scheindlin, *Wine, Women, and Death*
L. Weinberger, *Jewish Prince in Moslem Spain: Selected Poems of Samuel Ibn Nagrela*

CULTURAL LIFE

The cultural life of Spanish Jewry reached its peak during the period often referred to as the Golden Age of Spain (approximately 900–1200). It was at this time that Spanish Jewry began to produce remarkable and outstanding poets, philosophers, halakhists, historians, grammarians, and moralists. Muslim scholars, who were very much involved with poetry and grammar, exerted great influence on Arabic-speaking Jews, providing them with important resources. In addition, they provided Jewish scholars with a great deal of important philosophic source material.

Among the Jews of Muslim Spain, four outstanding poets stand out. Yehudah Halevi authored an important series of poems focusing on the theme of the Jews' attachment to Zion. Shmuel Ha-Nagid wrote poetry on religion, love, friendship, and war. Shlomoh ibn Gabirol wrote poems on both secular and religious themes, including the outstanding poem "Keter Malkhut," which Sephardic Jews include in the liturgy for Yom Ha-Kippurim. Moshe ibn Ezra wrote poetry about love, wine, and nature, but also poetry intended to serve as *shirei kodesh* (songs of holiness) in the synagogues.

Muslim Spain produced great philosophers, among them Yehudah Halevi and Moses Maimonides (Rambam). Halevi authored a work called the *Kuzari,* in which he presents a dialogue between the King of the Khazars and a philosopher, a Christian, a Muslim,

Statue of Rambam in Cordoba

and a Jew. The Jew is judged the winner, and from that point on has the opportunity to explain the Jewish views on knowledge, prophecy, free will, and other matters. Rambam's important work was the *Moreh Nevukhim*, or *Guide for the Perplexed*, in which he had two central goals: (1) to offer theological guidance to readers who were well-educated but troubled by certain religious and philo-sophical questions, and (2) to explain problematic passages in the Bible and Talmud. Among the topics treated by Rambam are cre-ation *ex nihilo* versus eternity of the world, miracles, prophecy, evil, *ta'amei ha-mitzvot* (the reasons for the various mitzvot), human free-dom, and human perfection.

In the area of halakhah, too, works of distinction were produced. The first of these was the *Hilkhot ha-Rif* by R. Yitzhak Alfasi, an abbreviated version of the Talmud. It contains only practical halak-hah; no aggadah is included, and no material irrelevant to the needs of everyday life, such as the laws of *korbanot* (sacrifices). The second great work was the *Mishneh Torah* of Rambam (Maimon-ides). Unlike Alfasi, he set out to create a systematic halakhic code that would encompass all of halakhah, not just the parts with prac-tical application. Thus it includes not only *Yesodei ha-Torah*, which takes in some of the most basic concepts of the Torah, but also the halakhot of *Biyat Mikdash,* which deal, albeit in limited fashion, with the laws of the Holy Temple in Jerusalem. It was Rambam's view that a reader with his work in hand would have no need to consult any other rabbinic sources.

Other important works include Ibn Daud's *Sefer ha-Kabbalah,* a history of Islamic Spain, Bahya ibn Pakuda's ethical work, *Hovot ha-Levavot,* and the grammatical works of Yehudah ibn Hayyuj and Yonah ibn Janach.

Texts

THE SUCCESSION OF THE RABBINATE

Prior to that, it was brought about by the Lord that the income of the academics which used to come from Spain, the land of the Maghreb, Ifriqiya, Egypt, and the Holy Land was discontinued. The following were the circumstances that brought this about.

The commander of a fleet, whose name was Ibn Rumahis, left Cordova, having been sent by the Muslim king of Spain, 'Abd ar-Rahman an-Nasir. This commander of a mighty fleet set out to capture the ships of the Christians and the towns that were close to the coast. They sailed as far as the coast of Palestine and swung about to the Greek sea and the islands therein. [Here] they encountered a ship carrying four great scholars, who were travelling from the city of Bari to a city called Sefastin, and who were on their way to a Kallah convention. Ibn Rumahis captured the ship and took the sages prisoner. One of them was R. Hushiel, the father of Rabbenu Hananel; another was R. Moses, the father of R. Hanok, who was taken prisoner with his wife and his son, R. Hanok (who at the time was but a young lad); the third was R. Shemariah b. R. Elhanan. As for the fourth, I do not know his name. The commander wanted to violate R. Moses's wife, inasmuch as she was exceedingly beautiful. Thereupon, she cried out in Hebrew to her husband, R. Moses, and asked him whether or not those who drown in the sea will be quickened at the time of the resurrection of the dead. He replied unto her: "The Lord said: I will bring them back from Bashan; I will bring them back from the depths of the sea." Having heard his reply, she cast herself into the sea and drowned.

These sages did not tell a soul about themselves or their wisdom. The commander sold R. Shemariah in Alexandria of Egypt; [R. Shemariah] proceeded to Fostat where he became head [of the academy]. Then he sold R. Hushiel on the coast of Ifriqiya. From there the latter proceeded to the city of Qairawan, which at that time was the mightiest of all Muslim cities in the land of the Maghreb, where he became the head [of the academy] and where he begot his son Rabbenu Hananel.

Then the commander arrived at Cordova where he sold R. Moses along with R. Hanok. He was redeemed by the people of Cordova, who were under the impression that he was a man of no education. Now there was in Cordova a synagogue that was called the College Synagogue, where a judge by the name of R. Nathan the Pious, who was a man of distinction, used to preside. However, the people of Spain were not thoroughly versed in the words of our rabbis, of blessed memory. Nevertheless, with the little knowledge they did possess, they conducted a school and interpreted [the traditions] more or less [accurately]. Once R. Nathan explained [the law requiring] "immersion [of the finger] for each sprinkling," which is found in the tractate Yoma, but he was unable to explain it correctly. Thereupon, R. Moses, who was seated in the corner like an attendant, arose before R. Nathan and said to him: "Rabbi, this would result in an excess of immersions!" When he and the students heard his words, they marvelled to each other and asked him to explain the law to them. This he did quite properly. Then each of them propounded to him all the difficulties which they had, and he replied to them out of the abundance of his wisdom.

Outside the College there were litigants, who were not permitted to enter until the students had completed their lesson. On that day, R. Nathan the Judge walked out, and the litigants followed him. However, he said to them: "I am no longer judge. This man, who is garbed in rags and is a stranger, is my master, and I shall be his disciple from this day on. You ought to appoint him judge of the community of Cordova." And that is exactly what they did.

The community then assigned him a large stipend and honored him with costly garments and a carriage. [At that point] the commander wished to retract his sale. However, the King would not permit him to do so, for he was delighted by the fact that the Jews of his domain no longer had need of the people of Babylonia.

The report [of all this] spread thoughout the land of Spain and the Maghreb, and students came to study under him. Morever, all questions which had formerly been addressed to the academies were now directed to him. This affair occurred in the days of R. Sherira, in about 4750, somewhat more or less.

R. Moses the Rabbi allied himself by marriage with the Ibn Falija family, which was the greatest of the families of the community of Cordova, and took from them a wife for his son R. Ḥanok. [Subsequently,] the daughter of R. Ḥanok was married to one of the Ibn Falija family. Because of this, they are called by the surname Ibn Falija to this day.

R. Moses acquired numerous disciples, one of whom was R. Joseph b. R. Isaac b. Shatnash, surnamed Ibn Abitur. He interpreted the whole of the Talmud in Arabic for the Muslim King al-Ḥakam. Because of his prominence and his learning, he rejected R. Ḥanok the Rabbi, who had occupied his father's post. Accordingly, after the death of the great nasi, R. Ḥisdai b. R. Isaac, the community was divided by a bitter dispute. (In the days of R. Ḥisdai there was not a man in the world who could have disputed the authority of R. Ḥanok.) Every day there used to go out of Cordova to the city of al-Zahra seven hundred Jews in seven hundred carriages, each of them attired in royal garb and wearing the headdress of Muslim officials, all of them escorting the Rabbi. A second faction would escort Ibn Shatnash. Finally, the party of the Rabbi gained the upper hand, excommunicated Ibn Shatnash and banned him. [At that point] the King said to him: "If the Muslims were to reject me in the way the Jews have done to you, I would go into exile. Now you betake yourself into exile!"

Ibn Daud, *Sefer he-Qabbalah*, 62–67

A MEDIEVAL CURRICULUM OF ADVANCED JEWISH AND SECULAR STUDIES
(LATE TWELFTH CENTURY)

Reading and Writing: The method of instruction must be so arranged that the teacher will begin first with the script, in order that the children may learn their letters, and this is to be kept up until there is no longer any uncertainty among them. This script is, of

course, the "Assyrian,"[1] the use of which has been agreed upon by
our ancestors. Then he is to teach them to write until their script is
clear and can be read easily. He should not however keep them
too long at work striving for beauty, decorativeness, and special
elegance of penmanship. On the contrary, that which we have already mentioned will be sufficient.

Torah, Mishnah, and Hebrew Grammar: Then he is to teach them
the Pentateuch, Prophets, and Hagiographa, that is the Bible, with
an eye to the vocalization and modulation in order that they may
be able to pronounce the accents correctly. Then he is to have them
learn the Mishna until they have acquired a fluency in it. "Teach
thou it to the children of Israel; put it in their mouths" (Deut.
31:19). The teacher is to continue this until they are ten years of
age, for the sages said, "At five years the age is reached for the
study of the Scriptures, at ten for the study of the Mishna" (Avot.
5:21). The children are then taught the inflections, declensions, and
conjugations, the regular verbs . . . and other rules of grammar.

Poetry: Then the teacher is to instruct his pupils in poetry. He
should, for the most part, have them recite religious poems and
whatever else of beauty is found in the different types of poetry,
and is fit to develop in them all good qualities.

Talmud: Then say the wise: "At fifteen the age is reached for the
study of Talmud" (Avot 5:21). Accordingly when the pupils are
fifteen years of age the teacher should give them much practice in
Talmud reading until they have acquired fluency in it. Later, when
they are eighteen years of age, he should given them that type of
instruction in it which lays emphasis on deeper understanding,
independent thinking, and investigation.

Philosophic Observations on Religion: When the students have
spent considerable time in study which is directed toward deeper
comprehension and thoroughness, so that their mental powers
have been strengthened; when the Talmud has become so much a
part of them that there is hardly any chance of its being lost, and
they are firmly entrenched in the Torah and the practice of its commands; then the teacher is to impart to them the third necessary
subject. This is the refutation of the errors of apostates and heretics

[1]What is meant is the Aramaic square script that has been standard for Hebrew for the
past two millennia.

and the justification of those views and practices which the religion prescribes.

Philosophic Studies: These studies are divided into three groups. The first group is normally dependent on matter, but can, however, be separated from matter through concept and imagination. This class comprises the mathematical sciences. In the second group speculation cannot be conceived of apart from the material, either through imagination or conception. To this section belong the natural sciences. The third group has nothing to do with matter and has no material attributes; this group includes in itself metaphysics as such.

Logic: But these sciences are preceded by logic which serves as a help and instrument. It is through logic that the speculative activities, which the three groups above mentioned include, are made clear. Logic presents the rules which keep the mental powers in order, and lead man on the path of clarity and truth in all things wherein he may err.

Mathematics, Arithmetic: The teacher will then lecture to his students on mathematics, beginning with arithmetic or geometry, or instruct them in both sciences at the same time.

Optics: Then the students are introduced into the third of the mathematical sciences, namely optics.

Astronomy: Then they pass on to astronomy. This includes two sciences. First astrology, that is, the science wherein the stars point to future events as well as to many things that once were or now are existent. Astrology is no longer numbered among the real sciences. It belongs only to the forces and secret arts by means of which man can prophesy what will come to pass, like the interpretation of dreams, fortune-telling, auguries, and similar arts. This science, however, is forbidden by God. . . . The second field of astronomy is mathematical. This field is to be included among mathematics and the real sciences. This science concerns itself with the heavenly bodies and the earth.

Music: After studying the science of astronomy the teacher will lecture on music to this students. Music embraces instruction in the elements of the melodies and that which is connected with them, how melodies are linked together, and what condition is required to make the influence of music most pervasive and effective.

Mechanics: This includes two different things. For one thing it aims at the consideration of heavy bodies insofar as they are used for measurements. . . . The second part includes the consideration of heavy bodies insofar as they may be moved or insofar as they are used for moving. It treats, therefore, of the principles concerning instruments whereby heavy objects are raised and whereby they are moved from one place to another.

Natural Sciences, Medicine: Let us now speak of the second section of the philosophic disciplines, that is, the natural sciences. After the students have assimilated the sciences already mentioned the teachers should instruct them in the natural sciences. The first of this group that one ought to learn is medicine, that is, the art which keeps the human constitution in its normal condition, and which brings back to its proper condition the constitution which has departed from the normal. This latter type of activity is called the healing and cure of sickness, while the former is called the care of the healthy. This art falls into two parts, science and practice.

After the students have learned this art the teacher should lecture to them on the natural sciences as such. This discipline investigates natural bodies and all things whose existence is incidentally dependent on these bodies. This science also makes known those things out of which, by which, and because of which these bodies and their attendant phenomena come into being.

Metaphysics: After this one should concern oneself with the study of metaphysics, that which Aristotle has laid down in his work, *Metaphysics*. This science is divided into three parts. The first part investigates "being" and whatever happens to it insofar as it is "being." The second part investigates the principles with respect to proofs which are applied to the special speculative sciences. These are those sciences, each one of which elucidates, along speculative lines, a definite discipline, as for instance, logic, geometry, arithmetic, and the other special sciences which are similar to those just mentioned.

Furthermore, this part investigates the principles of logic, of the mathematical sciences, and of natural science, and seeks to make them clear, to state their peculiarities, and to enumerate the false views which have existed with respect to the principles of these sciences. In the third part there is an investigation of those entities which are not bodies nor a force in bodies.

This is the first among sciences. All the other sciences, which are but the groundwork of philosophy, have this discipline in mind.

Joseph b. Judah Ibn 'Aknin, *Tibb al-Nufus,*
trans. Jacob R. Marcus, in
The Jew in the Medieval World, 374–77.

RAMBAM'S LETTER TO IBN TIBBON

Be assured that, when I saw the beauty of your style and noted the penetration of your intellect and that your lips utter knowledge clearly, I greatly rejoiced. I was surprised indeed to discover such talents, such a thirst for knowledge, such an acquaintance with Arabic (which I believe to be a partially corrupt dialect of Hebrew) displayed by one who has been born among 'stammerers'. I also admired your familiarity with the niceties of that language in abstruse subjects; this is indeed like a tender plant springing out of a dry ground. May the Lord enlighten your eyes with the light of His law, so that you may be of those that love Him, who are even as the sun when he goes forth in his strength. Amen.

The letters of your esteemed college, which God grant may ever increase in dignity and learning, reached me. I have carefully examined all the passages concerning the translation of which you entertain any doubt, and have looked into all those passages in which the transcriber has made any mistake, and into the various preliminary Propositions and Chapters which were not perfectly clear to you, and of which you sought elucidation.

Let me premise one rule. Whoever wishes to translate, and aims at rendering each word literally, and at the same time adheres slavishly to the order of words and sentences in the original, will meet with much difficulty; his rendering will be faulty and untrustworthy. This is not the right method. The translator should first try to grasp the sense of the passage thoroughly, and then state the author's intention with perfect clearness in the other language. This, however, cannot be done without changing the order of words, putting many words for one, or vice versa, and adding or taking away words, so that the subject may be perfectly intelligible in the language into which he translates. This method was followed by

Maimonides Commentary on the Mishnah—an Autographed Manuscript

Honein Is'hak with the works of Galen, and by his son Is'hak with
the works of Aristotle. It is for this reason that all their versions are
so peculiarly lucid, and therefore we should study them to the
exclusion of all others. Your distinguished college ought to adopt
this rule in all the translations undertaken for those honoured men

and the heads of the congregation. And may God grant that the spread of knowledge among the other communities of Israel be promoted by such works.

I now proceed to reply to your questions *seriatim*, to explain all those points which need explanation, to give the correct reading according to which you may amend the faults in your copy, arranged in the order of your epistle and embracing the three books of my work. [Here follow various explanations which refer to the most difficult portion of the 'Guide'].

God knows that, in order to write this to you, I have escaped to a secluded spot, where people would not think to find me, sometimes leaning for support against the wall, sometimes lying down on account of my excessive weakness, for I have grown old and feeble.

But with respect to your wish to come here to me, I cannot but say how greatly your visit would delight me, for I truly long to commune with you, and would anticipate our meeting with even greater joy than you. Yet I must advise you not to expose yourself to the perils of the voyage, for, beyond seeing me, and my doing all I could to honour you, you would not derive any advantage from your visit. Do not expect to be able to confer with me on any scientific subject for even one hour, either by day or by night. For the following is my daily occupation:

I dwell at Mizr [Fostat] and the Sultan resides at Kahira [Cairo]; these two places are two Sabbath days' journey distant from each other. My duties to the Sultan are very heavy. I am obliged to visit him every day, early in the morning; and when he or any of his children, or any of the inmates of his harem, are indisposed, I dare not quit Kahira, but must stay during the greater part of the day in the palace. It also frequently happens that one or two royal officers fall sick, and I must attend to their healing. Hence, as a rule, I repair to Kahira very early in the day, and even if nothing unusual happens. I do not return to Mizr until the afternoon. Then I am almost dying with hunger. . . . I find the antechambers filled with people, both Jews and Gentiles, nobles and common people, judges and bailiffs, friends and foes—a mixed multitude who await the time of my return.

I dismount from my animal, wash my hands, go forth to my patients, and entreat them to bear with me while I partake of some slight refreshment, the only meal I take in the twenty-four hours. Then I go forth to attend to my patients, and write prescriptions and directions for their various ailments. Patients go in and out until nightfall, and sometimes even, I solemnly assure you, until two hours or more in the night. I converse with and prescribe for them while lying down from sheer fatigue; and when night falls, I am so exhausted that I can scarcely speak.

In consequence of this, no Israelite can have any private interview with me, except on the Sabbath. On that day the whole congregation, or at least the majority of the members, come to me after the morning service, when I instruct them as to their proceedings during the whole week; we study together a little until noon, when they depart. Some of them return, and read with me after the afternoon service until evening prayers. In this manner I spend that day. I have here related to you only a part of what you would see if you were to visit me.

Now, when you have completed for our brethren the translation you have commenced, I beg that you will come to me, but not with the hope of deriving any advantage from your visit as regards your studies; for my time is, as I have shown you, excessively occupied.

Be careful not to study the works of Aristotle except with the help of his commentators, the commentary of Alexander, Themistius or Ibn Roshd.

As a general rule I may tell you, study only the works on logic composed by the learned Abunazar Alfarabi, for everything he has written is as fine flour. A man may indeed gain knowledge from his writings because he was a distinguished philosopher. So also Abubekr ben Alsaig was a great philosopher; all his writings are plain to him that understandeth, and right to them that find knowledge.

The writings of Aristotle are the foundations upon which all these philosophical works are based, and, as I have said above, they can only be understood by the help of their commentaries. . . . But other works besides those here enumerated, such as the writings of Empedocles, Pythagoras, Hermes and Porphyrius, all belong to ancient philosophy; it is not right to waste time upon them. He, Aristotle, indeed arrived at the highest summit of knowledge to which man can ascend, unless the emanation of the Divine Spirit be vouchsafed to him, so that he attain the stage of prophecy, above

126

which there is no higher stage. And the works of Ibn Sina, although they contain searching investigations and subtle thoughts, do not come up to the writings of Alfarabi. Still, they are useful, and it is right that you should study them diligently. I have now indicated to you the works you should study, and to which you should devote your mind.

May your happiness, my son and pupil, increase, and salvation be granted to our afflicted people.

Written by Moses, the son of Maimon, the Sephardi, on the 8th of Tishri 1511 according to the Seleucid era.

Kobler, *Letters of Jews Through the Ages*, 210–213

RAMBAM, INTRODUCTION TO THE *Mishneh Torah*

. . . And at this time there were significant historical problems, the hour exerted pressure on all, and the wisdom of our fathers and the understanding of our thoughtful ones was closed up—therefore those interpretations, halakhot, and responsa, which were composed by great rabbis [geonim] and seen by them to be clearly stated, became difficult in our days, with no one understanding them as they ought to be understood, except for a few in number. There is no need to mention the gemara itself, where lack of understanding applies to the Bavli [Babylonian Talmud] and the Yerushalmi [Jerusalem Talmud], the Sifra [halakhic midrash to Leviticus], the Sifri [halakhic midrash to Numbers and Deuteronomy], and the Tosefta [tannaitic beraitot supplementing the Mishnah]. Clear comprehension, a wise soul, and a long time are required—only after this will there be known from them the correct path in regard to those things which are forbidden and permitted, as well as the rest of the laws of the Torah.

On account of this, I washed my hands (I bound up my loins)—I, Moshe ben Maimon, the Sefardi—and I relied on the Almighty, May He Be Blessed. I analyzed all of these works, and I saw fit to compose matters which are clear from all of these works with regard to the *assur* [forbidden] and the *muttar* [permitted]; the *tamei* [impure] and the *tahor* [pure], with all the rest of the Torah laws, all of them in clear language and abbreviated form, until the entire

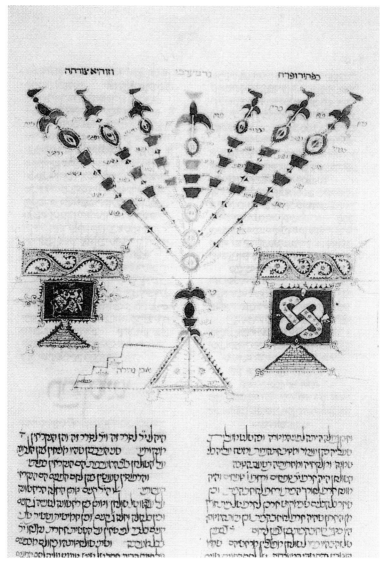

Manuscript of Rambam's Mishneh Torah

Torah she-be-al Peh [Oral Law] would be organized for everyone without questions or answers (i.e., without a full discussion). This one will not say thus, while the other says thus—rather clear formulations, accurate and well-formulated, in accordance with the law which emerges from all those compositions and interpretations, which are found from the days of Rabbenu Ha-Kadosh [R. Yehudah ha-Nasi, the compiler of the Mishnah] until now, so that all the laws are clear to big and small, with regard to every mitzvah, and with regard to all matters instituted by hakhamim [sages] and nevi'im [prophets].

The general purpose: that no one need any other composition in this world regarding any *din* [law] of *dinei Yisrael* [the laws of Israel], this composition will be a digest of the *Torah she-be-al Peh* in its entirely, with takkanot [rabbinic enactments], minhagot [customs], and gezerot [rabbinic prohibitions], which were made from the time of Moshe Rabbenu until the composition of the Talmud, as the rabbis have interpreted in all their works composed subsequent to the Talmud. For this reason I have called this work *Mishneh Torah* ["second Torah"]—since a man reads in the *Torah she-be-al Peh* first, and only afterwards he reads in this knowing from it the entire *Torah she-be-al Peh*. Thus he does not need to read any book between them, i.e., except these two.

Rambam, *Introduction to Mishneh Torah*, (trans. J. Bloomberg)

Questions on the Texts

IBN DAUD, "THE SUCCESSION OF THE RABBINATE"

1. Who are the central figures in Ibn Daud's account? Who might be the fourth captive?
2. What does the meeting between R. Moshe b. Hanokh and R. Natan indicate?
3. What major development in Spanish-Jewish history is Ibn Daud trying to explain?

IBN AKNIN, EDUCATIONAL CURRICULUM

1. Which elements in the program reveal Muslim influence?
2. Which parts are surprising in their inclusion? Why?
3. Which parts are excluded? Why?

RAMBAM, LETTER TO IBN TIBBON

1. What can be concluded from this letter regarding Rambam's daily pursuits?
2. What made Ibn Tibbon's translation effort important historically?

RAMBAM, INTRODUCTION TO *Mishneh Torah*

1. Where is there room to criticize Rambam's efforts?
2. Why does he feel the need for a different kind of work?
3. How does Rambam's effort differ from that of Alfasi?

Paper Topics

The Poetry of Yehudah Halevi: Themes, Poetic Structure, Religious/Secular Content

The *Kuzari* of Yehudah Halevi: Ideas and Concepts, Structure

The *Moreh Nevukhim*: Thematic Concerns, Conclusions, Structure

Rambam as Halakhist on *nevuah* (prophecy), *behirah hofshit* (freedom of will), and *kiddush hashem* (martyrdom)

Bahya ibn Paquda's *Hovot ha-Levavot*: Themes and Structure

Major Poets in Muslim Spain

Reference Works

E. Ashtor, *The Jews of Muslim Spain*
G. Cohen, *Sefer ha-Qabbalah (The Book of Tradition)*
J. Gerber, *The Jews of Spain*

MUSLIMS AND JEWS

The Jews of Spain enjoyed an atmosphere of tolerance. They served as diplomats, clerks, and financiers, holding considerable political power, with no office denied them. Although the Qur'an required justification for the employment of non-Muslims, this was overlooked with regard to the Jews, given the important functions which they served. The specific requirements of the Pact of 'Umar, which expected Jews to be humbled in status, were also ignored.

For the most part, the Spanish Jews were secure and fully integrated with the Muslim majority. Economic, political, and social factors came together to permit a degree of freedom unmatched anywhere in the world. Signs of tension between Muslims and Jews show up infrequently.

There were, however, some noteworthy instances of intolerance toward Jews. The earliest of these was the distinguished Muslim scholar Ibn Hazm (994–1064). Ibn Hazm argued that non-Muslims should be outside Muslim society—kept humble and, if necessary, humiliated. He wrote three works on Judaism and the Jews, of which two have survived. The first of these is the *Fisal* ("Studies about Religions, Opinions, and Sects"). This is the only extensive work on Judaism by a Muslim author, as well as the only anti-Jewish work authored by a great Muslim mind. Ibn Hazm's focus is on textual criticism of the Tanakh; it was not written to persuade Jews, but is directed at Muslims and intended to challenge their reverence for the Bible.

Ibn Hazm argues that careful consideration of certain passages in the Bible makes it clear that they were not divinely inspired and, therefore, that any claim of their ancient origin cannot be maintained. The Tanakh is filled with inconsistencies and contradictions, with shocking statements about the immoral conduct of Avraham, Yitzhak and Yaakov, anthropomorphisms, and assertions about plurality in God. The presence of so many forgeries and distortions in the Tanakh must lead Muslims to reject it.

The second important work by Ibn Hazm is the *Radd* ("Refutation"). Here he responds to a pamphlet composed by Shmuel ibn Nagrela against the Qur'an. Although Ibn Hazm had no copy of the pamphlet, he did have a refutation written by a Muslim.

In each of the eight chapters of the *Radd*, Ibn Hazm first defends the Qur'an and then presents a critique of relevant parts of the Tanakh. The major difference between this work and the *Fisal* is that here the Jews are attacked for dominating country, state, and resources, and Muslim kings are criticized for allowing this to happen.

Another work of great importance is the *Ifham al-Yahud* ("Silencing the Jews") by Samau'al al-Maghribi (ca. 1125–1175), a Jew of Baghdad who converted to Islam in 1163. The book has two major elements: criticism of Judaism and arguments in favor of Islam. In the section in which Judaism is critiqued, al-Maghribi contends, in line with Muslim thinking, that portions of the Tanakh have been "abrogated," withdrawn by God. He reviews and criticizes Jewish thought about tradition, the authorship of the Torah, the composition of the Talmud, and the differences between Rabbinic Judaism and the Karaism. He then, without much sympathy, explores the reasons for the ongoing existence of the Jewish people. His overall theme is that Judaism is a fossil whose continued existence cannot be justified. Reason and conscience, says al-Maghribi, should lead those who are honest to embrace Islam.

A final interesting source is a poem composed by Abu Izhaq al-Elbiri (d. 1067). Muslim rulers who have the audacity to appoint Jews to high office, writes al-Elbiri, can expect widespread discontent among their people. Jews should not be permitted to dominate Spain; the ruler himself is responsible for this evil. Appointing Jews is against the word of Allah. It is also a violation of the Pact of 'Umar, adhered to by the successors of Muhammad; the covenant with Allah is thus broken. Some see this poem as a decisive factor in the death of Joseph, the son of Shmuel ibn Nagrela, along with some 3,000 others, in 1066.

Texts

Ibn Hazm, Radd

. . . A man who was filled with hatred towards the Apostle—a man who is, in secret, a materialist, a free-thinker, a Jew—of the most contemptible of religions, the most vile of faiths . . . loosened his tongue . . . and became conceited in his vile soul, as a result of his wealth. His riches, his gold and his silver robbed him of his wretched senses; so he compiled a book in which he set out to demonstrate the alleged contradictions in the Word of God, the Koran . . . When I came to know of the affair, of the work of that accursed creature, I did not cease searching for that filthy book, so that, with the gift bestowed upon me by Allah, I might be of service by helping His faith with words and insight, and in defending His community with eloquence and knowledge. I was fortunate, and obtained a manuscript containing a refutation written by a Muslim. So I copied out the passages the polemist had reproduced from the work of that ignominious ignoramus. I proceeded at once, with God's help, to refute his evil thoughts. By God, his argumentation proves how poor is his knowledge, how narrow his mind, about which I already knew something. For I used to know him when he was naked, except for charlatanry, serene, except for anxiety, void except of lies.

It is my firm hope that God will treat those who befriend the Jews and take them into their confidence as He treated the Jews themselves. . . . (Koran injunctions against Jews and Christians) For wosoever amongst Muslim princes has listened to all this and still continues to befriend the Jews, holding intercourse with them, well deserves to be overtaken by the same humiliation and to suffer in this world the same griefs which God has meted out to the Jews, apart from their chastisement in the next world. Whosoever acts in this manner will be recompensed by suffering along with the Jews themselves, according to God's warning in their Torah, in the Fifth Book (Deuteronomy XXVIII.15–58, quoted in full). . . . On their own evidence, this is God's message, and the chastisement He has apportioned them . . . Then let any prince upon whom God has bestowed some of His bounty take heed . . . Let him get away from this filthy, stinking, dirty crew beset with God's anger and malediction, with humiliation and wretchedness, misfortune, filth and dirt, as no other people has ever been. Let him know that the garments in which God has enwrapped them are more obnoxious than war, and more contagious than elephantiasis. May God keep us from rebelling against Him and His decision, from honouring those whom He has humiliated, by raising up those whom He has cast down. . . .

M. Perlmann, "Eleventh-Century Andalusion Authors on the Jews of Granada," 282–283

Samau'al al-Maghribi, Ifham al-Yahud

Firstly, I was loath to mention a matter that could not be proved, lest the mind of the listener should be prompt to deny it as something extraordinary or unusual. For a sensible man is loath to expose himself to refutation, be it open or secret. Secondly, I was loath to have the report of the two dreams reach anyone in the land who was envious of me on account of the scholarship and esteem of God had bestowed upon me, let this report be used to stir up ill-will against me and contempt for my conduct, and lest the ill-wishers say: "He left his religion on account of a dream he had seen; he was deceived by jumbled dreams."

The reader of these pages should now understand that it was not the dream that had induced me to abandon my first faith. A sensible man will not be deceived about his affairs by dreams and visions, without proof or demonstration. But I had know for a long time the proofs and demonstrations and arguments for the prophethood of our master Muhammad . . . It was those proofs and demonstrations that were the cause for my conversion and for taking the right path. As to the dream, it served merely to alert and to prod me out of my procrastination and inertia.

The Jews assert that Muhammad had dreams indicating that he was to be the head of a state; that he traveled to Syria on business of Khadija (Muhammad's employer, later his wife), met rabbis and told them his dreams, and that they recognized that he was to be the head of a state. Then they attached to him as companion ¤Abdallah b. Salam (an early Jewish convert to Islam), who instructed him for some time in scholarship and jurisprudence of the Torah. They go so far in their claim as to ascribe the miraculous eloquence of the Koran to its compilation by ¤Abdallah b. Salam, and maintain that it was he who stipulated in the marriage law that a wife, after her third divorce from her husband, shall not be permitted to rewed him until she has been married and divorced from another man, the purpose being, in their contention, to make *mamzerim* of the children of the Muslims. This word is plural; its singular is *mamzer*. This is the term for an illegitimate child. For, in their law, if the husband takes back his wife after she has been married to another man, her children are considered illegitimate. Since abrogation is inconceivable to them, they conclude that this stipulation in the marriage law is an interpolation of ¤Abdallah b. Salam, by which he sought to turn Muslim children into what they consider *mamzerim* (cf. Koran 2:229–230).

M. Perlmann, "The Medieval Polemics Between Islam and Judaism," 116–7, 119

134

Abu Izhaq

Your lord has sadly erred
And his foes are rejoicing
He selected an infidel to be his Katib
Who, if you lord wished, could have been a believer . . .
It was not even of their own (the Jews') making
For from our midst arises the accomplice.

Many a pious Muslim is in awe of the vilest infidel ape.

Bring them down to their place
Return them to the most abject station.
They used to roam around us in their tatters
Covered with contempt, humiliation, and scorn.
They used to rummage amongst the dungheaps for
     a bit of filty rag
To serve as a shroud for a man to be buried in.

They divided up Granada, capital and provinces
And everywhere there is one of those accursed
They seize Granada's revenues
Biting into and crunching them.
They dress in exquisite garments
Whilst you the basest wear.

That ape of theirs had his home paved with marble
And made the purest of springs flow thither.
Our affairs are his charge
And we have to wait at his gate
While he ridicules us and our religion.

Therefore, haste to slaughter him as sacrifice
And offer him, fat ram that he is.

Do not consider that killing them is treachery
Nay, it would be treachery to leave them scoffing.

They are in charge of your secrets
But how can the faithless be trusted.

M. Perlmann, "Eleventh-Century Andalusion Authors on the Jews of Grenada," 285–287

Questions on the Texts

IBN HAZM, *Radd*

1. How does Ibn Hazm characterize Shmuel ibn Nagrela? (selection 1)
2. What "reward" should be expected by those who treat Jews well? (selection 2)
3. What is the tone of Ibn Hazm's remarks about ibn Nagrela? about Jews? (both selections)

SAMAU'AL AL-MAGHRIBI, *Ifham al-Yahud*

1. How does al-Maghribi account for his own conversion?
2. What role did 'Abdallah b. Salam play in Muhammad's education? How did he lead Muhammad astray? To whom do the Jews attribute the authorship of the Qur'an?

ABU IZHAQ

1. How are the courtiers of Spain described? How does Abu Izhaq's poetic language give additional emphasis?
2. What is Abu Izhaq's plan for action?

Paper Topics

Muslims and Jews in Spain
Muslim-Jewish Polemic in Spain
Ibn Hazm and Shmuel ibn Nagrela: A Confrontation
Poetry as a Weapon: Abu Izhaq and Joseph ibn Nagrela
Al-Maghribi and the Jews

Reference Works

E. Ashtor, *The Jews of Muslim Spain*
J. Gerber, *The Jews of Spain*
M. Perlmann, "Eleventh-Century Andalusian Authors on the Jews of Granada"
———, "The Medieval Polemics Between Islam and Judaism"
N. Stillman, *The Jews of Arab Lands*

ECONOMIC ACTIVITIES

'Abd-ar-Rahman I (756–788), Spain's Muslim ruler, chose Cordoba as his capital city, due to its central location and its fertile countryside, which made it a natural agricultural market. Cordoba reached its peak in the 10th century during the reign of 'Abd-ar-Rahman III (912–961), becoming the home of at least 100,000 residents of various nationalities and ethnic backgrounds. Some 700 mosques served this population, along with perhaps 3,000 public baths. The streets were paved and lit, and along the riverbanks were many luxurious villas, some of which even had indoor plumbing.

Cordoba became a major cultural center that attracted scientists, architects, physicians, translators, and others. The city had 70 libraries, with the personal library of 'Abd-ar-Rahman holding 400,000 volumes. Among the gems of its architecture was an enormous mosque that is now regarded as one of Spain's greatest architectural treasures. 'Abd-ar-Rahman III built a 400-room palace in honor of his favorite concubine, Zahra (and therefore called Madinat az-Zahra); it took twenty years to complete, and involved the labor of 8,000 workers and 1,000 mules.

Cordoba was also a major economic center built on a combination of agriculture, industry, and trade. Citrus fruits, bananas, cinnamon, almonds, and other produce was brought there from the East, and its markets were also filled with locally cultivated cotton, silk, flax, and wool. The active economy of Spain made gold and silver very important. Even alcohol did well, despite the well-known Islamic prohibitions. The enormous wealth of Cordoba is described by Hasdai ibn Shaprut in one of the sources quoted below.

To what extent were Jews involved in the commerce of the medieval Islamic world (both in Spain and beyond Spain)? The extensive Arabic travel literature in the 8th and 9th centuries led to expanded knowledge of travel routes as well as of modes of access to remote areas of the world. As a result, Jews found themselves able to travel from Spain to Sicily to Aden to the Indian Ocean; documents from the famous Cairo Genizah make it evident that Jews enjoyed unrestricted freedom of travel in the Muslim world.

Learned merchants were very important to medieval commerce.

The genizah collection contains around 300 letters from a Tunisian Jewish merchant-scholar named Nahrai ben Nissim. His career as a merchant lasted for 50 years. He commuted regularly between Tunisia and Egypt, and was involved in transactions dealing with merchandise from Spain, Egypt, North Africa, Sicily, Syria, and India. In addition to his role in trade, Nissim was regarded as a talented scholar and honored as such by communities in Egypt, Palestine, and North Africa.

Jews were important in commerce for other reasons as well. First, Jews were multilingual, with competence in Hebrew, Arabic, Persian, Greek, and other languages. Second, Hebrew was a language relevant to religious and intellectual discourse. Third, Jews saw themselves as bound by the authoritative legal code of the Talmud.

It should be added that there was considerable risk involved in long-distance commerce. Jews were frequently called upon to engage in the redemption of captives. In an 11th-century letter found in the Cairo Genizah, the Jews of Alexandria appeal to the elders of Fostat (Cairo) to redeem captive Jews from the hands of pirates.

The Jews of Spain were involved primarily in two professions: banking and medicine. Jews were important in banking and related pursuits because they were able to draw upon financial resources throughout the Islamic world. Jews were important in medicine because Muslims were willing to overlook their religious prejudices in order to obtain the best treatment available. The prominence of Jews in banking and medicine was sometimes the source of access to political power outside the Jewish community.

Other professional pursuits of the Jews included artisanship and crafts. Many Jews were goldsmiths and silversmiths. Interestingly, Jews avoided food production, transportation, and enterprises related to warfare. As is evident from the genizah documents, Jews avoided growing cereal crops and raising cattle, camels, horses, and pack animals. Moreover, they did not engage in the purchase or sale of arms. These may well have been regarded as overly sensitive areas of endeavor for Jews.

Texts

Letter of Hasdai

The land is rich, abounding in rivers, springs, and aqueducts; a land of corn, oil and wine, of fruits and all manner of delicacies;

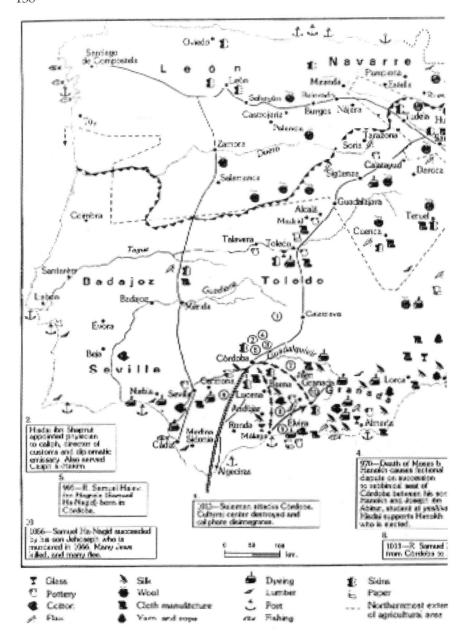

Muslim Spain: Economy and Centers of Jewish Settlement

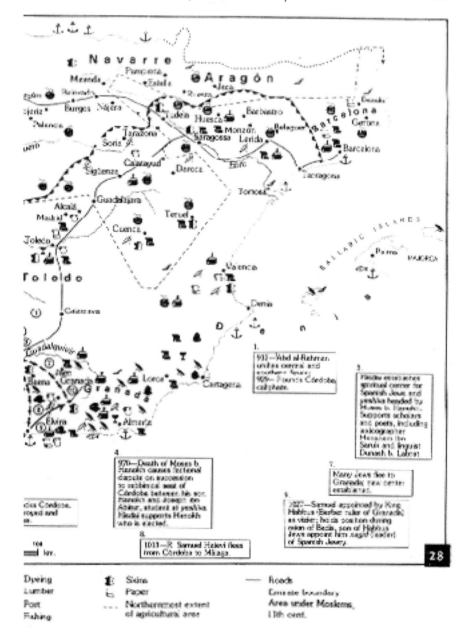

Muslim Spain: Economy and Centers of Jewish Settlement

it has pleasure-gardens and orchards, fruitful trees of every kind, including the leaves of the tree upon which the silkworm feeds, of which we have great abundance. In the mountains and woods of our country cochineal is gathered in great quantity. There are also found among us mountains covered by crocus and with veins of silver, gold, copper, iron, tin, lead, sulphur, porphyry, marble, and crystal. Merchants congregate in it, and traffickers from the ends of the earth, from Egypt and adjacent countries, bringing spices, precious stones, splendid wares for kings and princes, and all the desirable things of Egypt. Our King has collected very large treasures of silver, gold, precious things, and valuables such as no king has ever collected. His yearly revenue is about 100,000 gold pieces, the greater part of which is derived from the merchants who come hither from various countries and islands; and all their mercantile transactions are placed under my control.

N. de Lange, *Illustrated History of the Jewish People*, 162

Nahrai ben Nissim—the Merchant and his Business

1. Flax, exported from Egypt to Tunisia and Sicily.
2. Silk (from Spain and Sicily) and other fabrics, from Syrian or European (Rum) cotton to North African felt, and textiles of all descriptions, from robes to bedcovers.
3. Olive oil, soap and wax from Tunisia, occasionally also from Palestine and Syria.
4. Oriental spices, such as pepper, cinnamon, and clove, sent from Egypt to the West.
5. Dyeing, tanning, and varnishing materials such as brazilwood, lacquer and indigo (sent from East to West); sumac and gallnuts (from Syria to Egypt); saffron (from Tunisia to the East).
6. Metals (copper, iron, lead, mercury, tin, silver ingots), all West to East.
7. Books (Bible codexes, Talmuds, legal and edifying literature, grammars, and Arabic books).
8. Aromatics, perfumes, and gums (aloe, ambergris, camphor, frankincense, gum arabic, mastic gum, musk, betel leaves).
9. Jewelry and semiprecious stones (gems, pearls, carnelians, turquoises, onyxes, and the like).

10. Materials (such as beads, "pomegranate" strings, coral, cowrie shells, lapis lazuli, and tortoiseshell) used for ornaments and trinkets, items that loomed large in his papers.

11. Chemicals (alkali, slum, antimony, arsenic, bamboo crystals, borax, naphtha, sulfur, starch, vitriol).

12. Foodstuffs, such as sugar, exported from Egypt, or dried fruits, imported from Syria.

13. Hides and leather. Also furs and shoes. All coming from, or through, Tunisia and Sicily.

14. Pitch, an important article.

15. Varia, such as palm fiber, and items not yet identified with certainty.

S. Goitein, *A Mediterranean Society*, 1:154

The Radhanites (9th Century)

They speak Arabic, Persian, Greek, Frankish, Andalusian, and Slavonic. They travel from East to West and from West to East by both land and sea. From the West, they bring adult slaves, girls and boys, brocade, beaver pelts, assorted furs, sables, and swords. They sail from the Land of the Franks on the Western Sea (the Mediterranean) and set out for al-Farama (Pelusium). There they transport their merchandise by pack animal to al-Qulzum, which is twenty-five parasangs away. At al-Qulzum they set sail for al-Jar and Jidda, after which they proceed to Sind, India, and China. From China they bring musk, aloeswood, camphor, cinnamon, and other products obtained from those regions, as they make their way back to al-Qulzum. Then they transport it overland to al-Farama, there setting sail on the Western Sea once again. Some go straight to Constantinople to sell their merchandise to the Byzantines, while others go to the capital of the king of the Franks and sell their goods there.

Sometimes they choose to take their merchandise from the Land of the Franks across the Western Sea to Antioch, and thence overland on a three-day journey to al-Jabiya, from which they sail down the Euphrates to Baghdad, then down the Tigris to Ubulla. From Ubulla they sail to Oman, Sind, India, and China—in that order.

. . . .

As for their overland itinerary—those of them that set out from Spain or the Land of the Franks can cross over to the Further Sus, go from there to Tangier, and then across to Ifrīqiya (Tunisia), Egypt, Ramle, Damascus, Kufa, Baghdad, Basra, Ahwaz, Fars, Kirman, Sind, India, and finally, China. Sometimes they take the route behind the Byzantine Empire through the Land of the Slavs to Khamlıj, the capital of the Khazars. Then they cross the Sea of Jurjan (the Caspian) toward Balkh and Transoxania. From there they continue to Yurt and Tughuzghuzz, and finally to China.

N. Stillman, *The Jews of Arab Lands*, 163–4

Letter from Jews of Alexandria to Jews of Fostat(Cairo)

To the highly respected Rabbi Ephraim, member of the great assembly,[1] son of the R. Shemarya, of blessed memory, and the Elders, the noble and highly honoured men, may the Lord protect them, from your friends, the community of Alexandria, best greetings! . . . You are the supporters of the poor and the aid of the men in need, you study diligently, you rouse the good against the evil impulse. You walk in the right way and practise justice. We let you know that we always pray for you. May God grant you peace and security!

We turn to you today on behalf of a captive woman who has been brought from Byzantium. We ransomed her for 24 denares besides the governmental tax. You sent us 12 denares; we have paid the remainder and the tax. Soon afterwards sailors brought two other prisoners, one of them a fine young man possessing knowledge of the Torah, the other a boy of about ten. When we saw them in the hands of the pirates, and how they beat and frightened them before our own eyes, we had pity on them and guaranteed their ransom. We had hardly settled this, when another ship arrived carrying many prisoners. Among them were a physician and his wife. Thus we are again in difficulties and distress. And our strength is overstrained, as the taxes are heavy and the times critical. . . .

N. de Lange, *Illustrated History of the Jewish People*, 153

Questions on the Texts

LETTER OF HASDAI

1. What resources are identified as central to Cordoba? Why might this be?
2. To whom does Hasdai give credit for the great wealth of Cordoba? How has he obtained this information?

NAHRAI BEN NISSIM

1. Categorize the items specified here in the order of their importance.
2. Which items surprised you, and which did not? Explain why.

THE RADHANITES

1. What commodities do the Radhanites bring from the West? from the East?
2. Which routes are taken by sea? by land?

LETTER FROM THE JEWS OF ALEXANDRIA TO THE JEWS OF FOSTAT

1. What is the halakhic basis for *pidyon shvuyim*? (See Bava Batra 8:8 and Rambam, Mattenot Aniyim 8:10.)
2. Why were the Jews of Fostat expected to be generous even regarding those who came from outside their community?

Paper Topics

Cordoba: Center of Medieval Commerce
Economic Pursuits of the Jews of Spain
Jews in Medieval Commerce: Evidence from the Cairo Genizah
The Jews of Muslim Spain and the Slave Trade

Reference Works

E. Ashtor, *The Jews of Moslem Spain*
J. Gerber, *The Jews of Spain*
M. Gil, "The Radhanite Merchants and the Land of Radhan"

144

S. D. Goitein, *A Mediterranean Society*, vol. 1
————, "Jewish Society and Institutions Under Islam"
N. Gross, ed., *Economic History of the Jews*

MUSLIM SPAIN (711–1148)

711	Muslims conquer Spain Jews aid Muslim invaders
732	Charles Martel defeats Muslims at Tours
755	Ummayad regime in Cordoba founded by Abd ar-Rahman allows Jews to work in all occupations
916	Al-Tabari completes annals of Muslim political and religious leaders
929	Abd ar-Rahman III declares himself caliph
940	Hasdai becomes caliph's physician and leader of Jewish community
960	Menahem b. Saruq compiles first Hebrew dictionary; Dunash b. Labrat writes poetry in Hebrew
1027	Shmuel ibn Nagrela becomes vizier of Granada
1049	Shmuel ibn Nagrela completes *Hilkheta Gavrata* synthesizing talmudic law
1055	Shmuel leads Granada's army to victory over Seville
1085	Alfonso VI of Castile captures Toledo from Muslims; beginning of Reconquista
1088	R. Isaac Alfasi composes *Hilkhot ha-Rif*
1091	Alfonso VI withdraws Jewish civil rights
1139	Yehudah Halevi writes *Kuzari*, as well as some 800 Hebrew poems
1148	Almohad invasion of Spain When Cordova falls, Rambam's family leaves Spain

4

The Jews in Christian Spain

THIS UNIT DEALS with the history of the Jews in Spain from 1148, when the Christian kings of Aragon and Castile began to reconquer the country, to 1492, when the last Muslim stronghold was captured and the Jews were expelled.

The Jews of Spain were inevitably affected by the Reconquista, a series of wars between Christians and Muslims that lasted for nearly three centuries, with the borders of Christian Spain steadily shifting southward and the Muslims pushed further and further back. As the territories in which they resided came under Christian control, many of Spain's Jewish communities continued to function in the same way they had under Muslims. Changes were gradually introduced, however, depending very much on who was the king, since some Christian monarchs involved themselves in the affairs of the Jewish community and some did not.

Under Christian rule, unlike their experience under Islam, the Jews of Spain faced many challenges to their religion. Among these were the disputations at Barcelona and Tortosa, and the conversionary efforts of Franciscan and Dominican monks, which ultimately induced as many as 100,000 Jews to accept Christianity.

In the 15th century the Inquisition came to Spain, headed by Tomas de Torquemada, the inquisitor-general. The history of Spanish Jewry came to an abrupt end in 1492 when Ferdinand and Isabella issued the decree of expulsion.

Despite these hardships, the Jews of Christian Spain continued to have a rich cultural life. Its output included the Bible commentaries of Nahmanides and Don Isaac Abrabanel, classics of Jewish literature that are still studied today. It also produced outstanding halakhic works, including the talmudic commentaries of Nahmanides, Ibn Adret, and R. Asher ben Yehiel. In philosophy the outstanding figure was Nahmanides, but the 13th century also yielded the *Zohar*, which rapidly became the "Bible" of the Kabbalah.

Jews in Christian Spain enjoyed productive economic lives, pursuing many of the same occupations as during the Muslim period, such as tax-farming, finance, medicine, moneylending, commerce, and crafts of all kinds.

As we examine the history of the Jews in Christian Spain more closely, you will develop a much fuller understanding of this rich but tragic period in our history.

POLITICS AND COMMUNITY

During the Reconquista, Aragon, in the northeast, and Castile, in the northern and central part of the country, emerged as Spain's two most powerful Christian kingdoms. They steadily increased in size, strength, and wealth both by conquering Muslim territories and by absorbing smaller Christian principalities. Their union in the 15th century through the marriage of Ferdinand and Isabella resulted in the establishment of a single Spanish state. For the purposes of our study, it will be interesting to consider events in Aragon and Castile separately during the period before their union.

Castile in the 13th Century: Alfonso X

At the very beginning of his reign as king of Castile, Alfonso X (1252–84) set down rules governing both Christians and Jews. For Christians he prohibited any display of luxury and even indicated what would be regarded as acceptable forms of dress. As for Jews, he demanded extreme simplicity of dress and adornment. He sought to prevent Christians from associating with Jews and thus being exposed to Jewish religious teachings. The civil rights of Jews, Muslims, and heretics were limited; they could not inherit property from Christians or serve as their attorneys and executors of wills.

Alfonso produced a code of law known as *Las Siete Partidas*. This famous law code did not take effect until the 14th century, and its legislation regarding the Jews did not affect them much, but its ideology reveals a great deal about Alfonso's thinking. The code's provisions related to Jews clearly reflect church thinking on the issue. Jews are denied the right to hold public office, and Christians are forbidden to accept medical treatment from Jews. A special judicial procedure is prescribed for cases of the blood libel, despite this accusation having been disavowed by Pope Innocent IV. Still, a certain measure of humane treatment is given the Jews; it is forbidden to break into a synagogue, and Sabbaths and holidays are to be respected properly.

Other laws not included in the *Partidas* had great practical importance. The legal rate of interest on loans by Jews to Christians was set at 33 1/3 percent. The formula for the Jewish oath was fixed and included in the official law codes. The effort to abolish the *wergeld*—a penalty for injury and murder paid by the offender and his family to the victim or his next of kin—and replace it with a state-imposed penalty of personal monetary compensation was opposed by Christians wherever this change favored the Jews.

Alfonso supported the growth of Jewish communal autonomy. Thus the *aljamas* (Jewish communities) were granted criminal jurisdiction; Alfonso never limited this right. Disputes between Jews were judged by the administrative officers and rabbis of the Jewish communities, with each of the litigants reserving the right of appeal to the royal court. The king had the power to involve himself directly in lawsuits between Jews and refer them to his judges, although in such instances Jewish judges and rabbis had to sit with the king's judges and give advice about any decision. The Jewish judges decided in accord with Torah law and the views of contemporary authorities. The king could appoint, and sometimes did, a supervisor of Jewish legal affairs in a given locality. Such a position was occupied by R. Todros ben Joseph Halevi Abulafia in Toledo. Abulafia was a member of an aristocratic family distinguished for its wealth, learning, and piety. He was a mystic and an ascetic. Alfonso saw him as worthy of being the chief rabbi and justice of all the Jews in Castile. Abulafia is described in the literature of the time as the "prince of the Spanish diaspora."

The Jewish courtiers of Castile, of whom there were only a few, were something of an aristocracy. They organized the administration of taxes for the whole kingdom and managed its other finances. They were the ones who drew on the royal treasury to pay its bills. It was they who paid the knights their salaries, supplied food, clothing, and arms to the armies of the kingdom. They also managed the royal household.

The most powerful of the court Jews under Alfonso was Don Solomon ibn Zadok of Toledo. He was the chief collector of taxes and was highly regarded for his endowments of synagogues and charitable institutions. He held much property: houses, vineyards, olive groves, and warehouses full of goods. Todros Halevi knew Don Solomon well and praised him highly; Todros's own patron was Don Solomon's son, Don Isaac ibn Zadok.

Castile in the 13th Century: Sancho IV

Alfonso was succeeded by his son, Sancho IV (1284–95). Although Sancho imposed a heavier tax burden on the Jews, his treatment of them was very much like his father's. The Jews of Toledo administered Castile, their leader being Don Abraham el Barchilon, who paid the knights and the court personnel and purchased cloth for the court. The tax collectors of Castile had to present their accounts to him.

In June of 1287, Sancho gave Don Abraham a two-year lease on the crown's principal sources of revenue; the most important part of this was that he received the crown's right to mint the gold of the entire realm. The lease agreement included many other privileges, with Don Abraham becoming responsible for collecting the taxes on livestock, collecting debts owed by Jews to the crown, disposing of ownerless property, receiving fines imposed for violation of the crown's economic rules, collecting export duties, overseeing the income of the royal treasury, supervising the export of mercury, examining the accounts of earlier tax farmers, and collecting all arrears of payments due the crown. Thus he had concentrated in his hands the central fiscal administration of Castile; this appears to have been an attempt not simply to recoup budget deficits in Castile but also to introduce overall reform into Sancho's government.

Todros Halevi was a prominent figure at the court of Sancho as he had been at the court of Alfonso. Most other court Jews were from Toledo, but not all. Their number included Don Judah Abrabanel of Cordova, Don Samuel de Belorado, Don Joseph de Avila, Isaac de Faro, and Moses ibn Turiel of Murcia. There were also Jewish physicians mentioned in royal accounts, especially Isaac ibn Wakar and his brother, Abraham.

Aragon in the 13th Century: James I

As was the case with his predecessors on the throne of Aragon, James I (1213–76) took great advantage of the skills and talents of Jews. They participated actively in the Reconquest, and not just as diplomats, for Jews helped to parcel out the conquered land, with many taking possession of houses and estates located around the conquered city of Valencia, for example. Jews who settled in Majorca, Catalonia, and Valencia were offered charters of privilege, which included three or four years of tax exemption.

The churchmen advising James called upon him to enact laws that prohibiting Jews from holding any public office that would permit them to have judicial or penal authority over Christians. James did so, but apparently never felt bound to enforce such legis-

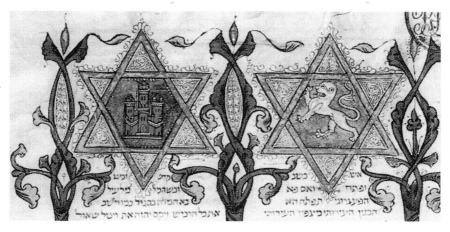

Coat-of-Arms of the United Kingdom of Castile and Leon

lation. Thus Jews were appointed as bailiffs; this was an office of power, since there was no line drawn between administrative and jurisdictional functions. Thus, a Jew named Bondia was the bailiff of Aragon, Abraham ben Saadia was the bailiff in Saragossa, Solomon Bonafos was the bailiff of Barcelona.

The most influential Aragonese Jew was Judah ben Lavi de la Cavelleria. In 1260 James authorized him to collect all state revenues and make all necessary expenditures on the crown's behalf. All the bailiffs in the kingdom had to turn over to him the monies they collected along with their accounts. It was his right to dismiss and replace incompetent officials. In 1263 Judah himself funded a fleet to fight against the Muslims. He also provided money needed by James for other military and political purposes. Eventually Judah became the bailiff of Valencia.

As was true in Castile, the *aljamas* were permitted to govern themselves, so long as they met their tax obligations. James was very much interested in the inner life of the Jewish communities. His charters to the communities regulated the elections of judges and rabbis, tax assessments, the administration of justice, and the general religious and moral conduct of community members. He gave communities the right to punish offenders by fine, ban, flagellation, or expulsion. In some parts of Aragon the local communities had the right to punish capital offenses.

Castile in the 14th Century

Although in Aragon policy toward the Jews changed dramatically in the 14th century, as we will see shortly, in Castile the trends of the 13th century continued. Jewish courtiers were involved in tax farming and held other posts in the royal chancelleries or the royal accounting system. Thus, for example, Don Judah Abrabanel provided funding for the battles against the Muslims during the Reconquest. In addition, Abraham ibn Shoshan and others were placed in charge of tax collection throughout Castile.

Some changes did take place in the inner life of the *aljamas*. Although the elders of each community, generally members of aristocratic families, were its leaders, leadership began to be taken over by overseers (*me'ayenim*), with whom were associated judges appointed annually to deal solely with legal matters. This development led to a downplaying of the influence of the powerful noble families.

In 14th-century Aragon, local communities administered themselves. In Castile, by contrast, the communities were brought together as one unified structure. The man in charge was the *rab de la corte*, or court rabbi, who served all the Jews of Castile, supervising the administration of their laws, finances, and taxes. In the first part of the 14th century (1305–28), the court rabbi was R. Asher ben Yehiel (Rosh), who had come to Toledo from Cologne, Germany, by invitation of the community, and rapidly gained a recognition as the greatest rabbinic scholar in all of Spain.

The court rabbi was the presiding officer when conferences of the local *aljamas* were convened. At these conferences the taxes for which the communities would be responsible would be divided among the local communities according to their financial capacity. In addition, general agreements would be adopted, and seen as binding upon all *aljamas*, regarding taxation, administration of justice, election of overseers and judges, education, laws on domestic relations, and other matters relating to religion and morals. In Castile the powers of criminal jurisdiction exceeded in great measure those granted the Jews in any other country; Jews were licensed to impose the death penalty on informers, murderers, and adulterers.

Castile in the 14th Century: Pedro the Cruel and Henry II

The years 1366–69 brought a civil war between Pedro the Cruel (1350–69) and Henry II (1369–79), his stepbrother. Each side brought troops from England and France into the conflict. Henry made much of the role and importance of Jews in Pedro's kingdom, and the Jews of Castile suffered greatly as a result. In the spring of 1366, the entire Jewish community of Briviesca, some 200 families, was massacred. When Henry took Burgos in April 1336, an enormous sum was demanded from the Jews; those who could not pay a share were sold into slavery; similarly, when Henry entered Toledo, he again demanded an enormous sum from the Jews, with payment required within two weeks. Burgos and Toledo became scenes of battle again later in the war; the Burgos and Toledo Jews again had to pay enormous sums, even if they had to sell themselves and their property to raise money. The battle for Toledo was a fierce one; some 8,000 Jews were killed during the siege. Pedro was killed as well, so Henry became the sole acknowledged king.

Henry's stated concern regarding the Jews related to their loans; thus he declared a moratorium on Jewish loans. There were other complaints about Jews, however. The Cortes, meeting at Burgos in February 1367, demanded that no Jewish officials or physicians be employed in the households of the king, queen, or princes. It also complained about new powers given to Jewish tax farmers. Although Henry was prepared to continue the moratorium, he did not agree to the latter demands.

Aragon in the 14th Century: James II

James II (1291–1327) set forth a policy on Jews that was followed by the kings of Aragon for nearly a century. His goal was to protect the Jews and confirm their privileges, but only to the extent that these were not in conflict with the principles of the church and the state. The economic and legal privileges of the Jews and their communal institutions were all protected, but the king reserved the right to become involved in internal communal affairs if he chose to do so.

This meant that Jewish authority in criminal cases was now more limited; after the death of R. Solomon ibn Adret there was no scholar with sufficient halakhic and moral authority to take charge and impose death sentences. The tax obligations of Jews were heavy, but no heavier than they had been before. In any case, money was demanded from Jews on the pretext that they had violated the usury laws. James made occasional inquiries about violations of the usury laws, usually placing the investigations in the hands of the clergy.

A critical change in the internal organizational life of Barcelona took place in 1327, as a series of important communal statutes (takkanot) that had been approved by James late in his reign were adopted. These statutes made it unacceptable for individuals to draw on privileges granted by the king to obtain communal posts; instead communal affairs were to be administered by thirty members elected from the best elements of the community, later to be known as the Council of the Thirty, or simply as The Thirty. This group was to appoint all communal officials: trustees, judges, accountants, and charity wardens. It would decide how taxes should be collected, draft takkanot, and appoint committees to deal with specific problems.

The trustees (*ne'emanim*) were empowered to call meetings of The Thirty at the synagogue or elsewhere and to fine latecomers and absentees. The council was elected every three years by the trustees and judges by majority vote, and members were eligible for reelection; the trustees, however, could serve for no more than two years and could not stand for reelection to successive terms. They served as the executive officers of the *aljama*, although their decisions had to be approved by The Thirty; any disagreements between trustees and individual community members about taxation were decided by a majority vote of the judges, from whose decision there could be no appeal. Within three days of the election the members were to take an oath to give honest and loyal service for the welfare of the community.

The takkanot regarding communal organization were read aloud in Barcelona's synagogue, and those who violated their terms were threatened with excommunication. From time to time the takkanot were passed on to the royal authorities to be ratified anew. Other communities, such as Valencia (1364) and Huesca (1374), adopted similar takkanot. In fact these takkanot were of such significance that they were discussed in this period's halakhic literature.

Aragon in the 14th Century: Pedro IV

Pedro IV (1336–87) cultivated close personal relationships with the Jews of Aragon. This was especially true regarding his loyal Jewish financiers and the Jewish physicians who attended his family. He also extended a wide scope of privileges to the *aljamas*, even beyond those given by James I; under Pedro the Jews had greater powers of criminal jurisdiction than ever before.

Pedro was very much interested in the internal arrangements of the *aljamas*, encouraging democratic tendencies in them as well as in the general community. Thus in 1386 there was movement toward democracy in both the municipality of Barcelona and the local Jewish community. A new communal constitution for the *al-*

jama of Barcelona, to take effect under a royal edict of April 2, 1386, was put together with the assistance of the royal treasurer.

The new constitution called for the Council of Thirty to be elected from representatives of the three estates. Five representatives of the three estates would join together with three trustees to form a smaller council. Ten councilors were to withdraw each year, with others taking their places. The trustees were to be elected annually, but could be reelected as trustees only after two years had passed.

The power of the trustees was limited, when compared with their power under the takkanot of 1327. They could not make decisions about tax farming without council approval, nor could they spend the *aljama*'s money without council approval. The tax appraisers were to be elected from among the three estates, and tax assessments were to be done jointly with the royal bailiff under his supervision.

Castile and Aragon in the 15th Century

The year 1391 was a time of catastrophe for the Jews of Spain. In 1378 a churchman in Seville, Ferrant Martinez, began a campaign against them. In his view, the way to solve the problem of the Jews in Seville—and elsewhere—included destroying Seville's 23 synagogues, establishing a ghetto for Jewish residence, in order to cut off contact between Jews and Christians, and removing Jews from all positions of influence. When both the archbishop and the king of Castile died in 1390, and Martinez became administrator of the diocese, Christians were called upon to destroy the synagogues of Seville. In addition, Martinez baptized all slaves owned by Jews and called all Jewish tax farmers to appear before his ecclesiastical court.

On June 4, 1391, the Jews of Seville were attacked; many Jews died, but many others converted. Seville's synagogues were converted to churches, and the Jewish quarter was settled by Christians. But Seville was just the beginning for the Jews of Castile. In Toledo, on June 20, R. Judah, grandson of R. Asher ben Yehiel, was martyred along with his family and students; others chose conversion. Toledo's famous synagogues fell into Christian hands; some were destroyed. In Madrid, most of the Jews were killed or baptized. In Burgos, the Jewish quarter was attacked, with many Jews taking refuge in the homes of Christians. Many Jews converted, and the few who remained Jews asked for a written guarantee of political and economic protection.

In Aragon, Valencia was the first community to be attacked. On July 9, a gang of youths appeared in front of the Jewish quarter, shouting: "The archdeacon is coming! The Jews must choose between baptism and death!" Fearing an attack, the Jews closed the gate of their quarter, but the Christians broke through. Around 250 Jews were killed; some were baptized by force, while others took refuge in the homes of Christians. Majorca was struck next, the disturbances beginning on August 2. Three hundred Jews were killed, and 800 escaped to the fortress. The conversions of Jews began on August 2, but the peasants forced the Jews to choose either death or conversion; the pressure they exerted led large numbers of Jews to become converts.

The news of attacks in Valencia and Majorca soon reached Barcelona. The city's Jews began to be concerned about their own fate. August 5 brought the attacks on Jews to Barcelona, and 100 of them were killed while another 100 took refuge in the so-called New Fortress. The attacks continued, however, as the peasants marched on the New Fortress, demanding that the Jews choose death or conversion. The looting and killing continued through the week, with about 400 Jews killed in total. More attacks followed in Gerona, in Lerida, in Tortosa.

Were the Jews of Spain able to restore their communities after these terrible events? In Castile, the major communities of Seville, Toledo, and Burgos had little to rebuild; most of their leaders, the courtiers, had been killed, baptized, or dismissed from their positions. In Aragon, the king and queen declared their intention to rebuild the communities of Barcelona and Valencia, with commitments made to exempt Jews from taxes and from payment of debts for a short time; Jews were reluctant to return to Barcelona and Valencia due largely to the strong opposition of Christians.

The Jews of Saragossa, led by R. Hasdai Crescas, became the leaders in the effort to rebuild. in June 1396 R. Hasdai drew up a series of takkanot that were approved by the queen and by the Saragossa community. Three years later, though, the queen suggested some revisions to these takkanot, largely in response to her

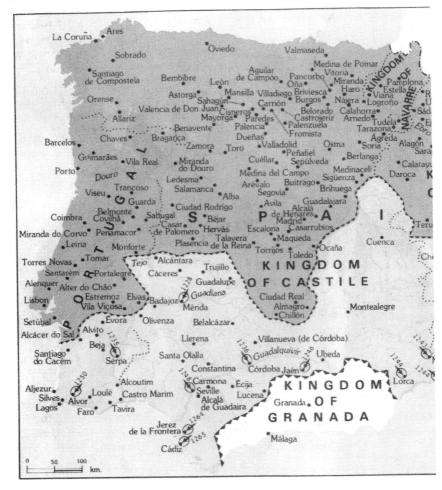

Jewish Communities in Spain and the Reconquest

perception that all three estates ought to be involved in the affairs of the community. Thus, for example, the trustees were to be elected by representatives of all three estates; the treasurer was to be elected by all community members, with the trustees having no privileged opinions. In addition, although R. Hasdai threatened anyone who attempted to change the takkanot with excommunication, the queen felt that the takkanot should be subject to review

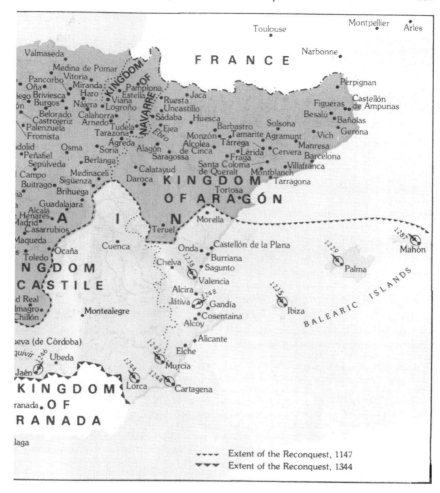

Jewish Communities in Spain and the Reconquest

after three years had passed. The revised takkanot were read to the community members and approved by the majority.

The years 1413–14 brought the famous Disputation of Tortosa, instigated by Vincent Ferrer, a preacher of penitence among the Christians who was successful in attracting uncertain Jews to the baptismal font. One outcome of Ferrer's agitation was that on January 2, 1412, Castile published a series of "reformatory laws" aimed

at undermining Jewish economic life, abolishing the political freedom of the *aljamas*, and making the Jews feel like outcasts. They
were to be confined to separate residential areas in all the towns
and villages so that they would have minimal social contact with
Christians. They were to dress differently from Christians, let their
hair and beards grow long, and could not be addressed with the
courtesy title of "Don." Jews were not permitted to be tax farmers,
or to hold government posts, or, if physicians, to treat Christians.
Ferrer took these anti-Jewish laws with him to Aragon and then to
Majorca.

The situation of the Jews looked bleak, but the Jews were the
fortunate beneficiaries of changes in the royal courts of Spain as
well as in the leadership of the Catholic Church. In Castile, Juan/
John II (1406–54) headed the government; in Aragon, Alfonso V
(1416–58) occupied the throne. Both Juan II and Alfonso V were
interested more in general culture than in antagonizing the Jews,
especially since they saw the restoration of the Jewish communities
beneficial to their kingdoms. Pope Martin V was supportive of
overturning the anti-Jewish edicts of 1419–22. As a result, the confiscated synagogues were returned to the Jewish communities, and
the social and economic restrictions were abolished.

Nonetheless, the post-1391 situation was not at all comparable
to the pre-1391 situation. In Aragon, the community of Saragossa
numbered about 200 families. Elsewhere, however, only small
groups remained—those who had survived both the sword and
the "temptation" of apostasy. As we have seen, the attempts to
reestablish communities in Barcelona and Valencia failed. This was
also the case in Gerona and Cervera. Jews paid taxes to the royal
treasury but had no influence in Aragonese political life; there were
no Jews in the service of the state. Jewish judges did not try criminal cases. The Jewish population of Aragon post-1391 was some
6,000 families.

Most of Spain's remaining Jews lived in Castile. There were
around 30,000 Jewish families in Castile at the time of the expulsion, and perhaps 10,000 *conversos*. Here, too, the major communities of Seville, Burgos, and Toledo had lost their prominence; now
the smaller towns became the focus of cultural and economic life.
Jews were engaged in various economic pursuits; they were mer-

chants and shopkeepers, artisans, physicians, tax collectors, and vineyard owners.

The municipalities and the *aljamas* did not enjoy the best relationships with one another. The towns were not pleased with the overturning of the 1412–15 edicts. In a number of towns, despite the overturning of the edicts, Jews were required to live in separate quarters and to wear the Jewish badge on their garments; they were deprived of synagogues and cemeteries, and efforts were made to convert them. In addition, Jews were excluded from the commercial centers of the towns. Yet, at the same time, there were Jews and Christians who related well to one another. Jewish doctors treated Christians, Jews farmed taxes, both royal and municipal. Jews served as lawyers and political advisers. During the rule of John II, Don Abraham Bienveniste held the post of supervisor of tax farmers for all of Castile and was the royal treasurer; these posts certainly carried some political influence.

In 1432, Bienveniste, who also held the posts of chief judge and chief rabbi of Castile, summoned the trustees and scholars of the communities to Valladolid. Working together with the communal representatives, he formulated takkanot to govern the communities. The statutes dealt with Torah study, selecting judges and other officials, cases of denunciation and slander, collecting taxes, dress restrictions, and other matters of concern. Although these takkanot do not seem to have been enforced, they help us to see what was on the minds of Jews in 15th-century Castile.

Ferdinand and Isabella

The marriage in 1469 of Ferdinand of Aragon (1479–1576) and Isabella of Castile (1474–1504) united Christian Spain's most powerful kingdoms. The joint reign of the "Catholic Monarchs," as Pope Alexander VI called them, seemed to foretell a period of stability after a time of political disarray and civil war. The Jews of Spain believed that their greatest hope for security was a strong central power that could keep order. This seemed to be the case now that Spain was ruled by two monarchs who were capable of restoring and maintaining order. Jews were appointed to the royal administration, among them Abraham Seneor and Isaac Abrabanel, as well as prominent *conversos* like Luis de Santangel and Gabriel Sanchez.

Isabella's own doctor was a Jew, Lorenzo Badoc. Ferdinand and Isabella intervened personally in cases of anti-Jewish violence, punishing those who had carried it out. They saw it as their obligation to defend and protect the Jews.

Before long, however, Ferdinand and Isabella brought the Inquisition to Spain and expelled its Jews. We will consider these topics in a separate section.

Texts

Alfonso X, *Las Siete Partidas*

Although the Jews are a people who do not believe in the religion of Our Lord Jesus Christ, the great Christian sovereigns have always permitted them to live among them. . . . we intend here to speak of the Jews, who insult His name and deny the marvelous and holy acts which He performed when He sent His Son, Our Lord Jesus Christ, into the world to save sinners. . . .

. . . a Jew should be very careful to avoid preaching to or converting any Christian, to the end that he may become a Jew, by exalting his own belief and disparaging ours. Whoever violates this law shall be put to death and lose all his property. We have heard it said that in some places Jews celebrated and still celebrate Good Friday, which commemorates the Passion of Our Lord Jesus Christ, by way of contempt, stealing children and fastening them to crosses and making images of wax and crucifying them, when they cannot obtain children. . . .

We also forbid any Jew to dare to leave his house or his quarter on Good Friday. They must all remain shut up until Saturday morning. . . .

. . . we forbid any Christian man or woman to invite a Jew or Jewess, or to accept an invitation from them, to eat or drink together or to drink any wine made by their hands. We also order that no Jews shall dare to bathe in company with Christians and that no Christian shall take any medicine or cathartic made by a Jew. He can take it by the advice of some intelligent person, only where it is made by a Christian, who knows and is familiar with its ingredients. . . .

No force or compulsion shall be employed in any way against a

Jew to induce him to become a Christian. Christians should convert him to the faith of Our Lord Jesus Christ by means of the texts of the Holy Scripture and by kind words, for no one can love or appreciate a service which is done him by compulsion. We also decree that, if any Jew or Jewess should voluntarily desire to become a Christian, the other Jews shall not interfere with this in any way. . . .

Many crimes and outrageous things occur between Christians and Jews because they live together in cities and dress alike. In order to avoid the offenses and evils which take place for this reason, we deem it proper and we order that all Jews male and female living in our dominions shall bear some distinguishing mark upon their heads so that people may plainly recognize a Jew or a Jewess. Any Jew who does not bear such a mark shall pay for each time he is found without it ten *maravedis* of gold. If he has not the means to do this, he shall publicly receive ten lashes for his offense.

Chazan, *Church, State and Jew in the Middle Ages*, 190–95

LETTER OF HASDAI CRESCAS (OCTOBER 19, 1391)

If I were to tell you here all the numerous sufferings we have endured, you would be dumbfounded at the thought of them; I will therefore set before you only in brief detail the table of our disaster set with poisonous plant and wormwood, giving you a bare recital of the facts so that you may satiate yourselves on the bitterness of our wormwood and drink from the wine of our grief. As I suppose that you have been told the story already, I will recount it as briefly as possible, commencing as follows:

On the day of the New Moon of the fateful month Tammuz in the year 5151 [July 1391] the Lord bent the bow of the enemies against the populous community of Seville, where there were between 6,000 and 7,000 heads of families, and they destroyed their gates by fire and killed in that very place a great number of people; the majority, however, changed their faith. Many of them, children as well as women, were sold to the Moslems, so that the streets occupied by Jews have become empty. Many of them, sanctifying the Holy Name, endured death, but many also broke the holy Covenant. From there the fire spread and consumed all the cedars of

Lebanon in the holy community of the city of Cordova. Here, too, many changed their faith, and the community became desolate.

And on the day of misery and punishment, on which the sufferings were intensified, the wrath of the Lord was discharged on the holy city, the source of learning and the word of the Lord, namely the community of Toledo, and in the temple of the Lord the priests and the learned were murdered. In that very place the rabbis, the descendants of the virtuous and excellent R. Asher, of blessed memory, together with their children and pupils, publicly sanctified the Holy Name. However, many who had not the courage to save their souls changed their faith here, too.

The country trembled even on account of these three communities, apart from the others in their neighborhood to the number of 70. And withal, we were in the greatest danger here, and had to be on the alert day and night. On the 7th of the month Av the Lord destroyed mercilessly the community of Valencia, in which there were about a thousand heads of families; about 250 men died, sanctifying the name of the Lord; the others fled into the mountain; some of these saved themselves but the majority changed their faith. From there the plague spread over the communities of glorious Majorca, which is situated on the shore of the sea. On the day of the New Moon of Elul, the bloodthirsty villains came there, profaned, plundered and robbed them and left them like a net in which there are no fish. There died, sanctifying the Holy Name, about 300 persons, and about 800 took refuge in the royal castle; the others changed their faith.

On the following Sabbath the Lord poured out His fury like fire, destroyed His sanctuary and profaned the crown of His teaching, namely the community of Barcelona, which was destroyed on that day. The number of murdered amounted to 250 souls; the rest fled into the castle, where they were saved. The enemies plundered all streets inhabited by Jews and set fire to some of them. The authorities of the province, however, took no part in this; instead, they endeavored to protect the Jews with all their might. They offered food and drink to the Jews, and even set about punishing the wrongdoers, when a furious mob rose against the better classes in the country and fought against the Jews who were in the castle, with bows and missiles, and killed them in the castle itself. Amongst the many who sanctified the Name of the Lord was my only son, who was a bridegroom and whom I have offered as a faultless lamb for sacrifice; I submit to God's justice and take comfort in the thought of his excellent portion and his delightful lot. Amongst them were many who slaughtered themselves and others who threw themselves down from the tower and whose limbs were already broken before they had reached halfway down the tower. Many also came forth and sanctified the Name of the Lord in the open street. All the others changed their faith, and only few found refuge in the towns of the princes; a child could register the names of these. However, these were precisely the most esteemed. Consequently, because of our many sins, there is none left in Barcelona today who still bears the name of Jew.

In the town of Lerida, too, many died and others changed their faith. There were only a few people who saved their lives. In the town of Gerona, where knowledge of the Law could be found combined with humility, the rabbis of that place sanctified the Name of the Lord publicly, and few only changed their faith. The majority of the community escaped to the houses of the citizens and are today in the castle.

In a word, in the state of Valencia not one single Jew remained with the sole exception of the place called Murviedro. In the province of Catalonia, too, not one single Jew remained except in the towns of the princes and administrators, who nowhere attacked them.

For us, however, who are still in the country of Aragon, there is no more trouble and complaint, because the Lord has taken pity on us and has preserved the remnant of us in all these places after vehement supplication, although nothing but our bodies is left after the distribution of our belongings. In spite of this, fear fills our hearts, and our eyes are directed towards the Father in heaven, that He may be merciful to us and may heal us of our wounds, and keep our feet from wavering. May this be his Will. Amen.

"I am the man that hath seen affliction by the rod of His wrath," Hasdai ben Abraham ben Hasdai ben Judah Crescas, who writes here in Saragossa, on the 20th day of the month Marheshvan in the year 5152 of the Creation.

Kobler, *Letters of Jews Through the Ages*, 272–5

SOLOMON IBN ADRET

Be advised that we (that is, the *kahal* of Barcelona), the *kahal* of Villafranca del Panades, the *kahal* of Tarragona, and the *kahal* of Montblanch, maintain a common chest and a common purse for the payment of taxes and imposts levied upon us by the crown. Whenever they wish to pass new regulations governing the assessment of taxes either by the tax assessors or by the submission of memoranda or by individual declaration, to meet the requirements of the king, we do not impose our will upon them, even though we are in the majority and the city is supreme in all matters. If we should take action without their counsel, they would not heed us. Sometimes we send our men to them, and at other times their representatives come to us with their resolutions. Only if they fail to do either of these things at our request do we compel them by the arm of the government to come to us or to adopt in their communities the measures that are in force in ours. In other places, however, the head community decrees for its dependencies and subjects them to its will.

Baer, *History of the Jews in Christian Spain*, 1:216–17

R. ASHER BEN YEHIEL

You have asked me a difficult question, involving a capital crime. In all the countries I have ever heard of, capital matters are not judged [by Jews] except here in Spain. I was greatly puzzled when I first came here, how it was possible to judge capital matters with the Sanhedrin not in existence. I was told that this was due to the royal will, and, what is more, the [Jewish] community judges with a view to saving life; a great deal more blood would be shed if such cases were judged by the Gentiles. I have therefore let the custom stand, though I have never agreed with them [the Jews of Spain] on the subject of taking life. Indeed, I note that all of you agree on the elimination of this evil from your midst. There can be no doubt that this man blasphemed openly and the matter is already known among the Gentiles. The latter being very strict with those who blaspheme against their law and faith, the blasphemy would assume greater proportions if in this case punishment were not meted out.

Baer, *History of the Jews in Christian Spain*, 1:323–24

ASHER BEN YEHIEL

Know ye, all who see this letter, that for some time now astounding cries, complaints and accusations have reached me against this man, Abraham. . . . It is charged that he has several times caused the forfeiture of Jewish money, public as well as private, to Gentiles; that he played a treacherous role in the cancellation of debts; that he constantly threatens Jews with confiscations and the desecration of their synagogues; that he mocks the words of our sages in the princely courts and seeks to disparage our faith in the eyes of the populace. . . . The communal leaders have already consulted me about him several times. . . . And now the distinguished R. Joseph Halevi, whose spirit the Lord has stirred with zeal, has taken action in the matter. Let all the notables who wield authority take to heart what I have written.

Baer, *History of the Jews in Christian Spain*, 1:325

Questions on the Texts

ALFONSO X, *Las Siete Partidas*

1. Alfonso is concerned about Jews "observing" Good Friday. Why did Christians believe such things about Jews? Do you think many of them shared Alfonso's concern?
2. Why is convincing Jews to convert through Scripture and "by kind words" superior to compulsion?
3. What was objectionable about Christians and Jews socializing? What was the concern about drinking wine made by Jews? About taking medicine made by Jews?

LETTER OF HASDAI CRESCAS

1. How many Jews were affected by the 1391 attacks according to Hasdai?
2. Hasdai tells us that many Jews converted to Christianity, thus escaping the attacks. Compare the response of the Jews of Ashkenaz when attacked during the First Crusade, and explain the difference.
3. Did all Christians participate in the attacks on Jews in Barcelona? Explain.

RESPONSUM OF IBN ADRET

1. When are the communities of Aragon subject to the decisions of the head community, Barcelona? When are they free to make their own decisions?
2. How does the king of Aragon involve himself in the tax policies of the *aljamas*?

RESPONSUM OF R. ASHER BEN YEHIEL

1. In the 14th century, Spanish Jews were empowered to adjudicate capital crimes, unlike Jews living in France or Germany. How did the Jews of Spain "justify" this difference?
2. How does R. Asher support his acceptance of local custom on this issue?

RESPONSUM OF R. ASHER BEN YEHIEL

1. Of what crimes is Abraham guilty?
2. What makes these offenses so serious in the community's eyes that "the communal leaders have already consulted me about him several times"?

Paper Topics

R. Hasdai Crescas and the Rebuilding of Spanish Communities after 1391

R. Asher ben Yehiel: A Community Leader in 14th-Century Castile

R. Isaac ben Sheshet Perfet: A Community Leader in 14th-Century Aragon

The Jewish Communities of Spain: The Powers of their Courts

Jews as Courtiers in Christian Spain

Reference Works

Y. Baer, *History of the Jews in Christian Spain*

J. Gerber, *The Jews of Spain*

J. F. O'Callahan, *A History of Medieval Spain*

JEWISH CULTURE

The culture of Spanish Jewry was many-faceted. There were major figures in Bible commentary, such as Nahmanides and Abrabanel, and in halakhah, again including Nahmanides, as well as Ibn Adret and Asher ben Yehiel. But Spain was also a center of kabbalah (Jewish mysticism) and Jewish philosophy.

Bible Commentators

Nahmanides' commentary on the Torah is a classic of Jewish literature, a work that continues to be studied. The words of the rabbis of the Talmud are prominent in it, whether pertaining to halakhah or aggadah (non-halakhic material), and Nahmanides attempts to interpret them. The comments of earlier medieval commentators like Rashi, Ibn Ezra, and Maimonides are considered. Sometimes they are seen as valid, sometimes they are rejected. While certainly concerned with *peshuto shel mikra*, the plain sense of the biblical text, Nahmanides is far more interested in the Torah's philosophical and theological ideas. But the greatest innovation is his introduction of ideas derived from the kabbalah into a commentary intended to be disseminated widely, even to ordinary, unlearned Jews; thus his commentary to the Torah became a major contribution to the spread of kabbalistic thought.

A second major figure in Spanish Bible commentary was Don Isaac Abrabanel, who contributed commentaries on Torah, Nevi'im (Prophets), and some parts of Ketuvim (Writings), as well as three books on the subject of the Messiah.

Five major features characterize Abrabanel's commentaries: (1) the biblical books are divided into chapters and questions are posed to the text; (2) the main focus is on content, i.e., ideas and concepts, rather than grammar and philology; (3) philosophical-allegorical interpretation is rejected; (4) there are no kabbalistic interpretations; and (5) the comments are lengthy and frequently repetitious.

Abrabanel's commentaries are innovative. He attempts to draw comparisons between society in biblical times and in Christian Spain; thus, for example, he compares the institution of kingship in ancient Israel and in Spain. He provides lengthy introductions to the books of the prophets, considering such matters as content, authorship, and date of composition. Finally, he makes use of Christian Bible interpretations, rejecting whatever he finds unconvincing, especially interpretations used to make the case that Jesus was the Messiah, but accepting interpretations that reflect valid understandings of the text.

Halakhah

Spain was also a center for the study of halakhah. Beyond representing the Jews at the Barcelona Disputation and being the author of a classic Bible commentary, Nahmanides was a great halakhist. In the yeshivot of today, his *Milhamot ha-Shem* commentary on the Talmud is a standard text used by advanced students; his *Hiddushei ha-Ramban* is also consulted and studied by advanced students.

The greatest of Nahmanides's students was R. Solomon ibn Adret (Rashba), although he regarded R. Jonah ben Abraham Gerondi as his principal teacher. Ibn Adret wrote *Hiddushei ha-Rashba*, still studied in the yeshivot of today, but he is better known for the more than 1,000 responsa he authored. These responsa are important in halakhah, as they became a major source for its authoritative codification, the *Shulhan Arukh*; they are important as well for what they reveal about the history of Christian Spain. Ibn Adret also authored a work called *Torat ha-Bayit*, a standard text used by advanced students in the study of certain ritual observances.

A third major figure in the area of halakhah was R. Asher ben Yehiel. R. Asher was born and grew up in Germany, where he became the outstanding student of R. Meir of Rothenburg, the greatest rabbinic authority of 13th-century Germany. In 1303 he left Germany to avoid being imprisoned as R. Meir had been, in an effort by Emperor Rudolph to compel Germany's Jews to pay taxes beyond those required by their local rulers. Welcomed to Spain by Ibn Adret, R. Asher settled in Toledo.

There he contributed a commentary to the Talmud, the text of which is found at the end of each tractate. He also wrote a collection called *Tosafot ha-Rosh*, published as separate volumes and ordered by tractate of Talmud. His responsa number more than 1,000; they too served as a major source for the *Shulhan Arukh*.

A Spanish Synagogue

Kabbalah

What is Kabbalah? It is Jewish mysticism in the special forms it took from the 12th century on. Kabbalah began in Provence in Southern France, where the major figure, the "father" of Kabbalah, was R. Isaac the Blind, the son of a notable halakhist, R. Abraham ben David (Raavad). Raavad's writings show some familiarity with mysticism, and his impact on the beginnings of Kabbalah should not be underestimated. R. Isaac, however, was the first to devote himself entirely to kabbalistic ideas, writing a commentary on *Sefer Yezirah* ("The Book of Creation"), a work describing the process of creation that was written in the time of the Talmud.

R. Isaac believed that the teachings of the Kabbalah should be kept secret. They should not be talked about openly, nor should books on kabbalistic mysticism be published; there was too much danger, he thought, that such material would confuse and mislead readers who lacked the background to understand the Kabbalah's profound and difficult concepts.

Nonetheless, Kabbalah spread to Spain. There, in Gerona, lived two great disciples of R. Isaac, R. Ezra and R. Ezriel. They did not share his concern about spreading the teachings of the Kabbalah to those who might not grasp its profundities. In the same Gerona there lived another great kabbalist, Nahmanides, who, as mentioned above, incorporated kabbalistic teachings into his commentary on the Torah, making them the property of the ordinary Jew.

The central and fundamental teaching of Kabbalah is the doctrine of the sefirot. According to kabbalistic doctrine, there are two "sides" of God. The first of these cannot be understood and grasped by man at all; God's ineffable aspect is called Ein Sof. God's second aspect, which can be understood by man, comprises the sefirot. There are ten sefirot, all of them emanated from Ein Sof, one after the other: *keter* ("supreme crown"), *hokhmah* ("wisdom"), *binah* ("intelligence"), *hesed* ("love"), *gevurah* ("power"), *tiferet* ("beauty"), *nezah* ("lasting endurance"), *hod* ("majesty"), *zaddik* ("righteous one"), and *malkhut* ("kingdom"). The sefirot are fundamental aspects of God, the means by which He reveals Himself in the created world and is active in it, and the means by which man can come to know God.

The 13th century brought the appearance of the classic work of

Kabbalah known as the *Zohar*; this work quickly became the "Bible" of Kabbalah. The traditional view holds that the author of the *Zohar* was R. Shimon bar Yohai, who lived in Israel in the mid-2nd century. This view is difficult to support, however, as has been pointed out by the great scholar of the history of Jewish mysticism, Gershom Scholem. The Aramaic of the Zohar is an artificial literary language, not a spoken language. It does not reflect any known spoken dialect of Aramaic, tends to misuse Aramaic conjugations, and translates medieval Hebrew words. The descriptions of Palestine's mountains make it clear that the author has never been there; the descriptions fit the mountains of Castile—but not those of Palestine. There are allusions to Arab rule over Eretz Yisrael, which did not begin until the Muslim conquest in the 7th century, and there are reflections of medieval Christian society and its customs. The description and criticism of Jewish life fit very well into 13th-century Spain.

Who then was the author of the *Zohar*? In Scholem's view, it was Moses de Leon, who lived in Spain in the 1280s. The style, vocabulary, and sources of the *Zohar* parallel those found in works unquestionably known to have been written by de Leon. He uses the same wrong constructions, the same incorrect verb inflections, and so on.

Jewish Philosophy

Christian Spain was a major center of Jewish philosophy, with the two major figures being R. Hasdai Crescas at the end of the 14th century and R. Joseph Albo in the first half of the 15th. Albo was in fact a student of Crescas. Let us consider each of them.

Crescas was a rabbinic leader in Saragossa and played an active role in the effort to rebuild Spain's Jewish communities after the tragic events of 1391. But Crescas was also a philosopher. His most important philosophical work was called *Or Adonai* ("The Light of God"); its stated purpose was to replace the work of Maimonides in halakhah and philosophy.

Crescas argued that Maimonides had misconstrued Judaism; the goal of the life of a Jew is to attain fear and love of God, not what Maimonides called "knowledge of the intelligibles." Knowledge of the mitzvot leads to their performance, and thus is validated by its leading to religious observance. Knowledge of the mitzvot, says Crescas, must meet three conditions if its purpose is to be served: (1) each mitzvah must be precisely defined; (2) each mitzvah should be easily understood; and (3) each mitzvah should be preserved in the Jew's memory. Crescas reiterated what other critics, such as R. Abraham ben David of Provence (Raavad), had already said about the *Mishneh Torah*: that Maimonides did not cite sources or provide reasons for his decisions, and thus failed to provide substantive knowledge of the mitzvot.

Moreover, argued Crescas, in his *More Nevukhim* ("Guide to the Perplexed"), Maimonides had been caught in the web of Aristotelian thought. Crescas devoted all of Book I of *Or Adonai* to a refutation of Aristotle's basic principles. Book II considers the bases/foundations of the Torah; Book III deals with other beliefs that must accompany acceptance of the Torah; and Book IV discusses ideas that can or cannot be accepted.

To what degree were these criticisms of Maimonides well received? Crescas was not at all successful in his attempt to criticize Maimonides. Neither his rejection of the Rambam's philosophical thought nor his rejection of his main concepts in halakhah was well received by readers of *Or Adonai*.

The second prominent figure in Jewish philosophy in Spain was R. Joseph Albo, a student of Crescas. Albo was a participant in the Tortosa Disputation of 1413–14; his major work, *Sefer ha-Ikkarim*, was written at the time of the debate and should be regarded as relating to it. *Sefer ha-Ikkarim* was an attempt to establish the fundamental beliefs of the Jewish faith. Albo sought to integrate Mosaic law into the framework of political law in human society.

Book I presents Albo's main ideas, especially his famous view that there are only three principles of Jewish belief: God's existence, revelation, and reward and punishment. Books II, III, and IV, written at the request of Albo's friends, spell out the three principles, adding a few additional points of clarification.

Spain was the host to three religions, each of which asserted its own superiority. Cannot the Torah be supplanted by Christianity or Islam? Albo wrote that a law that is genuinely of divine origin can be recognized by two criteria: (1) its content, in which the three principles mentioned above must figure and nothing may be in conflict with them, and (2) the messenger or lawgiver who transmitted the law. One must be absolutely certain that the transmitter of the law was a true prophet and that he was sent by God to give the law to mankind. The performance of miracles by a supposed prophet establishes that he was a prophet.

Christianity, says Albo, contradicts the principle of divine unity, thereby failing the first criterion, because it speaks of a Trinity; thus Catholicism cannot claim to be of divine origin. As for Islam, Muhammad was not a true prophet because he did not satisfy the second criterion, and thus he could not transmit authentic religious teachings. Only Moshe was a true messenger who could meet both criteria.

Texts

NAHMANIDES ON LEVITICUS 19:2

YOU SHALL BE HOLY

. . . It is my view that this abstinence is not simply refraining from improper relationships as Rashi has interpreted; instead it is the separation intended everywhere in the Talmud, where those who practice this self-control are called *perushim*. The meaning of this is that the Torah has forbidden improper relationships and the consumption of forbidden foods but permitted sexual intercourse between man and wife and the consumption of certain meat and wine. Thus the one who is tempted will find opportunity to become consumed with sexual passion for his wife (or many wives), to drink wine and eat meat without restraint, and to speak all profanities; thus he will become a scoundrel within the realm of what the Torah permits! Therefore, having first presented those practices which are forbidden unconditionally, the Torah presents a broader command to be moderate even with those practices which are permitted . . . This is the manner of the Torah, to present certain specific prohibitions and then include all of these in a general imperative. . . .

(Translation: J. Bloomberg)

NAHMANIDES ON DEUTERONOMY 6:18

AND THOU SHALT DO THAT WHICH IS RIGHT AND GOOD IN THE SIGHT OF THE ETERNAL . . .

. . . Our Rabbis have a beautiful *Midrash* on this verse: "[*That which is right and good*] means compromise and going beyond the requirements of the law." They mean by this that at first Moses stated that one is obligated to keep His statutes and testimonies as He commanded. Now he states that even where He has not commanded you, be sure to do that which is good and right in His eyes, for He loves the good and the right. This is a fundamental principle, for it is impossible to mention in the Torah all aspects of a man's conduct with neighbors and friends, all his business transactions and all the rules by which societies are governed. Since many of these have been mentioned, such as: *Thou shalt not go up and down as a talebearer; Thou shalt not take vengeance, nor bear any grudge; neither shalt thou stand idly by the blood of thy neighbor; Thou shalt not curse the deaf; Thou shalt not rise up before the hoary head* , etc., He stated in more general terms that, in all matters, one should do what is good and right, including even compromise and going beyond the requirements of the law. . . .

(Translation: J. Bloomberg)

ABRABANEL ON DEUTERONOMY 17:14

It ought to be considered whether kings are an obligation and a necessity in their own right or whether kings are not a necessity at all. The philosophers have seen kings to be a necessity and have seen the political service of the king to the nation as comparable to the role played by the heart in the body and the First Cause to the universe. If these thinkers believe that monarchy assures the three things which are necessary to the effective functioning of society, i.e., unity, continuity, and absolute power, they are mistaken, for it is certainly conceivable that a society could be governed by leaders who meet and share opinions and decide as one as to how to govern, without there being any monarch. . . .

Even were it to be argued that kings are a necessity . . . kings deal with three areas: defense of the nation, ordering society by establishing its rules, and preserving order within society. The Jewish people needs none of these: The Jewish people rely on God to defend them. . . . Order in society is assured by the guidance of the Torah. . . . Responsibility for preserving social order is that of Jewish courts. . . .

Listen now to my interpretation of the section of the Torah about kings. . . There is no mitzvah in this at all. . . . It is instead an anticipation of the desires of the Jewish people when they have entered Eretz Yisrael to have a king like all other nations.

(Translation: J. Bloomberg)

RESPONSUM OF R. ISAAC BEN SHESHET

I also informed you that my teacher, R. Peretz ha-Kohen, of blessed memory, did not speak of or recognize such sefirot (divine emanations). I also heard from him that R. Samson of Chinon, who was a greater master than all of his contemporaries, and of whom I also have memories even though I did not actually see him, was wont to say, "I pray with the knowledge of a child," to distinguish himself from the kabbalists who sometimes pray to one sefirah and sometimes to a different one, according to the content of the prayer. They claim that this is the meaning of the statement by the Rabbis of blessed memory (Bava Batra 25b): "One who wishes to become wise [should turn] to the south; to become rich [should turn] to the north." That is to say, one should direct himself to the attribute of the right or to the attribute of the left. Also, in the Shemoneh Esreh prayer, they direct each blessing to a particular sefirah. All this is extremely bizarre in the eyes of one who is not a kabbalist as they. They consider this to be a secondary belief. I have heard one of the philosophers speak disparagingly of the kabbalists and remark that the Christians believe in a Trinity while the kabbalists believe in a Decem-Unity (ten sefirot). It happened to me while I was in Saragossa that there came to the city the venerable scholar Don Joseph ibn Susan of blessed memory, whom I had already seen in Valencia. He was knowledgeable in the Talmud and had seen philosophical works; he was a kabbalist and a very saintly man, meticulous in [observing] the commandments. There was a great love between us. I once asked him, "How is it that you kabbalists direct one blessing to one sefirah and another blessing to a different one? Furthermore, are the sefirot so endowed with divinity so that one should pray to them?" He answered me, "Far be it that prayers be other than to God, blessed be He, the Cause of all causes. . . . One directs his thought . . . to the sefirah associated with the matter he is requesting. For example, in the blessing of *al-ha-Zaddikim* (on behalf of the righteous), one should think of the sefirah known as *hesed*, which is the attribute of mercy, and in the blessing of *al-ha-minim* (against heretics), one should think of the sefirah known as *gevurah*, which is the attribute of justice."

This was explained to me by the aforementioned pious person regarding the kabbalists' intentions, and it is [a] very good [explanation]. But who forces us to enter into all of this? It is better to pray to God alone with concentration, and He will know the way to fulfill that which is requested, as the verse states, "Commit your way unto God; trust in Him and He will bring it to pass" (Psalms 37:5).

Bleich, *With Perfect Faith*, 257–59 (Trans. E. Kanarfogel)

R. HASDAI CRESCAS, *Or Adonai*

. . . the argument based on reward and punishment [in the Torah]—if man were compelled and forced in his deeds, reward and punishment would be an injustice of God—appears to be a strong argument against any kind of necessity. However, a close examination shows that it can be easily dissipated. For, if reward and punishment follow from the [obedient] deeds and sins in the way that effects follow from causes, there would be no injustice attributable to God; no more than there is an injustice if someone is burned when he approaches fire, even if his approach is involuntary. . . .

[We shall now provide] an additional explanation of this view by means of the solution of a very difficult problem about which our predecessors have never ceased to be perplexed: how can divine justice with respect to reward and punishment be reconciled with necessity? [Moreover], if a reconciliation is feasible, what is the difference between the necessity by virtue of causality in which there is no feeling of force and compulsion and the necessity in which there is such a feeling? It might be thought that if the doing of the command or the transgression is the cause, whereas the reward or the punishment is their necessary effect, it would be inappropriate to distinguish the necessity without the feeling of compulsion from the necessity with such compulsion if the reward and punishment are the effects of one but not the effects of the other; for in either case there is an ineluctable necessity. [That is, where there is felt compulsion the reward and punishment are not, one might argue, genuine effects of the deeds.] [Furthermore], even if we were to admit that there is such a difference [such that] where force or compulsion is felt there is no reward or punishment, since in that case the person is not a voluntary [agent], whereas where the person does not feel force or compulsion he is called a voluntary agent, even if he is necessitated, how can [we speak of] reward and punishment in the domain of beliefs concerning the foundations of the Torah? It is evident from tradition that the punishment in these matters is severe, as of it the [rabbis] have said, "But heretics and apostates who deny [the divinity of] the Torah and [the belief] in resurrection of the dead" [Rosh Hashanah 7a]; or "The following are those who have no portion in the World to Come" [Mishnah Sanhedrin 10].

Bleich, *With Perfect Faith*, 479, 484 (Trans. S. Feldman)

R. Joseph Albo, *Sefer ha-Ikkarim*

We now desire to investigate whether it is possible that a given divine law of a given people should change in time, or whether it cannot change but must be eternal.

It would seem that a divine law cannot change, for reasons based upon a consideration of the giver, of the recipient, and of the law itself. Considering the giver, it would seem inconceivable that God, who is the giver, should desire one thing at one time and then change His will and desire its opposite at another time. It cannot be that God should desire right at one time and wrong at another. Why then should God change His law for another?

Considering the recipient, we cannot see why, since the nation is the same, the law should change in the course of time. We cannot use the analogy of the individual and say that just as the rules of health for a child are different from those of a young man, and those of a young man are different from those of an old man, as the time changes from childhood to youth and from youth to old age, so the rules of divine law must change with the times. For while it may be true in the case of an individual that his behavior is bound to change as the period of his life changes, the rule does not apply to a political group in which there is no such change from childhood to youth and to old age, for the convention of law is that all the times are the same. Hence we cannot see that divine law should change by reason of the recipient.

Now if we consider the law itself, it would seem that since the purpose of the divine Torah is to teach men intellectual conceptions and true opinions, there can be no reason for its changing at any time. For true opinions can never change. Monotheism cannot be true at one time and dualism or trinitarianism at another, anymore than it is possible that a thing that has already been should change and not have been. It seems clear, therefore, that there can be no change in a divine law, whether we consider the law itself, the giver, or the recipient. . . .

In this way we can reply to our opponents, who argue from the verse in the Torah: "I will raise them up a prophet from among their brethren, like unto thee; and I will put My words in his mouth, and he shall speak unto them all that I shall command him." This verse signifies, they say, that a law will be given through the new prophet as it was given through Moses; also that "from among their brethren" means from the brethren of Israel and not from Israel itself. Our reply to these men is that granting that, according to the verse quoted, a prophet will come to give a law, as Moses did before, the expression, "I will raise them up a prophet . . . like unto thee," signifies that his "raising up" and the verification of his prophetic mission, which is a fundamental dogma of divine law, as we have seen, must be of the same kind as the verification of Moses' prophetic mission, which took place in the presence of 600,000 people, so that there was no doubt and no suspicion of any kind.

Bleich, *With Perfect Faith*, 404, 414 (Trans. I. Husik)

Questions on the Texts

NAHMANIDES ON LEVITICUS 19:2

1. Where do Rashi and Nahmanides disagree about the command of *kedoshim tihyu* ("You shall be holy")?
2. What does Nahmanides mean by *naval be-reshut ha-Torah*?

NAHMANIDES ON DEUTERONOMY 6:18

1. How does Nahmanides interpret the midrash on this verse, *Ve-asita ha-yashar ve-ha-tov* ("And thou shalt do what is right and what is good")? How can compromise and going beyond the requirement of the law be seen as "doing the right and the good"? Isn't this taking things too far?

ABRABANEL ON DEUTERONOMY 17:14

1. Where have the philosophers gone wrong regarding kings and their functions in society?
2. Is the appointment of kings a mitzvah of the Torah? If not, how should the passage in Deuteronomy be understood?

RESPONSUM OF R. ISAAC BEN SHESHET

1. How does the prayer of the kabbalist differ from that of one who is not a kabbalist?
2. How did Don Joseph ibn Shushan respond to the questions posed to him by R. Isaac ben Sheshet?

HASDAI CRESCAS, *Or Adonai*

1. Can God be seen as acting unjustly in regard to reward and punishment? Explain.
2. What problem is Crescas addressing in this passage? Why is this problem especially challenging in respect to what Crescas calls the "foundations of the Torah"?

JOSEPH ALBO, *Sefer ha-Ikkarim*

1. Albo seeks to prove that divine law must be eternal. Explain how this view is confirmed with regard to each of the three "players."
2. How does Albo refute the claim that Moses has been succeeded by later prophets, i.e., Jesus and Muhammad?

Paper Topics

Major Themes in the Commentary of Nahmanides
Major Themes in the Commentary of Abrabanel
Rabbi Isaac the Blind: A Biography
Gerona: A Center of Kabbalah in Christian Spain
The *Zohar*
Prophecy in the Writings of Crescas, Albo, and/or Abrabanel
Miracles in the Writings of Crescas, Albo, and/or Abrabanel
The Messiah in the Writings of Abrabanel and/or Albo
Reward and Punishment in the Writings of Albo

Reference Works

Y. Baer, *A History of the Jews in Christian Spain*
J. Gerber, *The Jews of Spain*
G. Scholem, *Kabbalah*
C. Sirat, *A History of Jewish Philosophy in the Middle Ages*

JEWS AND CHRISTIANS

Antisemitism steadily increased in Christian Spain from the 13th to the 15th century. During this period new monastic orders were established, Jews were confronted with disputations and conversionist sermons, and many Jews converted, becoming *conversos* (New Christians). The Jews of Spain were more fortunate than the Jews of Ashkenaz in certain respects, for the kings valued their economic contributions and administrative ability and treated them accordingly; moreover, Spain had a history of religious tolerance, having been home to three different religions. Nevertheless antisemitism was inescapable, as will become evident when we examine Jewish-Christian relations during this period.

Mendicant Orders

Pope Innocent III was greatly concerned about heresy; he saw the sect of the Cathari as a serious threat to Christian orthodoxy. He opposed the establishment of new orders of monks and instead placed his reliance on the Cistercians and the Benedictines, who were models of the ideals of the church but favored living in rural monasteries and withdrawing from society. St. Dominic and St. Francis, the founders of the Dominican and Franciscan orders, favored living in urban society while still practicing poverty, remaining obedient to Rome, and preaching and teaching Christian orthodoxy; these ideals were enough to gain Innocent's approval, particularly at a time when cities were developing in Europe and a middle class was emerging.

The Dominicans and Franciscans were missionaries and became a decisive element in molding the church during this period. Both orders were active in the Inquisitions of Northern Europe and Spain. The inquisitor-general of Spain, Torquemada, was a Dominican monk. The impact of both new orders was profound; their impact on attitudes toward and treatment of Jews was enormous.

Disputations

As was the case in France, the Jews of Spain were compelled to participate in public disputations. The first of these took place in Barcelona in 1263, the second in Tortosa in 1413–14. Let us consider each of them.

The 1240s brought an intensified campaign by the monks to convert Jews. Their missionizing saw the Jews as a major focus of their efforts for a number of reasons: Jews were easily identifiable and "available" for conversionist sermons and debates; Jews were good evidence for successful missionizing work—if they were converting, it was thought, the missionizing must be working well; and many former Jews were anxious to be involved in proselytizing. The leader of Christian missionary work was Raymond de Penaforte, the master-general of the Dominicans.

The peak of the monks' missionary work was reached at the Barcelona disputation. The main participants were a Dominican monk, Pablo Christiani, who had converted from Judaism, and R. Moses ben Nahman (Nahmanides). Christiani had had a number of private "debates" with Nahmanides, the most highly regarded and respected rabbi in 13th-century Spain; it was now thought that if Nahmanides was "defeated" at Barcelona in a public debate, many more Jews would be inclined to convert. Christiani urged King James I of Aragon to order Nahmanides to appear at the palace and participate in a public disputation. James assured Nahmanides that he could speak freely, even to attack Christian dogma.

At the Paris disputation, the Talmud was attacked and eventually burned; Christiani, however, advocated the use of the Talmud as a missionary tool. He was a learned apostate, one who was quite capable of discussing and debating talmudic texts. His entire life, after his conversion, was devoted to attacking the Jewish people and their religious literature.

Three questions formed the agenda of the disputation: (1) Has the Messiah come? (2) Is the Messiah human or divine? and (3) Who keeps the true Torah, Jews or Christians (i.e., are the mitzvot still in effect)? The discussion and debate lasted four days, until James I called it to a halt, fearing that the mobs would attack Jews.

Did Barcelona succeed in attracting Jews to Christianity? Certainly not in the numbers hoped for. The debate was a failure largely because Christiani was not sufficiently familiar with midrashim and aggadot; familiar enough, that is, to debate with Nahmanides! In addition, he did not have the full support of King James; the debate was stopped, but James never declared Christiani the winner! James is supposed to have remarked to Nahmanides: "Never have I seen anyone who was in the wrong argue so well as you have."

The Tortosa disputation was initiated by Pope Benedict III, who ordered the Jews of Spain to send delegates to Tortosa in January of 1413. The disputation itself began in February 1413 and was conducted in the presence of the pope in a large auditorium draped in ecclesiastical purple. Also present were cardinals, archbishops, and bishops, along with burghers and nobles. At times there were as many as 2,000 in attendance.

Once again, the spokesman for Christianity was an apostate Jew, Geronimo de Santa Fe, a learned man and a powerful opponent of Judaism. The Jews were represented by several individuals, including R. Astruc Halevi, R. Zerahiah Halevi, and R. Joseph Albo, author of *Sefer ha-Ikkarim*. Although the outcome of the disputation could never be in doubt, the Jewish spokesmen were not permitted to see the texts to be used against them or to meet and discuss what they would say in order to coordinate their responses.

The discussion focused on two issues: the Messiah and the Talmud. Geronimo attempted to prove from the Talmud that the Messiah had already come. He also tried to show that the Talmud was full of mistakes, heresy, and abuse of Christianity. The rabbis were permitted to respond, but the rules of procedure always gave Geronimo the last word.

The disputation lasted from February 1413 until November 1414; there were some 69 sessions. Enormous pressure was exerted upon Jews to convert. Many did, including members of some prominent Jewish families. Many Jewish communities disappeared entirely as their members embraced Christianity.

The Conversos

Spanish Jews who converted to Christianity are usually called Marranos ("pigs"); it is better to call them conversos or New Christians, labels which are far more neutral. In Hebrew they are called *anusim* (forced converts).

There were three major waves of conversions: (1) after the 1391 outbreaks; (2) during the time of Vincent Ferrer's activism (1411–12); and during and after the Tortosa disputation (1413–15). The sources indicate that by the time of the Expulsion some 600,000 Spanish Jews had converted to Christianity!

Although we might have expected otherwise, hostility and tension characterized relations between Old Christians and New Christians. There were a number of reasons for this. First, there were suspicions that many of the Jewish converts had just gone through the motions but did not really see themselves as Christians. While some of the conversos were undoubtedly sincere, the vast majority became Christians under compulsion and continued to believe secretly in Judaism and to practice its rituals as much as they were able (and as much as they knew how to do). In some communities, conversos continued to live in the Jewish quarters; in others they did not.

Second, the Old Christians were jealous of the social and economic successes of the New Christians. Having become Christians, the conversos found many new professional and economic opportunities that had never been available to them as Jews: government posts, university chairs, even influential positions in the church hierarchy! Competition between New and Old Christians became a major source of tension.

Third, the ancestral hatred of Old Christians for Jews refused to disappear. Old Christians contended that one who was born a Jew could not be a true Christian. Connected with this was a new concept, *limpieza de sangre* ("purity of blood"). One who was a Christian by birth had *limpieza de sangre*; one who had been born as a Jew did not. Pope Nicholas V disavowed this concept, declaring that "all Catholics are one in body according to the teaching of our faith." Nevertheless ordinary Catholics embraced the concept, and in 1451, the kings of Spain lent their approval to municipal regulations distinguishing between Old and New Christians on the basis of *limpieza de sangre*.

Fourth, many Spaniards began to feel contempt for the ease with which the Jews had left their ancestral faith when threatened only by physical harm.

Until 1449 things remained quiet, with Old and New Christians living in relative peace. New Christians began to hold positions of influence and it appeared that they would assimilate successfully into Spanish society. In January of 1449, however, there were violent clashes in Toledo between Old and New Christians. The initiators of the clashes came from the lower class, but it was not long before they received support from the nobility. The houses of prominent New Christians were burned. Some of the conversos were themselves caught and set on fire, accused of secretly practicing Judaism and engaging in extortion of Old Christians. The council of Toledo imposed a ban on conversos holding positions of influence and serving as witnesses in the city or its suburbs.

The Toledo outbreaks failed to reduce the influence of conversos in Spanish society. The struggle between the two groups continued, and the tensions continued even after the expulsion of the Jews.

There were also tensions between Jews and conversos. The problem confronted by the Jews of Spain was to determine the degree of the conversos' loyalty to Christianity on the one hand and to Judaism on the other. The conversos were of several types. Some were enthusiastic Christians. Others were only Christians on the outside but observed mitzvot (commandments) in private. Others were Christians but with mixed feelings about what they had chosen to do. Still others claimed that although they acted as Christians, they remained Jews on the inside.

Some Jews criticized the conversos for not having left Spain; the opportunity to leave Spain had been available to them but only some had seized it. Others simply rejected the defense that one's Judaism should be measured from the inside out, that one's actions mattered less than one's thoughts and feelings.

The converso phenomenon greatly complicated the life of Spanish Jewry and presented many different types of challenges.

Texts

THE BARCELONA DISPUTATION (1263)

I said to them, "I do not wish to have to submit to your judgement on that , but to speak as I wish on the matter under dispute, just as you say all that you wish; and I have understanding to speak with moderation on the matters of dispute just as you do, but let it be according to my own discretion." So they all gave me permission to speak freely.

Upon this I replied, "There is dispute between Gentiles and Jews on many points of religious practice in the two religions which are not essential for religious belief. In this honored court, I wish to dispute only on matters which are fundamental to the argument."

They all replied, "You have spoken well." And thus we agreed to speak first on the subject of the Messiah, whether he has already come as Christians believe, or whether he is yet to come as Jews believe. And after that we would discuss whether the Jews still possess the true law, or whether the Christians practice it.

Then Fray Paul opened and said that he would show from our

186

The Barcelona Haggadah—mid 14th Century

Talmud that the Messiah about whom the prophets testified had already come.

I replied, "Before we argue about this I should like you to instruct me by telling me how this is possible. For ever since Fray Paul went around in Provence and in many other places, I have heard that he has been saying something like this, and I found it very surprising. Let him answer me this: does he wish to say that the Sages of the Talmud were believers in Jesus' Messiahship, and that they believed that he was not merely human, but truly divine, as Christians think? Is it not a well-known thing in truth that the affair of Jesus took place in the time of the Second Temple, and he was born and killed before the destruction of the Temple, while the Sages of the Talmud, such as Rabbi Akiva and his associates, were after the destruction? And those who composed the Mishnah, Rabbi [Yehuda ha-Nasi] and Rabbi Nathan, were many years after the destruction, all the more so Rav Ashi, who composed the Talmud and wrote it down, for he lived about 400 years after the destruction. And if these Sages believed in the Messiahship of Jesus and that his faith and religion were true, and if they wrote the things from which Fray Paul says he will prove this, if so how did they remain in the original religion and practice of Judaism? For they were Jews and remained in the Jewish religion all their lives and died as Jews, they and their sons and their pupils who listened to all their words from their own mouths. Why did they not become converted to Christianity, as Fray Paul did when he understood from their sayings that Christianity is the true faith, and he went and became converted according to their words?

[Fray Paul] then began, "Scripture says (Genesis 49:10), 'The sceptre shall not depart from Judah . . . until Shiloh come.' Shiloh is the Messiah and the prophet says that Judah will always have power until the coming of the Messiah who goes forth from him. And if so, today when you have not a single sceptre or a single ruler, the Messiah who is of the seed of Judah and has the right of rulership must have come."

I replied, "The prophet does not mean that the kingdom of Judah would continue without any interruption, but that it would never pass away from him [Judah] and cease forever. And he means that whenever Israel does have a royal ruler, he has to be a member of the tribe of Judah, and if their kingdom should lapse for a while because of sin, when it returns it must return to Judah . . .

I stood on my feet and said, "Hearken and listen to my voice, Jews and Gentiles. Fray Paul asked me in Gerona whether I believed in the Trinity. I said, 'What is the Trinity? Does it mean that the deity has three physical bodies such as those of human beings?' Said he, 'No.' 'Does it mean, then, that the deity has three refined entities, such as souls or angelic beings?' Said he, 'No.' 'Does it mean one entity derived from three, as bodies are derived from the four elements?' Said he, 'No.' 'If so, what is the Trinity?' Said he, 'Wisdom, will and power.' So I said, 'I agree that God is wise and not foolish, that He wills and is not inert, that he is powerful and not powerless, but the expression 'Trinity' is a complete mistake, for wisdom in the Creator is not an accidental quality, but He and His wisdom are one, and He and His will are one, and He and His power are one. Thus wisdom, will and power are all one. . . .

Then Fray Paul stood up and said that he believed in a perfect Unity, and together with it there is a Trinity, and that this is a matter so deep that even the angels and princes on high do not understand it. . . .

Then our Lord the King stood up, and they descended from the Ark, and they departed. And on the following day, I stood up before our lord the King, and he said to me, "Return to your city in life and peace." And he gave me 300 dinars, and I took my leave of him with great love. May God make me worthy of the life of the World to Come. Amen.

H. Maccoby (ed.), *Judaism on Trial*, 102–4, 105, 144–6

DECREE OF KING JAMES I (1242)

Whenever the archbishops, bishops, Dominicans or Franciscan monks, visit towns or localities inhabited by Saracens [Muslims] or Jews and wish to espouse the word of God to those Jews or Saracens, the latter shall foregather at such calls and patiently listen to these persons. Should they refuse to come voluntarily, our officials shall compel them to do so without subterfuge.

J. Gerber, *The Jews of Spain*, 105

Solomon Alami, *Iggeret Musar*

If we ask ourselves why all this happened to us, then we have to accept the truth: we ourselves are at fault. . . . We and our iniquities caused this evil to happen. Our sages were jealous of each other and disrespectful . . . there was much quarreling among the wise men. . . . Then there were those scholars who attempted to interpret the Scriptures in the Greek manner and clothe it in Greek dress. They believed that Plato and Aristotle had brought us more light than Moses our master. . . . Now, if a man should not be able to "live by his faith," why should he suffer death for it and endure the joke and the shame of dispersion among the nations? It serves no good purpose to quote Scriptures as support for philosophical opinions: the way of reason and the way of faith are too far apart and will never meet. . . . Those who read a few columns in a book of Greek philosophy will soon tear to shreds the scroll of the Torah. . . . The next line of decadence were the leaders of the communities and those favored and trusted by the kings. Their riches and their high position made them forsake humility. . . . They acquired costly wagons and horses, dressed in precious garments. . . . They gave up study and industry and cultivated idleness, vainglory, and inordinate ambition. . . . Everyone chased after coveted positions; envy estranged a man from his fellow and they did not mind denouncing one another before the court. . . . The burden of taxation they shifted to the poorer classes. In the end, the court itself found them despicable and removed them from their power. . . .

There is no communal spirit among us. People quarrel over trifles; they hold banquets, listen to music, imitate the gentiles in their clothes and hairdress.

J. Gerber, *The Jews of Spain*, 116–7

Limpieza de sangre

We declare the so-called conversos, offspring of perverse Jewish ancestors, must be held by law to be infamous and ignominious, unfit, and unworthy to hold any public office or any benefice within the city of Toledo, or land within its jurisdiction, or to be commissioners for oaths or notaries, or to have any authority over the true Christians of the Holy Catholic Church.

J. Gerber, *The Jews of Spain*, 127.

Inquisition Testimony against Pedro de la Cavelleria (1450)

Silence, fool! Could I, as a Jew, ever have risen higher than a rabbin-
ical post? But now, see, I am one of the chief councillors (*jurado*) of
the city. For the sake of the little man who was hanged (Jesus), I
am accorded every honor, and I issue orders and decrees to the
whole city of Saragossa. Who hinders me—if I choose—from fasting on Yom Kippur and keeping your festivals and all the rest?
When I was a Jew I dared not walk as far as this (i.e., beyond the
prescribed limits of a Sabbath day's walk); but now I do as I please.

Baer, *History of the Jews in Christian Spain*, 2:277

Responsum of Solomon ben Simon Duran

Solomon, the son of Simon son of the sage Zemah, of blessed memory, [gives the following answer with regard to] the uncircumcised
children of those apostates who are called *anusim* [i.e., conversos]
who come to return in repentance. It is necessary to make the law
with regard to them clear in the matter of their repentance and
their circumcision and their ritual bathing. . . . [R. Solomon] says
that their status is Jewish in all their relations. It is a basic law in
Israel that a Jewish apostate, even though he has sinned, is still a
Jew, as the Talmud says (Sanhedrin 44b) and his marriages are
valid marriages. His children have the same status as he has, provided, of course, the children are born of a female apostate (i.e.,
not of a Gentile mother). . . .

Now do not say that [the enduring Jewish status] applies only to
a Jewish-born apostate. It applies also to a [Gentile-born] proselyte
who returns to his original religion. . . . to the end of time we count
him as a Jew. . . .

Therefore children of these apostates, as long as their mother is
of Israel, even over many generations and even if it was a Gentile
man who married this apostate woman, are to the end of all generations, Jewish. . . .

Since it is now clear that these [conversos] are not to be considered proselytes, we do not need therefore to enumerate to them all
the commandments and their punishments . . . because he is already in duty bound to fulfill them just as we are. . . .

Since he is an Israelite, he does not need the ritual bath nor formal acceptance, for he is already in duty bound to obey all the commandments.

Freehof, *Treasury of Responsa*, 88–92

Questions on the Texts

BARCELONA DISPUTATION

1. On what basis does Nahmanides challenge the Christian claim that Jesus was the Messiah?
2. How does Fray Paul interpret Genesis 49:10? How does Nahmanides refute this interpretation?
3. Belief in the Trinity is fundamental to Christianity. How does Fray Paul explain it? Which explanations does he reject as Nahmanides challenges them?

DECREE OF KING JAMES I

1. Do you think conversionist sermons were an effective tool for encouraging conversion? Why? Why not?
2. Jews were expected to come voluntarily and "patiently listen" to the churchmen. What does this show us about 13th-century Aragon?

SOLOMON ALAMI, *Iggeret Musar*

1. Which groups are to be blamed for the conversions among the Jews of Spain? Where has each of these groups gone astray?
2. Do you find Alami's analysis of the conversion question convincing? Why? Why not?

LIMPIEZA DE SANGRE

1. What benefits and privileges are to be denied the conversos of Toledo?
2. Why should conversos be denied any authority over the "true Christians of the Holy Catholic Church"?

Inquisition Testimony against Pedro de la Cavelleria (1450)

1. Pedro was a learned Jew. How does he attempt to justify his conversion to Christianity?
2. Does Pedro appear to be a sincere convert?

Responsum of R. Solomon ben Simon Duran

1. Rephrase the question posed to R. Solomon.
2. In his opinion, what is the status in halakhah of a returning convert?

Paper Topics

The Barcelona (or Tortosa) Disputation
The Role of the Dominicans/Franciscans in Christian Spain
Jewish Apostates in Christian Spain
Conversos in Christian Spain

Reference Works

Y. Baer, *A History of the Jews in Christian Spain*
R. Chazan, *Barcelona and Beyond*
J. Cohen, *The Friars and the Jews*
J. Gerber, *The Jews of Spain*
B. Netanyahu, *The Marranos of Spain*

INQUISITION AND EXPULSION

The Inquisition

The Inquisition was a papal judicial and investigative institution established in 1233 to deal with the problem of heresy. The pope's desire was to standardize procedures for uprooting heresy. The methods used by the Inquisition included torture, accepting testimony offered in secret, convicting on the basis of testimony offered by only two witnesses, and denying the accused any right to counsel. It is ironic that despite these methods, the Inquisition saw itself as "working out of love," expressing its love by preventing the sinner from sinning and bringing others to sin.

While the Inquisition was active in other parts of Europe over the years, it was not brought to Spain until the 15th century. At that time, increasing concern that many of the New Christians were insincere and were secretly judaizing led the Spanish clergy to advise Ferdinand and Isabella, especially Isabella, that an Inquisition was needed. Moreover, they insisted, what was needed was an Inquisition that would be *less* compassionate than the Inquisition of the pope! Persuaded that rooting out heresy among the New Christians would strengthen their regime, the Catholic Monarchs, in 1478, asked, and were granted, the pope's permission to bring the Inquisition to Spain.

In 1481, the Inquisition began its work in Seville with a dramatic auto-da-fe ("act of faith") in which dozens of members of some prominent converso families were burned at the stake. In 1483 a Dominican monk, Tomas de Torquemada, was appointed inquisitor-general of Aragon and Castile. It was Torquemada who determined the special methods and unique character of the Spanish Inquisition. Under his supervision the Inquisition turned its attention to the rest of Spain, touching the lives of tens of thousands of New Christians. Within ten years 700 people had been burned at the stake just in Seville; by the end of the 15th century, as many as 30,000 conversos were killed.

The Inquisition gave special attention to conversos who were courtiers and financial agents of the crown. The family of Luis Santangel, chief supporter of Christopher Columbus, were among the earliest victims. Some were burned alive, others were burned symbolically. On July 17, 1491, Santangel's son and namesake was forced to appear publicly in a *sambenito*, a distinctive hooded cloak that was the special garb of penitents accused of judaizing.

Inquisitional investigations began with a 30–40 day period of grace starting on the day when the Inquisition established itself in a town or province. During this time it would accept confessions and evidence offered voluntarily. Generally, conversos suspected of secretly practicing Judaism would try to get off by confessing to some minor offense. Neighbors and acquaintances would then share their suspicions about them: perhaps charging that "There is

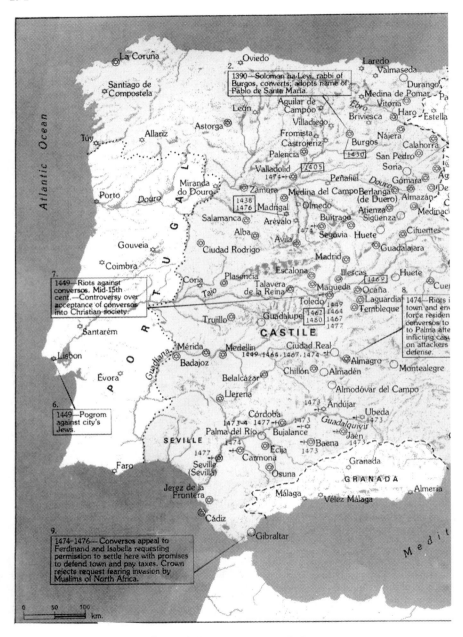

2.
1390—Solomon ha-Levi, rabbi of Burgos, converts; adopts name of Pablo de Santa María.

7.
1449—Riots against conversos. Mid-15th cent.—Controversy over acceptance of conversos into Christian society.

8.
1474—Riots in town and env force residen conversos in to Palma afte inflicting cas on attackers defense.

6.
1449—Pogrom against city's Jews.

9.
1474-1476—Conversos appeal to Ferdinand and Isabella requesting permission to settle here with promises to defend town and pay taxes. Crown rejects request fearing invasion by Muslims of North Africa.

Spanish Jewish Communities—15th Century

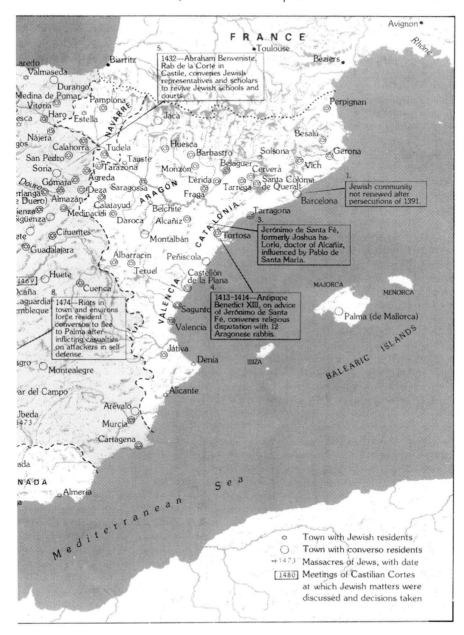

Spanish Jewish Communities—15th Century

no smoke in the chimney on the Sabbath" or "Those who live in the house buy large quantities of vegetables before Passover."

The "trial" of the accused converso came next. Those who did not confess during the grace period but were later found to have been judaizing were subjected to a long and painful interrogation that included the water torture and rope-hanging for which the Inquisition was so well known; at least in theory the purpose of these tortures was to draw a confession from the accused and thus save his or her soul. Those who were found guilty were burned at the stake.

In order to make it abundantly clear that judaizing was a terrible crime, public celebrations and processionals preceded the burnings. The sentences of the offenders would be pronounced before an enormous crowd, including thousands of peasants who had come from the rural areas to witness the events. Following behind the inquisitors and the clergy, the guilty persons would be led through the city's main square, carrying tapers and dressed in yellow *sambenitos* and tall miters decorated with the Cross of St. Andrew.

The processional would end at a specially prepared scaffold in the square. A cross would be raised and the people would take an oath to defend the faith. A high official of the church would then deliver a fiery sermon condemning the accused and their practices. Each of the accused would then be given his own sentence; this part sometimes took an entire day. The guilty would then be burned at the stake, with the "honor" of lighting the fire being extended to a distinguished guest such as a bishop or a visiting member of the royal family.

The Expulsion

On January 2, 1492, the flag of Ferdinand and Isabella was raised over the Alhambra, the palace fortress of Granada, the last Muslim principality in Spain. The entire country was now united under the Catholic Monarchs. That same month Ferdinand and Isabella signed a decree expelling all Jews from Spain. There was a close relationship between these two events. With the Reconquest of Spain finally completed, the only remaining impediment to national unity was the Jews. They were a problem, first, because they were not Christians, and second, because by their continued presence they were, in effect, a subversive element tempting New Christians to return to their former faith.

But what really lay behind the decision to expel the Jews? Was it in fact religious piety alone that motivated Ferdinand and Isabella? Perhaps there were other considerations that entered their thinking.

The Jews played a critical role in the economy of Spain. They were tax collectors and tax farmers. They paid high taxes and were successful businessmen. Thus expelling the Jews was foolish.

The Jews also held important political posts in Spain. A good example of this is Don Isaac Abrabanel, who was a prominent figure at the court of Ferdinand and Isabella. Along with Don Abraham Seneor, he tried to dissuade them from expelling the Jews. Thus expelling the Jews was foolish in this regard.

It seems, then, to have been considerations of religious belief which determined the fate of Spanish Jewry. The expulsion decree declared that its purpose was to prevent further damage to Spain's Christians from the efforts of the conversos to turn them into disloyal Christians. Other means of dealing with the conversos had been attempted, such as residential segregation, Inquisition, and expulsion from Andalusia (the southern part of Castile), but none had succeeded. Expulsion from all of Spain was the last alternative.

The decree was signed in January but announced only in May, due largely to efforts by influential Jews to have it set aside. The Jews began to leave in May, with the last one leaving Spain on July 31, 1492, the seventh day of Av. Approximately 175,000 Jews left Spain; another 100,000 chose to convert. This brought a tragic end to the history of the Jews in Spain.

Texts

THE DECREE OF EXPULSION

We are informed by the Inquisitors and by many other religious persons, ecclesiastical and secular, [that] it is evident and apparent that great damage to the Christians has resulted from and does result from the participation, conversation, and communication that they have had with the Jews, who try to always achieve by whatever ways and means possible to subvert and to draw away faithful Christians from our holy Catholic faith and to separate them from it, and to attract and pervert them to their injurious belief and opinion, instructing them in their ceremonies and observances of the Law, holding gatherings where they read unto them and teach them what they ought to believe and observe according to their Law, trying to circumcise them and their children, giving them books from which to read their prayers, and declaring the fasts that they ought to fast, and joining with them to read and teach them the histories of their Law; notifying them of Passover before it comes, advising them what they should observe and do for it, giving them and taking unto them the unleavened bread and the [ritually] slaughtered meats with their ceremonies, instructing them on the things they should stay away from, thus in the foods as in other matters, for observance of their Law, and persuading them as much as they can there is no other law nor truth besides it. This is evident from the many declarations and confessions, [obtained] as much from the Jews themselves as from those perverted and deceived by them, which has redounded to the great injury, detriment, and opprobrium of our holy Catholic faith. . . .

Therefore, we, with the counsel and advice of some prelates, grandees, and cavaliers of our kingdoms and other persons of knowledge and conscience of our Council, having had much deliberation upon it, resolve to order all and said Jews and Jewesses out of our kingdoms and that they never return nor come back to any of them.

Raphael, *The Expulsion 1492 Chronicles*

ABRABANEL AND SENEOR MEET WITH FERDINAND AND ISABELLA

On that day, Don Isaac Abrabanel was given permission to speak and to defend his people. There he stood, like a lion in wisdom and strength, and in the most eloquent language he addressed the king and queen. Don Abram Seneor, too, addressed the monarchs, but eventually all agreed not to pursue the matter any more. Then the two sages decided to write their words down and to send them to Queen Isabella, for they thought that maybe by this means the queen might consent to their plea. Thus Don Isaac Abrabanel sent a letter to Queen Isabella, in which he chastised her mercilessly and showed no respect for her rank. He then arranged to have the letter delivered to the queen while he fled for his life.

Raphael, *The Expulsion 1492 Chronicles*

Eliyahu Capsali on the Expulsion

As we mentioned, when Queen Isabella had seen how the city of Granada refused to surrender, she made a vow. Now that Granada had indeed fallen to Spain, she decided to keep that vow in full. Actually, Isabella had always hated the Jews, and had been involved in an ongoing argument with her husband, Ferdinand, for ever since her marriage she had been asking him to exile the Jews of Spain. In this she was spurred on by the priests. When, however, she saw that the king was reluctant to take such a step, she told him: "You no doubt love the Jews, and the reason is that you are of their flesh and blood. In fact, the reason the Jews arranged for you to marry me is so that you would act as their protector." When the king heard this terrible thing, he took his shoe off and threw it at the queen, hitting her. She then fled the room and the hatred between them continued for a long period of time.

Raphael, *The Expulsion 1492 Chronicles*

Torquemada on the Expulsion

In Spain there was a priest [Torquemada] who had tremendous hatred for the Jews, and the rule is that whoever afflicts the Jews becomes a leader by doing so. He was the confessor to the queen, and he instigated the queen to force the Jews to convert. If they would not, they were to be put to the sword. The queen pleaded to the king and begged him to do this.

Some time later the king gave in and decreed, at the advice of his wife, that all the Jews had to convert, and those that did not had to leave his kingdom. This was issued as a royal decree.

Solomon ibn Verga, *Shevet Yehudah*, 44th conversation

Questions on the Texts

THE DECREE OF EXPULSION

1. What were the prime considerations underlying the decree? Bring evidence from the decree to support your answer.
2. What other considerations might have entered into the decree?

ABRABANEL AND SENEOR MEET WITH FERDINAND AND ISABELLA

1. Why might the monarchs have been especially responsive to Abrabanel? to Seneor?
2. What makes Abrabanel think that he can get the decree canceled? What arguments do you think he might have used?

CAPSALI ON THE EXPULSION

1. What motivated Isabella's hatred of the Jews? (Didn't they bring major economic benefit to Spain? Weren't their financial talents useful?)
2. Why was Ferdinand so "soft" on the Jews?

TORQUEMADA ON THE EXPULSION

1. Was Torquemada a major contributor to the expulsion of the Jews or just a secondary player? Bring support for your position from the document.
1. Did Torquemada draw a distinction between Old Christians (those who were Christians by birth) and New Christians (those who came through conversion)?

Paper Topics

Torquemada and the Inquisition
"The Holy Child of La Guardia" (1490–91): The Blood Libel in Christian Spain
The Inquisition: Its Methods and Approaches
The Power and Influence of Don Isaac Abrabanel in 15th-Century Spain

The Expulsion: Were There Alternative Solutions to Spain's "Jewish Problem"?

Reference Works

Y. Baer, *History of the Jews of Christian Spain*, vol. 2
J. Gerber, *The Jews of Spain*
H. C. Lea, *A History of the Inquisition in Spain*
D. Raphael, *The Expulsion 1492 Chronicles*
C. Roth, *The Spanish Inquisition*

ECONOMIC ACTIVITIES

The Jews of Christian Spain involved themselves in a wide variety of economic pursuits. Some engaged in agriculture, some were in finance, some were moneylenders, some sold garments, some practiced medicine, some were tax-farmers, some were silversmiths or craftsmen. Let us take a closer look at some of the economic activities of Jews in Christian Spain.

Castile of the 13th century found the Jews of Toledo, Seville, and Cordova in various parts of the local economies. Some were tax-farmers and financiers whose responsibilities extended to all of Castile; among them, too, were those who owned textile shops in their own communities. Others were small shopkeepers and artisans, frequently silversmiths and shoemakers. Toledo of the 14th century even had a street in the Jewish quarter called Shoemakers' Lane. There were Jews in Castile who were manufacturers of cloth and many who were growers of grapes.

The well-known town of Avila was home to some fifty Jewish families, mostly small shopkeepers and artisans, among whom were blacksmiths and dyers. Jews also owned land which they cultivated and on which they herded sheep and cattle. On occasion they would extend loans at interest to Christian residents of the town. Don Joseph of Avila was the town's outstanding figure; he was one of the leading tax-farmers during the rule of Sancho IV. A 14th-century document from the town of Segovia indicates that most of its Jewish residents were weavers, shoemakers, tailors, furriers, blacksmiths, saddlers, potters, and dyers, but there were also a few merchants, a physician, and one toreador.

In 13th-century Aragon the picture was similar to that of Castile. Of special importance were the cloth merchants of Saragossa, Huesca, and Calatayud, who were seen as the founders of commerce in the cities and thus enjoyed high social standing, second only to that of the courtiers. Artisans were also prominent in Aragon: shoemakers, weavers, and tailors, among others. Many of the merchants and artisans owned fields and vineyards; the yearly grape harvest was an important event in Aragon.

The 14th century, in the wake of the 1348 Black Death, was a difficult period for the Jews of Spain. The economic picture, however, did not alter significantly. At least half the Jews in Barcelona were artisans: weavers, dyers, tailors, shoemakers, engravers, blacksmiths, silversmiths, bookbinders, workers in coral, and porters. There were many skilled physicians, two of whom served the royal family. In Saragossa, most of the Jews were small shopkeepers and artisans. Thus there were cloth merchants, furriers, coatmakers, wool washers, tanners, saddlers, shopkeepers, engravers, coppersmiths, ironsmiths, blacksmiths, and embroiderers; the bishop of Saragossa had his own Jewish tailor! Just as was the case in the 14th century, the cloth merchants were held in high esteem. As in Barcelona, there were also a number of Jewish doctors who achieved the highest regard for their services to the royal family.

Majorca, the capital of the largest of the Balearic Islands, was something of a special case. When the island came under the rule of Pedro IV of Aragon, and was no longer subject to the oppressive rule of its devout Christian majority, the local Jewish community became very prosperous. Much of the wealth and prosperity of Majorca came from its involvement in maritime trade. It was said of the Jews of Majorca that they had all sorts of valuables in their homes: "great stocks of silver and merchandise and secret treasures, gems and pearls, and caves filled with golden dinars. If a man lacked all these, even though he had possession of jewels and thousands of gold pieces and a good profession whereby he earned his livelihood and more, he was considered poor."

The tragic events of 1391 did not bring about major changes in the economic pursuits of Spain's Jews. As was the case before 1391, almost everywhere Jews were merchants and shopkeepers, but many more were artisans of various types. In just about every community there were physicians, tax collectors, and financiers connected with the local government, the nobles, and/or the bishops.

It is instructive to consider the communities of 15th-century Navarre, a small area which borders on Aragon in the east and Castile in the west. Jews there engaged in a wide variety of economic pursuits. In addition to being shopkeepers and artisans of various types—clothiers, hosiery makers, weavers, furriers—they were also involved in medicine, agriculture, tax-farming, and moneylending.

Thus Jewish economic activity in Spain did not vary greatly during the period we are here considering. Those who were in the lower classes were shopkeepers, ironsmiths, silversmiths, and blacksmiths. Those who were in the upper classes were tax-farmers, physicians, and financiers. In some cases Jews exercised some influence in the royal courts of Christian Spain; in others they simply strove to make a living.

Texts

RESPONSUM OF R. ASHER BEN YEHIEL (KELAL 6:10)

Reuben is an artisan, a dyer or saddler, and has an annual expense in the form of gifts to the judges and officials, to keep them from trumping up charges against him—the usual contribution that craftsmen are required to make out of their handiwork. Now the community also subsidizes the judges when resorting to their courts, and it demands of Reuben that he contribute his share. But Reuben replies, "What have I to do with you, that you have come to me when you are in trouble?"

Answer: It would seem to me that if the community gives a contribution to a judge in order that he be their protector and defender whenever his help is needed—as has become necessary for us in our exile to bribe the officials of each community—then Reuben is also obligated to participate and cannot separate himself from the community, for he must do this to serve his own personal needs as an artisan. If, however, the payment is made only to give aid to those who must appear in their courts, and Reuben does not need this himself, he is not obligated to participate.

(Trans. J. Bloomberg)

Responsum of R. Asher ben Yehiel (Kelal 89:11)

As to your question regarding two who were partners in saddle-making but split the partnership, with one of them leaving, a certain individual came to the one partner who remained, saying, "I gave my material to your partner to make a saddle for me. Return it to me, for you are his partner!" The remaining partner's response was, "Go and submit a claim against him, for I do not know whether you gave him something or not." The partner was then asked whether he had seen such material in his shop, to which he responded that he had, indeed, but did not know what had been done with the material. "I did not take it," he said, "and I do not know whether he did or not."

Answer: The customer has no claim against the remaining partner, for even though they were partners and even though he saw the material in the shop—so what! It is typical for one partner to leave working material in the shop, while his partner pays no attention to it. And if he, the other partner, left it there, the remaining partner has no obligation, and no claim can be made against him.

(Trans. J. Bloomberg)

Responsum of R. Asher ben Yehiel (Kelal 104:5)

Reuben gave Simon material from which to weave a garment, but claimed against Simon that he had exchanged the material submitted for inferior material. Simon conceded that he had but said that this had been done without his [Simon's] knowledge. Simon demanded that Reuben take an oath regarding the extent of inferiority and then take it [the product]. Reuben claimed that he did not know how much change was made and thus demanded that Simon take an oath and pay. Simon responded that he could not evaluate the difference.

Answer: Simon is obligated to take an oath but cannot; thus he should pay, for he admitted the change but could say how much change. This is comparable to "Fifty I know; fifty I do not." Thus Simon should pay to the degree that the experts agree that the garment is inferior.

(Trans. J. Bloomberg)

Solomon Alami, *Iggeret Musar* (1413–14)

And of late we have been beset by evil up and down the provinces of Castile and Catalonia in 1391, where many communities were destroyed, both small and large. And twenty-two years thereafter [i.e., in 1412] those that still remained in Castile were a byword and a mockery . . . for they were forced to change their manner of dress and to refrain from commerce, tax-farming and handicrafts. . . . They who had abode securely in their homes were driven out from their pleasant palaces to dwell in tombs and places of concealment. O worm of Jacob! They who were brought up in scarlet now embrace dunghills! Summer and winter, all Israel's citizens shelter in tabernacles, in everlasting contempt. As for our oppressing taxgatherers, no sooner were they deprived of farming the taxes than the majority of them left their religion, for none was master of a handicraft by which to earn his livelihood. And in the face of ruin, hardship and confinement, many artisans, too, left the fold, for when they saw the mischance and the travail, they could no longer stand in the presence of vicissitude. Such, too, was the case with the remaining communities in the Kingdom of Aragon, where a new king arose to issue new decrees. Who hath heard the like! Sucklings at their mothers' breasts cry for hunger and thirst, and barebodied children perish in snow and frost.

Baer, *History of the Jews in Christian Spain*, 2:239–40

Don Isaac Abrabanel on Deuteronomy 23:21

There is nothing unworthy about interest . . . because it is proper that people should make profit out of their money, wine, and corn, and if someone wants money from someone else . . . why should a farmer . . . who received wheat to sow his field not give the lender 10% if he is successful, as he usually should be? This is an ordinary business transaction and correct. . . . Interest-free loans should only be given to the coreligionist, to whom we owe special kindness.

Encyclopaedia Judaica, s.v. "Moneylending"

Responsum of Ibn Adret

[I have been asked regarding the] large expenditures made by the communities in the interests of public welfare and safety, namely, protection-money paid during the Christian festivals and like items, municipal improvements, expenses in connection with the king's order to wear a broad badge, and to return to the Christian debtors the interest collected above the legal rate [20%] and suffer forfeiture of the principal upon investigation by two Christians. The community made large expenditures to obtain mitigation of such measures. The size of the badge was reduced by half, and the badge is not required when one wears a cape. Also the excessive interest has to be returned but the principal is not forfeited.

Baer, *History of the Jews in Christian Spain*, 1:160

Questions on the Texts

R. ASHER BEN YEHIEL, KELAL 6:10

1. What responsibility is Reuben trying to escape? What argument does he make in his own favor?
2. What is R. Asher's response to the problem presented by Reuben?

R. ASHER BEN YEHIEL, KELAL 89:11

1. Summarize the issue presented to R. Asher and his answer to the question.
2. What inferences can be drawn about Jewish economic activities in Spain from this one responsum?

R. ASHER BEN YEHIEL, KELAL 104:5

1. Summarize the issue presented to R. Asher and his answer to the question.
2. Are the weavers and saddlemakers (text 2) from the upper classes? From the lower classes? Explain your conclusion.

SOLOMON ALAMI, *Iggeret Musar*

1. How does R. Alami "evaluate" the professions in which 15th-century Spanish Jews are involved?
2. Do you find Alami's comments illuminating and/or convincing regarding the conversions of so many Spanish Jews? Explain.

Don Isaac Abrabanel, Deuteronomy 23:21

1. How does Abrabanel justify moneylending? When must loans be made without interest? Explain.
2. Do you find Abrabanel's comments convincing? Why/Why not?

Responsum of Ibn Adret

1. How might the community of this text have attempted to combat these regulations?
2. What can be learned from this text about Jewish life in 13th-century Spain?

Paper Topics

Tax-Farming among the Jews of Christian Spain
Maritime Trade in Majorca
Moneylending among the Jews of Christian Spain
Social Status and Choice of Profession in Christian Spain
The Attacks on Spanish Jewry in 1391: Impact on Occupational Choices
The Conversos: Are They More/Less Successful in Their Occupational Pursuits?

Reference Works

Y. Baer, *A History of the Jews in Christian Spain*
B. Gampel, *The Last Jews on Iberian Soil*
J. Gerber, *The Jews of Spain*
N. Gross, *Economic History of the Jews*

CHRISTIAN SPAIN (1148–1492)

1161	Abraham ibn Daud writes *Sefer ha-Kabbalah*
1176	Jews referred to as *servi camerae* for first time
1185	Maimonides completes *Mishneh Torah*

1195	Maimonides completes *Moreh Nevukhim*
1232	Solomon bar Avraham bans study of philosophy and reading of *Moreh Nevukhim*
1236	Ferdinand III of Castile captures Cordoba
	Edict of Valencia grants Jews rights and protections
1263	Barcelona Disputation; *Las Siete Partidas* of Alfonso X
1270	Nahmanides completes his Torah commentary
1279	Jews required to attend sermons; anti-Jewish riots
1280	Catalonian revolt against Pedro III
	Jewish officials given responsibility for taxes and finances, arms supply, judicial appointments
1286	Moses de Leon composes *Zohar*
1302	Ferdinand IV of Castile resists opposition to Jewish courtiers
1305	Shlomo ibn Adret and 36 rabbis, supported by R. Asher, prohibit study of philosophy and natural sciences until age 25
1348	Alfonso XI of Castile prohibits Jews and Muslims from lending at interest and collecting debts
	Isaac ben Sheshet composes vast number of responsa
1391	Anti-Jewish riots in Seville and throughout Spain
1410	Hasdai Crescas writes *Or HaShem*
1413–1414	Disputation of Tortosa
1428	Yosef Albo writes *Sefer ha-Ikkarim*
1449	Violent clashes between Old and New Christians in Toledo
1470	Isaac Arama writes *Akedat Yitzhak*
	Ferdinand and Isabella organize Inquisition
1483	Torquemada appointed inquisitor-general
1492	Christian Reconquest completed with conquest of Granada
	Jews of Spain expelled

5

Jewish Women in the Middle Ages

MUCH CAN AND should be written about women and their lives and experiences in the Middle Ages. This is a subject whose surface has barely been scratched. In this final chapter, I will try to help you reach some preliminary conclusions.

Several basic questions must be raised. Were women fully integrated into Jewish society? Did they identify with it and participate in it, or did they lead lives apart? Were equal educational opportunities available to men and women? Did women pursue occupations and professions? What can be said about their social status? Were they happily married? What was the quality of their spiritual lives?

THE MIDDLE EAST AND NORTH AFRICA

Our major source for the status of women in the Middle East and North Africa in the 10th to 13th centuries is the treasure trove of documents discovered in the Cairo Genizah. A remarkable five-volume work by S. D. Goitein, *A Mediterranean Society*, assembles and brilliantly interprets this material. What we are able to say today about the women of this period emerges largely from Goitein's reading of the genizah documents.

Names

The names people give their children are always revealing; the name parents give a child are a good indicator of what they wish for the child. Analysis of the genizah documents shows a complete absence of biblical and other Hebrew names given to women. Surprisingly, the prevailing theme in the names chosen was ruling, overcoming, victory; names of women were introduced with the word *sitt*, meaning "mistress" or "female ruler." The themes of chastity and fertility, however, are almost completely absent, despite the obvious desirability of these traits.

Marriage and Divorce

Marriages were arranged for young Jewish women by their parents, ordinarily when the young woman was thirteen or fourteen. Marriage was usually to an older man, in order to obtain financial security for the young bride. This security was enhanced by the *ketubbah*, or marriage contract, which obligated the husband to provide his wife with food, clothing, and shelter. Talmudic law required a commitment to pay the wife 200 zuz (silver coins) in the event of the husband's death or a divorce. The bride brought with her a dowry, ordinarily worth considerably more than was the *ketubbah*.

An additional complication may have presented itself to the couples we know about from the genizah, for since they did not live in Ashkenaz, they were not bound by the 11th-century ban on polygamy attributed to Rabbenu Gershom. This may have been a source of tension in a marriage where the husband had more than one wife. The truth is, though, that the society of the genizah remained essentially monogamous.

Divorce was another threat that had to be confronted. The genizah documents contain much evidence that divorce was more common in this time than one might have imagined. The matchmaking of some families was not always successful. Moreover, genizah society required much mobility. Young men often had to leave their wives for months or years to pursue their business needs. This was clearly a factor that might undo a marriage relationship.

Widows

Widowhood is always tragic. It was especially tragic for the widows of the genizah period, for when their husbands died they lost everything but the remnants of the dowry, other personal possessions, and the promised late marriage gift—all of which were uncertain and insufficient assets. Widowhood brought a certain freedom, but only if some provision had been made for supporting the widow. Many widows were fortunate enough to have been designated executor and guardian of the husband's estate. Those who were not so designated found themselves at the mercy of the heirs, and were left in a very weak economic position, sometimes becoming involved in lengthy court cases concerning who was entitled to what.

Professions

The main area of women's employment was textiles. Women were involved in the production of textiles and in their sale. Female merchants sold textiles, threads, perfumes, or flour to Jewish women, but also to Muslim women. Some even had access to the harems of Istanbul.

Women owned real estate, which they could buy and sell. They could rent or lease houses, stores, and flour mills, thus taking real charge of their properties. The documents from the genizah tell us that some women were doctors, while others were teachers.

The professions open or specific to women, however, provided only a limited, small income. The possessions of most women were acquired only derivatively through gift, dowry, inheritance, or charity. Some women were on the public welfare lists, but they had to register with the community in order to be eligible. Private charity differed in that women appealed to communal leaders, judges, welfare officials, family members—but not to strangers.

Religious Education

Formal education of women and significant learning among women appear to have been rare in the time of the genizah. This is very much in line with traditional rabbinic attitudes and with the attitude of the surrounding Muslim environment. As with every rule, though, there are exceptions. Thus it is reported that Samuel b. Eli, the gaon of Baghdad between 1164 and 1193, had a daughter so expert in Tanakh and Talmud that she instructed her father's students. She would stay inside the building, while they stood outside so that they could hear her but not see her! One scholar of the period describes his daughter as "a scholar of Torah and a righteous woman."

Women at Home

Women had active lives at home. They bought bread at the market, they washed and cleaned, they reared children. The most common occupation at home was embroidery; although there were certainly professional embroiderers, the woman at home did much of this work on her own. There were also occasions when women left their homes. Some went to the synagogue, some went to see families and friends. As in every society there were births, weddings, and funerals.

ASHKENAZ

Marriage and Divorce

The young women of Ashkenaz were often betrothed at the age of eight or nine, with the marriage taking place at eleven or twelve. The young woman's new husband would be almost the same age.

What might have led families to let their children marry at such a young age? Perhaps it was concern that the family's financial situation might deteriorate and make it impossible to provide an adequate dowry. But it might instead have been religious considerations, as parents desired to relieve young people of the tensions engendered by sexual desire. Economic concerns might have entered as well; a young couple with some capital resources provided by parents could support themselves and gradually be introduced to the business world. Finally, there might have been social concerns, for when a marriage was arranged, it enhanced the prestige of the young woman's family by proving her desirability.

As in the society represented in the genizah documents, so too in Ashkenaz, key elements in any marriage were the ketubbah (marriage contract) obligations to provide food, clothing, and shelter and the dowry. The dowry usually comprised a substantial portion of the bride's parents' property, but its size would vary in accordance with the family's wealth.

The communities of Ashkenaz decided that the ketubbah commitment had to be more than the talmudic 200 zuz, which by medieval times was no more than a token sum. It had to be a serious financial commitment to the bride. Thus it was determined that 100 pounds of silver would become the standard ketubbah amount—enough to buy 100 average-sized vineyards. This new degree of obligation went very far toward raising the status of the Jewish woman in the communities of Ashkenaz.

Marriage at such a young age, as well as other problems of marital relationships, such as childlessness, incompatibility, and long absences of husbands from the home, made divorce a reality in Ashkenaz. A reading of the responsa of the time indicates that divorce was rather common. Rabbenu Gershom's ruling that no woman could be divorced against her will placed wives in a position of greater strength. Rabbenu Gershom had also ruled that polygamy was forbidden; this too strengthened placed the wife's position, for it was she alone that the husband had to support.

Widows

The responsa literature of Ashkenaz from the 11th to the 13th century Ashkenaz show us that most of the widows in this period were self-sufficient and economically active; widows who were poor are mentioned only rarely in the literature. Widows who had their own resources had some security, with little or no need to rely on the contributions of others. Many of the widows of Ashkenaz worked to support themselves.

Professions

The women of Ashkenaz were certainly adept at the essential domestic skills of spinning and weaving, but they were involved in much more than this. When their husbands were absent from the home for extended periods, women would do business with feudal princes and with other merchants, Jewish and Gentile, this despite the halakhah's requirements of modesty. Jewish women also engaged in moneylending. The men proffered large loans to Christian men, but their wives extended smaller loans to Christian women in exchange for pawns of some value. Some women were able to manage and administer large agricultural properties completely on their own.

Religious Education

Our earlier look at Jewish culture showed that the men of Ashkenaz made major and lasting contributions. Rashi's commentaries are indispensable tools for the student of the Torah, as are his commentaries on the Talmud. The Tosafot are likewise indispensable for the student of Talmud. Did the women of Ashkenaz share the benefits?

As far as can be ascertained from our sources, Jewish women did not share the benefits. Perhaps they received elementary instruction as children, but rarely did they go beyond the elementary level. This is not to say, however, that their lives had no spirituality or religious meaning. Some exceptional women, especially those who came from families distinguished for learning, did have access to what might be called higher culture. Thus it is reported that one of the daughters of Rashi recorded one of her father's responsa; this would be an extraordinarily difficult task for someone unfamiliar with talmudic style and language and with the concepts and categories of the halakhah.

MUSLIM AND CHRISTIAN SPAIN

Names

The names given to Jewish girls in Spain are very interesting. Sometimes they were biblical (e.g., Esther, Miriam), but more often they were Arabic (e.g., Aljofar, Belor, Jamila, Yamen) or of Romance origin (e.g., Astruga, Bona, Dolso, Ora). These names, whether Arabic or Romance, reflected the parents' wishes for their child to be beautiful (Jamila) or happy (Yamen) or wealthy (Ora, which means "gold").

Marriage and Divorce

As was the case in Ashkenaz, betrothal took place at the age of eight or nine, with marriage occurring at eleven or twelve. Early marriage for males, however, was out of the question in Spain.

The commitments of the new husband were listed in the ketubbah, which obligated him to provide food, clothing, and shelter. The contribution of the new bride was her dowry, which, as in Ashkenaz, was usually far in excess of the 200 zuz that the husband or his estate would be obligated to pay her in the event of death or divorce.

As in most societies, marriages sometimes ended in divorce, although the sources do not tell us how often this was the case in Spain. The grounds for divorce may have included childlessness, incompatibility, adultery, or any number of other things. For example, R. Yom Tov Alsabili, in a responsum, ruled on the question of whether a woman whose husband was losing the family's resources in gambling had a basis for divorce in this alone.

Marriage offered some special challenges to Spanish Jews. The first of these was polygamy, which, as mentioned earlier, was permitted because Sephardim were not bound by the ban of R. Gershom. Some men would take a second wife due to childlessness. Others would do so in an effort to remedy an unhappy marriage. Generally it was the wealthier men who took a second wife, as they could handle the increased expenses, but men of all classes, poorer and richer, had this option available to them. The unhappy first wife usually had to turn to outsiders—family members, the community, or even the king—for help. The rabbis of Spain were often supportive of the wife, but the truth is that one of Spain's most prominent rabbis, R. Hasdai Crescas, had more than one wife, and it is quite unlikely that voices of protest were raised against him.

A second challenge was the institution of concubinage. This meant that a woman entered into a permanent, stable nonmarital relationship with a man and was known to "belong" to him alone. For Muslims this was a tolerated practice at best, while for Christians it was only permitted to a bachelor. Jews followed the trends of their host society, so in Muslim Spain they had concubines and in Christian Spain they had concubines. The rabbis were not comfortable with the practice but tolerated it, concluding that to object would be counterproductive, undermining their efforts to bring about reform.

A third challenge was presented by prostitution. To be sure, prostitution was not adultery, so long as the prostitute was not a married woman. Prostitution was certainly a problem in both Muslim and Christian Spain, but it was treated as acceptable; Jews living in Aragon and Castile emulated the practices of their countrymen.

Widows

Spanish Jewish widows were usually self-sufficient. Their dowries and remaining marriage gifts allowed them some freedom and independence. The Jewish community of 14th-century Toledo was tempted to allow local custom to determine inheritance law rather than the law of the Talmud, but R. Asher b. Yehiel (Rosh) refused to permit this. The halakhah mandated, he said, that a wife could not inherit from her deceased husband.

Professions

Most Jewish women in Spain were illiterate, but this did not stand in their way. They supported themselves by engaging in spinning, knitting, or weaving. Women in the big cities had limited options beyond these, but women in villages and small towns could and did pursue other paths. The poorer ones might sell chickens, eggs, and wine in the market; the wealthier became merchants and moneylenders. One of the great surprises in the sources is that there were women who practiced medicine; some even had royal licenses to practice.

Religious Education

The sources available on the education of women are minimal. Nevertheless we do know that there were some exceptionally learned women in Spain. The wife of Dunash ibn Labrat (mid-10th cent.) was an excellent poet who corresponded with her husband in beautiful Hebrew poetry; she was clearly a master of meter, rhyme, and Hebrew literary sources. Shmuel ha-Nagid (mid-11th century), whose contributions to the culture of Muslim Spain as poet, Talmud scholar, and community leader were discussed in an earlier chapter, had a daughter, Qasmuna, who was a talented poet. Both the wife and daughter of Yehudah ha-Levi (12th cent.) were learned women. It is likely that other women received enough instruction to be able to read, recite the tefillah (prayers), and properly observe practical Jewish law and ritual.

Texts

A BETHROTHAL AGREEMENT FROM THE CAIRO GENIZAH

1. Should separation occur, the [divorce] document freeing Sitt al-Dalal [Lady Bold] will be produced by her husband without delay.
2. She is trustworthy in her statements concerning everything and no oath of any kind may be imposed on her.
3. He will not marry another wife (or keep a slave girl disliked by her).
4. He will not beat her.
5. He will not leave Fostat and travel anywhere [except with her consent].
6. Before setting out on a journey he will write her a conditional bill of divorce and deposit the delayed installment of her marriage gift as well as the sums needed for her maintenance during his absence.
7. The young couple will live in her parents' house. The husband owes yearly rent of 6 dinars and will never be late in paying it.
8. He will not separate her from her parents as long as the latter are alive and cannot force her to live anywhere else.
9. A fine of 90 dinars is imposed on him in case he fails to fulfill any of the preceding conditions.

Goitein, *A Mediterranean Society*, 3:144

A LETTER FROM THE CAIRO GENIZAH

Abundant greetings and wishes for speedy salvation come from East and West to my pure and chaste wife. Now I know how good your doings are, although I have no mouth to express this in words. I am sure you are well, but my well-being is bitter, because of my separation from you and from the eyes of the boy, my dear, beloved and most cherished son. I weep and groan and cry, day and night, and lift my eyes unto the four quarters of the world, but there is no one who has mercy upon me, except the Holy One, Blessed be He. Although you need no admonition from me, please lift your eyes to Heaven and act for the sake of your soul by taking the utmost care of our cherished and dear boy, and do not neglect him. This will be the best proof of your love.

Goitein, *A Mediterranean Society*, 3:220

THE EULOGY OF R. ELEAZAR B. JUDAH OF WORMS FOR HIS MARTYRED WIFE, DULCIA

Crown of her husband, daughter of nobles . . . her husband's heart trusted in her, she fed him and clothed him in honor to sit with the elders of the land and garner Torah and good deeds. . . . All the time she was with him, she made him books from her toil . . . she sought for white wool to spin fringes . . . she spun thread for phylacteries, scrolls and books. She was swift as a deer to cook for her children, and to do the will of the students . . . she sewed together about forty Torah scrolls . . . adorned brides and brought them [to the wedding] with honor. Her hands stitched clothes for the students and repaired torn books. She opened her hands to the poor and gave food to her sons and daughters and husband. She made wicks [for the candles of the] synagogue . . . and recited Psalms. She sang hymns and prayers. . . . in all the cities she instructed women and sang sweetly, coming early to the synagogue and staying late. Throughout the Day of Atonement she stood singing and taking care of the candles . . . she opened her mouth with wisdom and knew what is forbidden and what is permitted. . . . On the Sabbath day she would sit inquiring, absorbing her husband's words. . . . Wise in speech was she . . . buying milk for those who studied and hiring teachers by means of her toil. . . . She ran to visit the sick . . . fed her sons and urged them to study . . . rejoicing to perform her husband's will, and never at any time angering him.

Ben-Sasson, *A History of the Jewish People*, 523

SEFER HASIDIM, SEC. 669

A certain man, leaving on a journey, told his wife: "On such and such a day, I shall return and be with thee." The woman, knowing the time of her husband's return, prepared for his return by going to the ritual bath. Her husband thereupon said: "Since you've bathed in anticipation of my return, I shall present you with a gold piece with which to buy a garment." The woman replied: "Allow me, with that gold piece, to purchase a book or to hire a scribe to copy a book for lending to students, enabling them to pursue their studies." Subsequently the woman became pregnant and gave birth to a boy. While all of the brothers of the boy were devoid of learning, that boy himself was the exception.

Wistinetzki and Freimann, *Sefer Hasidim*

R. SOLOMON IBN ADRET

What the full intention of Rabbenu Gershom was I do not know, but it would seem to me that he did not intend to make his ban universal . . . and in the case of a wife who remained childless for ten years after marriage, where the husband is required (by divine precept) to marry a second wife in order to beget progeny, I do not believe that Rabbenu Gershom meant to forbid him to do so. In any case, whatever its author's intention was, this enactment was not accepted in our realm nor have we heard of its acceptance in Provence, which borders on France. In fact, there are a number of men in our community, among them scholars and communal leaders, who married a second wife while wedded to the first, and no one has ever questioned the propriety thereof.

Baer, *History of the Jews in Christian Spain*, 1:254

R. JONAH GERONDI, *SHA'AREI TESHUVAH* 3:94, 131–33

"Degrade not thy daughter by making a harlot of her, lest the land fall into harlotry, and the land become full of lewdness" (Leviticus 19:29). The rabbis explain (Sanhedrin 76a) that herein one is warned not to permit his daughter to enter into sexual relations not sanctioned by wedlock . . . for concubinage, without formal wedlock, was permitted only to the king, whose authority effectively restrained others from having converse with his concubine, so that the king's relation to her was tantamount to marriage. Beyond this royal privilege, the rabbis decreed that relations with one's bride are forbidden until the marriage benedictions have been pronounced. Intercourse with a slave woman is a capital sin, for the sinner defiled the holiness of God by loving and possessing "the daughter of an alien god" (Malachi 2:11). His alien offspring will be a snare to him and a reminder of his sin. The father shall bear guilt because of the son; he betrayed the Lord by begetting alien children.

Baer, History of the Jews in Christian Spain, 1:256

R. Jonah Gerondi, Iggeret ha-Teshuvah

We can derive from these words that women are the reason [that] study of Torah and fear of God [exist]. These modest women [by their encouragement] help their husbands to escape the burden of their work, which causes them at times to forget to devote time to Torah study. It is the obligation of the women to remind their husbands to study Torah, and not to indulge in idle activity. . . . The woman should be mindful of praying morning, noon, and night. At the end of her prayers, her main supplications should be for her sons and daughters, that they should be observant Jews, and that her sons should be successful in Torah study, because the main merit of the woman in the World to Come is when her children worship God. And when she has passed on, and her children are observant in Torah and possess the fear of God, it is considered as if she is alive, and she is on the highest rungs in the World to Come.

Zolty, "And All Your Children Shall Be Learned", 149

Questions on the Texts

A Betrothal Agreement from the Cairo Genizah

1. Why must the husband write a conditional bill of divorce before he leaves on a trip? Why must he commit himself to provide a divorce document "without delay"?
2. What other concerns of the bride-to-be are addressed here?

A Letter from the Cairo Genizah

1. Compare what the husband says about his wife with what he says about their son. What does this comparison show you?
2. "This will be the best proof of your love." What do you think the husband means by this?

Eleazar b. Judah's Eulogy for Dulcia

1. Describe Dulcia's religious and spiritual life as presented in this text. Was Dulcia a knowledgeable teacher of women? Bring support from the document.
2. Do you think R. Eleazar loved his wife? Support your answer from the document.

Sefer Hasidim, sec. 669

1. The wife accepts her husband's gold piece as a gift. What does she say she will do with it? What does this show about her life priorities?
2. Do you think the wife was a learned woman? Defend your answer from the text.

R. Solomon ibn Adret

1. In what case or cases did Rabbenu Gershom not forbid polygamy? Why?
2. What is Ibn Adret's evidence that the polygamy ban was not intended to be universal?

R. Jonah Gerondi, *Sha'arei Teshuvah*

1. To whom is concubinage permitted? On what basis?
2. How are we to understand the widespread Jewish practice of concubinage? How might people at the time have justified it?

R. Jonah Gerondi, *Iggeret ha-Teshuvah*

1. What does R. Jonah think should be the foci of a Jewish woman's religious life?

2. What should be the foci of the religious life of her family? Is she
   an enabler or an individual with a full spiritual life of her own?
   Bring evidence and support from the document.

Paper Topics

The Cairo Genizah as a Historical Source
Rabbenu Gershom's Takkanot (Ordinances) on Polygamy/on Divorce Without the Wife's Consent
Homosexuality in Muslim/Christian Spain
Homosexuality in Spain's Hebrew Poetry
Gambling in Muslim/Christian Spain
Professions of Jewish Women in Medieval Europe/Egypt
Jewish Women and Moneylending in Medieval Europe
Marriage/Divorce in Egypt/Spain/Ashkenaz
Women and Torah Study in Medieval Europe
Women in the Jewish Courts of Egypt/Spain/Ashkenaz

Reference Works

I. Agus, *The Heroic Age of Franco-German Jewry*
J. Baskin, *Jewish Women in Historical Perspective*
Y. Baer, *A History of the Jews in Christian Spain*
N. de Lange, *The Illustrated History of the Jewish People*
S. D. Goitein, *A Mediterranean Society*
A. Neuman, *The Jews of Spain*
S. Zolty, *"And All Your Children Shall Be Learned"*

Bibliography

Abarbanel: Commentary on the Torah. Jerusalem: Bnei Arabel, 1963.

Agus, I. *Rabbi Meir of Rothenburg.* New York: KTAV Publishing House, 1970.

———. *The Heroic Age of Franco-German Jewry.* New York: Yeshiva University Press, 1969.

Altmann, A. (ed. and trans.). *Three Jewish Philosophers.* New York: Harper Torchbooks, 1965.

Ashtor, E. *The Jews of Moslem Spain.* Philadelphia: Jewish Publication Society, 1973.

Baer, Y. *A History of the Jews in Christian Spain.* 2 vols. Philadelphia: Jewish Publication Society, 1978.

Barnavi, E. (ed.). *A Historical Atlas of the Jewish People.* New York: Alfred A. Knopf, 1992.

Baron, S. W. *A Social and Religious History of the Jews.* 15 vols. New York: Columbia University Press, 1952–72.

Baskin, J. (ed.). *Jewish Women in Historical Perspective.* Detroit: Wayne State University Press, 1991.

Beinart, H. (ed.). *The Sephardi Legacy.* Jerusalem: Magnes Press, 1992.

Ben-Sasson, H. H. (ed.). *A History of the Jewish People.* Cambridge, Mass.: Harvard University Press, 1976.

Bleich, J. D. (ed.). *With Perfect Faith.* New York: KTAV Publishing House, 1983.

Brody, R. *The Geonim of Babylonia and the Shaping of Medieval Jewish Culture.* New Haven: Yale University Press, 1998.

Chavel, C. (trans.). *Ramban: Commentary on the Torah.* New York: Shilo, 1976.

———. *Ramban: Writings and Discourses.* New York: Shilo, 1978.

Chazan, R. *Barcelona and Beyond: The Disputation of 1263 and Its Aftermath.* Berkeley: University of California Press, 1992.

———. "The Blois Incident of 1171." *Proceedings of the American Academy for Jewish Research* 36 (1968).

———. *European Jewry and the First Crusade.* Berkeley: University of California Press, 1987.

———. *Medieval Jewry in Northern France: A Political and Social History.* Baltimore: Johns Hopkins University Press, 1973.

——— (ed.). *Church, State and Jew in the Middle Ages*. New York: Behrman House, 1980.

——— (ed.). *Medieval Jewish Life*. New York: KTAV Publishing House, 1976.

Cohen, G. D. (ed.). *Sefer ha-Qabbalah (The Book of Tradition) by Abraham ibn Daud*. Philadelphia: Jewish Publication Society, 1967.

Cohen, J. *The Friars and the Jews*. Ithaca, N.Y.: Cornell University Press, 1982.

Cohen, M. R. *Under Crescent and Cross: The Jews in the Middle Ages*. Princeton: Princeton University Press, 1994.

Dan, J. *Jewish Mysticism and Jewish Ethics*. Seattle: University of Washington Press, 1986.

de Lange, N. (ed.). *The Illustrated History of the Jewish People*. New York: Harcourt, Brace, 1997.

Dinur, B. Z. *Yisrael ba-Golah*. Jerusalem: Bialik Institute, 1972.

Encyclopaedia Judaica. Jerusalem: Keter, 1972.

Feldman, L. (ed.). *Ancient and Medieval Jewish History*. New Brunswick, N.J.: Rutgers University Press, 1972.

Finkelstein, L. *Jewish Self-Government in the Middle Ages*. New York: Jewish Theological Seminary, 1924.

Freehof, S. B. *A Treasury of Responsa*. Philadelphia: Jewish Publication Society, 1963.

Gampel, J. *The Last Jews on Iberian Soil*. Berkeley: University of California Press, 1989.

Gerber, J. *The Jews of Spain*. New York: Free Press, 1992.

Gil, M. "The Radhanite Merchants and the Land of Radhan." *Journal of the Economic and Social History of the Orient* 17 (1974): 299–328.

Gilbert, M. *Atlas of Jewish History*. New York: Dorset, 1984.

Goitein, S. D. *A Mediterranean Society*. 5 vols. Berkeley: University of California Press, 1978.

———. "Jewish Society and Institutions under Islam." In *Jewish Society Through the Ages*, ed. H. H. Ben-Sasson and S. Ettinger. New York: Schocken, 1971.

Gross, N. (ed.). *Economic History of the Jews*. New York: Schocken Books, 1975.

Grossman, A. *Hakhme Ashkenaz ha-Rishonim*. Jerusalem: Magnes Press, 1988.

Haberman, A. M. *Sefer Gezerot Ashkenaz ve-Zarfat*. Jerusalem, 1945.

Jeffrey, A. (ed.) *Islam, Muhammad and His Religion*. New York: Bobbs-Merrill, 1958.

Jordan, William Chester. *The French Monarchy and the Jews*. Philadelphia: University of Pennsylvania Press, 1989.

Kanarfogel, E. *Jewish Education and Society in the Middle Ages*. Detroit: Wayne State University Press, 1992.

Kobler, F. (ed.). *Letters of Jews Through the Ages*. Philadelphia: Jewish Publication Society, 1952.

Lea, H. C. *A History of the Inquisition in Spain*. 4 vols. New York, 1906–7.

Lewis, Bernard. *The Jews of Islam*. Princeton: Princeton University Press, 1984.

Maccoby, H. *Judaism on Trial*. Washington: Littman Library, 1993.

Mann, V. (ed.). *Convinvencia: Jews, Muslims, and Christians in Medieval Spain*. New York: George Braziller, 1992.

Marcus, I. *Piety and Society: The Jewish Pietists of Medieval Germany*. Leiden: E. J. Brill, 1981.

Marcus, J. R. (ed.). *The Jews in the Medieval World: A Source Book, 315–1791*. New York: Atheneum, 1973.

Nemoy, L. (ed.). *A Karaite Anthology*. New Haven: Yale University Press, 1952.

Netanyahu, B. *The Marranos of Spain*. New York, 1966.

———. *The Origins of the Inquisition*. New York: Random House, 1995.

Neuman, A. *The Jews in Spain: Their Social, Political and Cultural Life During the Middle Ages*. 2 vols. Philadelphia, 1942.

O'Callahan, J. F. *A History of Medieval Spain*. Ithaca: Cornell University Press, 1975.

Perlmann, M. "Eleventh-Century Andalusian Authors on the Jews of Granada," *Proceedings of the American Academy for Jewish Research* 18 (1948–49).

———. "The Medieval Polemics Between Islam and Judaism." In *Religion in a Religious Age*, ed. S. D. Goitein. Cambridge, Mass.: Association for Jewish Studies, 1974.

Rahman, F. *Islam*. London, 1966.

Raphael, D. (ed.). *The Expulsion 1492 Chronicles*. North Hollywood, Calif., 1992.

Rapoport-Albert, A. and Zipperstein, S. (eds.). *Jewish History: Essays in Honour of Chimen Abramsky*. London: Peter Halban, 1988.

Roth, C. *The Spanish Inquisition*. London, 1937.

Scheindlin, R. P. *Wine, Women, and Death: Medieval Hebrew Poems on the Good Life*. Philadelphia: Jewish Publication Society, 1986.

Scholem, G. *Kabbalah*. New York: Schocken, 1974.

———. *Major Trends in Jewish Mysticism*. 3rd rev. ed. New York: Schocken, 1964.

Sirat, C. *A History of Jewish Philosophy in the Middle Ages*. Cambridge: Cambridge University Press, 1985.

Stillman, N. *The Jews of Arab Lands: A History and Source Book*. Philadelphia: Jewish Publication Society, 1979.

Stow, K. *Alienated Minority: The Jews of Medieval Latin Europe*. Cambridge, Mass.: Harvard University Press, 1992.

Urbach, E. *Baalei ha-Tosafot*. Jerusalem: Bialik Institute, 1968.

Weinberger, L. J. *Jewish Prince in Moslem Spain: Selected Poems of Samuel Ibn Nagrela*. University, Ala.: University of Alabama Press, 1973.

Wistinetski, Y., and J. Freimann (eds.). *Sefer Hasidim*. Frankfurt-am-Main, 1924.

Zolty, S. *"And All Your Children Shall Be Learned"*. Northvale, N.J.: Jason Aronson, 1993.

Agus, I. *Rabbi Meir of Rothenburg*. New York: Jewish Publication Society, 1942.

———. *The Heroic Age of Franco-German Jewry*.

Altmann, A. (ed. and trans.). *Three Jewish Philosophers*. New York: Harper Torch-books, 1965.

Ashtor, E. *The Jews of Moslem Spain*. Philadelphia: Jewish Publication Society, 1973.

Baer, Y. *A History of the Jews in Christian Spain*. 2 vols. Philadelphia: Jewish Publication Society, 1978.

Barnavi, E. (ed.). *A Historical Atlas of the Jewish People*. New York: Alfred A. Knopf.

Baron, S. W. *A Social and Religious History of the Jews*. 15 vols. New York: Columbia University Press, 1952–72.

Baskin, J. (ed.). *Jewish Women in Historical Perspective*.

Ben-Sasson, H. H. *A History of the Jewish People*.

Bleich, J. D. (ed.). *With Perfect Faith*.

Brody, R. *The Geonim of Babylonia and the Shaping of Medieval Jewish Culture*. New Haven: Yale University Press, 1998.

Chavel, C. (trans.). *Ramban: Writings and Discourses*. New York: Shilo, 1978.

Chazan, R. *European Jewry and the First Crusade*.

———. *Medieval Jewry in Northern France: A Political and Social History*.

——— (ed.). *Church, State and Jew in the Middle Ages*.

———. "The Blois Incident of 1171." *Proceedings of the American Academy for Jewish Research* 36 (1968).

———. *Medieval Jewish Life*.

———. *Barcelona and Beyond: The Disputation of 1263 and Its Aftermath*. Berkeley: University of California Press, 1992.

Cohen, G. D. (ed.). *Sefer ha-Qabbalah by Abraham ibn Daud*. Philadelphia: Jewish Publication Society, 1967.

Cohen, J. *The Friars and the Jews*.

Cohen, M. R. *Under Crescent and Cross: The Jews in the Middle Ages*. Princeton: Princeton University Press, 1994.

Dan, J. *Jewish Mysticism and Jewish Ethics*. Seattle, 1986.

de Lange, N. (ed.). *The Illustrated History of the Jewish People*.

Dinur, B. Z. *Yisrael ba-Golah*.

Encyclopaedia Judaica. Jerusalem: Keter, 1972.

Feldman, L. (ed.). *Ancient and Medieval Jewish History*.

Finkelstein, L. *Jewish Self-Government in the Middle Ages*. New York: Jewish Theological Seminary, 1924.

Freehof, S. B. *A Treasury of Responsa*.

Gampel, J. *The Last Jews on Iberian Soil*.

Gerber, J. *The Jews of Spain*.

Gil, M. "The Radhanite Merchants and the Land of Radhan." *Journal of the Economic and Social History of the Orient* 17 (1974): 299–328.

Gilbert, M. *Atlas of Jewish History*. New York: Dorset, 1984.

Goitein, S. D. *A Mediterranean Society*. 5 vols. Berkeley: University of California Press, 1978.

———. "Jewish Society and Institutions under Islam." In *Jewish Society Through the Ages*, ed. H. H. Ben-Sasson and S. Ettinger.

Gross, N. (ed.). *Economic History of the Jews*.

Grossman, A. *Hakhme Ashkenaz ha-Rishonim*.

Haberman, A. M. *Sefer Gezerot Ashkenaz ve-Zarfat*. Jerusalem, 1945.

Jeffrey, A. *Islam, Muhammad and His Religion*. New York, 1958.

Kanarfogel, E. *Jewish Education and Society in the Middle Ages*.

Kobler, F. (ed.). *Letters of Jews Through the Ages*. Philadelphia: Jewish Publication Society, 1952.

Lea, H. C. *A History of the Inquisition in Spain*. 4 vols. New York, 1906–7.

Lewis, B. *Salo Wittmayer Baron Jubilee Volume*. Jerusalem, 1975.

Maccoby, H. *Judaism on Trial*.

Marcus, I. *Piety and Society: The Jewish Pietists of Medieval Germany*.

Marcus, J. R. (ed.). *The Jews in the Medieval World: A Source Book, 315–1791*. New York: Atheneum, 1973.

Nemoy, L. (ed.). *A Karaite Anthology*. New Haven: Yale University Press, 1952.

Netanyahu, B. *The Marranos of Spain*. New York, 1966.

Neuman, A. *The Jews in Spain: Their Social, Political and Cultural Life During the Middle Ages*. 2 vols. Philadelphia, 1942.

O'Callahan, J. F. *A History of Medieval Spain*.

Perlmann, M. "The Medieval Polemics Between Islam and Judaism." In *Religion in a Religious Age*, ed. S. D. Goitein. Cambridge, Mass.: Association for Jewish Studies, 1974.

Perlmann, M. "Eleventh-Century Andalusian Authors on the Jews of Granada," *Proceedings of the American Academy for Jewish Research* 18 (1948–49).

Rahman, F. *Islam*. London, 1966.

Raphael, D. (ed.). *The Expulsion 1492 Chronicles*.

Roth, C. *The Spanish Inquisition*. London, 1937.

Scheindlin, R. P. *Wine, Women, and Death: Medieval Hebrew Poems on the Good Life*. Philadelphia: Jewish Publication Society, 1986.

Scholem, G. *Major Trends in Jewish Mysticism*. 3rd rev. ed. New York: Schocken, 1964.

———. *Kabbalah*. New York: Schoken, 1974.

Sirat, C. *A History of Jewish Philosophy in the Middle Ages*.

Stillman, N. *The Jews of Arab Lands: A History and Source Book*. Philadelphia: Jewish Publication Society, 1979.

Stow, K. *Alienated Minority: The Jews of Medieval Latin Europe*.

Urbach, E. *Baalei ha-Tosafot*.

Weinberger, L. J. *Jewish Prince in Moslem Spain: Selected Poems of Samuel Ibn Nagrela*. University, Ala.: University of Alabama Press, 1973.

Wistinetski, Y., and J. Freimann (eds.). *Sefer Hasidim*. Frankfurt-am-Main, 1924.

Zolty, S. *"And All Your Children Shall Be Learned"*. Northvale, N.J.: Jason Aronson, 1993.